DeBabelizer
The Authorized Edition

LISE DESPRES AND PAUL VACHIER

Hayden
Books

Hayden Books

President
Richard Swadley

Associate Publisher
John Pierce

Publishing Manager
Laurie Petrycki

Managing Editor
Lisa Wilson

Marketing Manager
Stacey Oldham

Acquisitions Editor
Michelle Reed

Development Editor
Brad Miser

Production Editor
Michael Brumitt

Copy Editors
Larry Frey
Michael Brumitt

Technical Editors
Chris Caracci, Richard
Frick, Carolyn Guy, Will
Kelly, Greg Marr, Will
Smithee, Michelle Szabo,
Leslie Tilling

Publishing Coordinator
Karen Flowers

Cover Designer
Ann Jones

Book Designer
Ann Jones

Manufacturing Coordinator
Brook Farling

Production Team Supervisors
Laurie Casey
Joe Millay

Production Team
Tricia Flodder, Mary Hunt,
William Huys Jr, Malinda
Kuhn, Daniela Raderstorf,
Christy Wagner

Indexer
Kevin Fulcher

DeBabelizer: The Authorized Edition

©1997 Lise Despres and Paul Vachier

Library of Congress Catalog Number: 96-77854

ISBN: 1-56830-324-6

Copyright © 1997 Hayden Books

Printed in the United States of America 1 2 3 4 5 6 7 8 9 0

Warning and Disclaimer

About the Authors

Lise Despres

Lise Despres began her career in publishing as a Managing Editor at MecklerMedia. She then moved into the growing industry of multimedia when she was hired by the Center for Creative Imaging, formerly known as the Kodak Center, in Camden, Maine. At CCI, Lise was in charge of the multimedia lab. She assisted experts who came to CCI to teach classes in multimedia.

After leaving CCI, she worked on several multimedia titles including titles for clients such as Microsoft, Simon & Shuster, and Grolier. She currently teaches multimedia in Connecticut. She also works on various multimedia projects in the metropolitan area. You can reach her at LDespres@CT2.NAI.net.

Paul Vachier

Paul Vachier is a freelance graphic artist, Web developer, and founder of Transmit Media in San Francisco, as well as a member of the Blue Platypus Internet team. He has also worked as a designer for online magazines such as *Word*, *Salon* and *PCWorld Annex* in the past and was recognized recently by *The Net* magazine as a noted Web designer. He has taught Internet topics at San Francisco State University's Multimedia Studies Program and is a founding member of the Noend Internet user's group in San Francisco.

Paul is a longtime computer graphics user, having been involved in computer graphics since 1988. Originally working in desktop publishing, he spent many years in prepress, honing his production skills before making the transition to design. He began using DeBabelizer as a multi-media tool while studying at SFSU's Multimedia Studies Department. With the advent of the Web, he found DeBabelizer became an even more important utility and has been particularly focused on its uses for optimizing Web graphics over the last two years.

Paul also recently co-authored the book, *Plug-N-Play JavaScript*, published by New Riders Publishing.

Trademark Acknowledgments

All terms mentioned in this book that are known to be trademarks or services marks have been appropriately capitalized. Hayden Books cannot attest to the accuracy of this information. Use of a term in this book should not be regarded as affecting the validity of any trademark or service mark. **DeBabelizer** is a registered trademark of **Equilibrium**. **ProScripts**, **SuperPalette**, **BatchList**, **WatchMe**, and **ActionArrow** are trademarks of **Equilibrium**.

Acknowledgments

Lise Despres' thank yous...

Many, many thanks go to Matt LeClair and Lynda Weinman for their generous support and belief in me.

Thanks to the folks at Equilibrium, who allowed Paul and me into their top secret vaults!! With a particular thanks to Richard Frick, Greg Wishart, and Leslie Tilling.

A big thanks to my partner in crime, Paul Vachier. I was lucky when the fickle finger of fate chose you—someone who understands Mercury Retrograde.

Thanks to the folks at Hayden, specifically but not exclusively, Michelle Reed, Steve Mulder, Michael Brumitt, and the irreplaceable Brad Miser.

Thanks to David L. Rogelberg for your sage advice.

I'd like to thank my family for their support and understanding through the years. I couldn't have done it without you.

I'd would also like to thank my friends. Colleen Abbott for sliding the chocolate shakes under the door and for not making fun of me for not knowing what Birefly meant... Thanks to Ed Kim for letting me borrow anything and everything. Thanks to Jessica Perry for your support and encouragement. Thanks to Susan Whitaker and Brenda Garcia for your emails, my one source of entertainment when deep in my writer's cocoon. Thanks to Bridget Abbott for the occasional sanity test. And big thanks to Bubba, just for being you.

Thanks to Gordon Cox and Mark Leaman for acting as PC support.

Many thanks go to the Artists at VSI, past and present, for keeping me busy with DeBab questions and for helping me blow off steam at the Savoy!

And lastly, thanks to all the people I have worked with over the years. I have continually learned from you all. You have generously shared your knowledge with me and have stepped up my game.

And now for Paul's...

In no particular order:

Kevin Ready and the Blue Platypus crew, the Noend community, Caleb Clark, Elise Bauer, Blake Kritzberg, Vikki Vaden, Jaime Levy, Greg Wishart, Bruce Falck and Simon Smith, Bruno Ybarra, Lewis Communications, Michelle Reed, Mark Richer, and my mom.

Hayden Books

The staff of Hayden Books is committed to bringing you the best computer books. What our readers think of Hayden is important to our ability to serve our customers. If you have any comments, no matter how great or how small, we'd appreciate your taking the time to send us a note.

You can reach Hayden Books at the following:

Hayden Books

201 West 103rd Street

Indianapolis, IN 46290

317-581-3833

Email addresses:

America Online: `Hayden Bks`

Internet: **`hayden@hayden.com`**

Visit the Hayden Books Web site at **`http://www.hayden.com`**

Foreword

Multimedia and Web authoring are some of the hardest disciplines today's digital artists and producers face. In order to make appealing graphics, one has to become fluent in a new, complex vocabulary of terms and techniques. One of the great ironies of this type of work is what looks easy to the end user—graphical interfaces, sound, movies, and interactivity—is the often hardest to create. What's easiest to use at the back-end is almost always the hardest to develop at the front-end.

DeBabelizer was developed specifically for multimedia and Web authors to help automate complex production tasks. Although any serious multimedia or Web developer owned the product and often sang its praises, it was universally regarded as a "difficult" program to master because of its confusing and unusual interface. For this reason, the need for a DeBabelizer book has existed for a long time.

The new version of DeBabelizer has improved greatly over the last year. It will unquestionably be much easier to learn and use. You might wonder if you'll really need a book to learn the program now. Regardless of how easy DeBabelizer has become, its features are so deep and so rich that its manual could not possibly cover the full range of potential tips and techniques. What's great about this book is that the authors have "been there, done that." They know first-hand how you'll want to use DeBabelizer and how to unleash its deeper powers.

Sadly, computer books are often just as confusing as computer programs. That's because they're commonly written by technical writers instead of true end-users. The fact that this book is written by two authors who are in-the-trenches multimedia and Web artists is a great asset. This book has the perfect blend—complex subject matter with training written by knowledgeable, experienced people who talk in plain English instead of technobabble. It should empower many new and old DeBabelizer users to get the full benefits of this remarkable program, and focus on multimedia and Web content instead of difficult tools and concepts.

Multimedia and the Web are exciting new publishing mediums that invite anyone to become an author. Programs like DeBabelizer and books like this stand to make a huge impact on the advancement of these industries, by enabling "mere mortals" (non-programmers!) to create compelling content. If you want to do this type of work, or already make your living doing this work, this book will serve as a treasured resource.

—Lynda Weinman

Author of *Designing Web Graphics*, *Deconstructing Web Graphics*, and co-author of *Coloring Web Graphics*

`http://www.lynda.com`

Contents at a Glance

Table of Contents

Introduction

When the idea of this book was first proposed, I thought to myself, "Great, I need a book like that." Many times when using DeBabelizer Toolbox and earlier versions, I wanted to look up something, but of course, no books on DeBabelizer had been published and articles were few and far between—I know, I checked.

NOTE

> Throughout this book, we refer to the current shipping Macintosh product as DeBabelizer Toolbox. DeBabelizer Toolbox refers to the Macintosh product version 1.6.5 and earlier. DeBabelizer Pro, to which most of this book is dedicated, refers to the new interface currently only available for Windows 95/NT (but expected for Macintosh later in 1997).

DeBabelizer is a program that every multimedia firm I've worked for has used, but there is no documentation about it, besides the manual, which lacks in description and readability. After searching, I started asking people I have worked with, "How do *you* use DeBabelizer?"

The answers I got were pretty standard—creating palettes, flattening QuickTime movies, saving GIFs and JPEGs for the Web, and, of course, file conversions. I then started to rip apart the program, delving deeper and deeper into it. I decided the program was like an onion; DeBabelizer has layer upon layer of functionality hidden beneath the onion skin—the challenging and rather quirky user interface. Then Equilibrium did something marvelous; they created a Windows version with an elegant new user interface, and peeling away the onion skin became much easier.

The purpose of this book is to help you navigate through the layers. DeBabelizer is an immensely powerful tool. It can act like a entire production team if you know how to use it to its fullest capabilities. Now, it is no longer an exclusive Macintosh program; with the advent of DeBabelizer Pro for Windows, PC users can harness much of the power Macintosh users have enjoyed.

Cross-Platform Availability

Occasionally on mailing lists, you used to see pleas for a DeBabelizer-like tool for the PC platform. Now, PC users can harness DeBabelizer power with the Windows version, DeBabelizer Pro. DeBabelizer Pro fills a hole for PC users looking for a program with DeBabelizer 1.6.5's scope and capabilities, but Mac users too can look forward to the new interface being implemented later in 1997, with DeBabelizer Pro for the Macintosh. Equilibrium has done a good job addressing the user interface difficulties in the previous version, and both PC and Mac users will benefit.

Just as DeBabelizer is available for both platforms, this book is also for both PC and Macintosh users. It mainly covers DeBabelizer Pro for Windows, but it also provides chapters on DeBabelizer 1.6.5 for the Macintosh, for those who still use the older version. Equilibrium intends to continue to fully support DeBabelizer 1.6.5. The two current versions offer similar functionality but use very different user interfaces. Although DeBabelizer Pro's interface is more user-friendly, the functionality is very similar to DeBabelizer 1.6.5. For example, using the Merge function does the same process on both platforms.

That said, what is different between DeBabelizer Toolbox and DeBabelizer Pro? In a nutshell:

- **DeBabelizer Toolbox (Macintosh only):** DeBabelizer Toolbox has a wider number of capabilities than DeBabelizer Pro, but its interface can be tricky. It's well-integrated into the Macintosh operating system but still has the limitation of only allowing one file to be open at a time. Part II of this book is dedicated to DeBabelizer Toolbox and helps you navigate through some of the trickier parts of the interface.

- **DeBabelizer Pro (Windows 95/NT):** DeBabelizer Pro has streamlined functionalty and an elegant user interface. Its capabilities are almost as extensive as Toolbox. The areas of difference in functionality are the Batch Automations offered and less support for reading and writing specific file formats. For example, DeBabelizer Pro does not currently support the QuickTime file format, but a future version supporting this is anticipated in 1997. An important difference is the capability to open an unlimited number of files and its new interface offers quicker access to file information. For example, you can access an image's Log directly from the Image window. Equilibrium has overhauled DeBabelizer Pro's own internal files such as palettes, scripts, and BatchLists and made these into stand-alone file formats that can be saved and opened by themselves. The

Windows version also offers elegant integration with the Windows operating system, allowing drag and drop between system windows and the Windows Explorer. It is also designed as a 32-bit app, fully compatible with both Windows 95 and Windows NT 4.0.

What DeBabelizer Toolbox and DeBabelizer Pro Can Do for You

DeBabelizer Toolbox and DeBabelizer Pro are valuable tools in any production environment. The new media industry is constantly changing—just when you think you've got one area covered, along comes a new advancement sending your production life into a whirl. If it is anything, the industry is dynamic. DeBabelizer Toolbox and DeBabelizer Pro can bring order to the chaos involved in putting a project together.

File Conversions

Both versions are often referred to as "Software Can Openers." In this day of cross-platform accessibility, computer artists can use DeBabelizer to create art on one platform and port it to another to do the programming. Without DeBabelizer, this kind of transfer involves a few hoop tricks. DeBabelizer Toolbox and DeBabelizer Pro support over 60 different file formats so that converting your files to a specific format is a simple affair.

The alphabet soup of file formats continues to grow as the new media industry expands, creating the need for more file formats to be used and supported. Converting files so that other programs can use them is just one of the many functions DeBabelizer can accomplish.

Image Manipulation

DeBabelizer Pro offers many different ways to manipulate your images. You can crop, rotate, resize, and set the dpi resolution, to name a few. You can also adjust the intensity or colors in the image. Coupling these manipulations with a batch run is an incredibly efficient process. You can create a script to implement any of the image manipulations.

Palette Management

Creating custom palettes for your artwork is a wonderful thing. Both DeBabelizer Toolbox and DeBabelizer Pro enable you to create SuperPalettes, which is a custom palette based on all the files in your project, regardless of format. You can include still images, QuickTime movies, or AVIs (depending on the platform version) to create the SuperPalette. Converting 24-bit images by using palettes decreases the size of your files and increases end-user enjoyment.

SuperPalettes are a great way to optimize Web graphics and with the growth of the Internet, this function is more important than ever. Creating SuperPalettes is also important in producing CD-ROM titles.

You are no longer limited to the conventional colors of a system palette, although you can also use one of the standard palettes and conform all your files to it. Anything and everything you would like to do to a palette can be done in DeBabelizer. You can even change the colors in a palette or merge two palettes together.

Batch Automations and Batch Processes

Equilibrium has taken common scripts and turned them into Batch Automations for DeBabelizer Pro and Batch Processes for DeBabelizer Toolbox. These Batch Automations and Batch Processes automate routinely used program functions, such as creating a SuperPalette that is available as a batch function in both Macintosh or Windows versions.

Scripts

DeBabelizer Toolbox and DeBabelizer Pro enable you to create your own custom scripts. A *script* is a list of DeBabelizer functions you can apply to a series of files, which can be carried out while the computer is unattended.

Equilibrium's ProScripts

You can point your browser to Equilibrium's home page (www.equilibrium.com) to download new ProScripts.

DeBabelizer by Discipline

This book includes chapters dedicated to using DeBabelizer Pro by a specific new media discipline: Web graphics, digital video and animations, and CD-ROM publishing. Chapter 8, "Working with Web Graphics," illustrates the many ways you can optimize your Web graphics using DeBabelizer Pro. Chapter 9, "Working with Digital Video and Animations," identifies ways to apply DeBabelizer Pro to your files. Chapter 10, "CD-ROM and Multimedia," illustrates ways to get the most out of DeBabelizer Pro when putting a title together.

Extra Tools

DeBabelizer Toolbox and DeBabelizer Pro offer a number of other tools to use on your files. If your files were digitized with a blue screen, you can remove it from your files, and Photoshop's third-party plug-ins can be accessed to run filters or to export/import files. You can also apply NTSC or PAL standards to files you intend for video or TV broadcast.

Who Uses DeBabelizer?

Anyone involved in the new media industry can use DeBabelizer. No matter what facet you are in—whether it is CD-ROM development, Web graphics, animation, or game development—DeBabelizer Toolbox and DeBabelizer Pro are an important part of project management and production.

How the Book Works

The book is divided into two main parts: the first part is on DeBabelizer Pro and the second provides a general view of DeBabelizer Toolbox. Each software version is explained in its respective part.

The book's chapters break down the software version's functionality and group together functions that are similar. For example, you will find all the palette functions for DeBabelizer Pro listed in Chapter 5. Many different functions in DeBabelizer Toolbox and DeBabelizer Pro can be used in more than one way. This book tries to provide the most common and productive uses.

You are also given examples of functions and sidebar tips throughout the book. Appendix A, "File Formats Supported by DeBabelizer Pro and DeBabelizer Toolbox," lists all the file formats both software versions support, and lastly, Appendix B, "Glossary of Terms," helps with some of the terminology used. In Appendix C, "DeBabelizer Toolbox 1.6.5 Interviews," interviews with industry professionals are included, asking them to share their secrets and insights into DeBabelizer to give you a feeling as to how well regarded DeBabelizer is in the industry and how indispensable a tool it is. Also, included on the accompanying CD-ROM are color versions of the figures for Chapters 4, 5, and 10.

This book suggests some of the ways you can use DeBabelizer Toolbox and DeBabelizer Pro in your day-to-day new media life. It has been designed to appeal to users of different skill levels.

The Future

Equilibrium plans to release new versions for both Macintosh and PC platforms sometime in late 1997. There has also been talk of an SGI port. The Macintosh version will incorporate the DeBabelizer Pro for Windows interface and both will support added functionality. Equilibrium plans aggressive updates to DeBabelizer Pro and increased functionality over time; stay tuned to Equilibrium's Web page at http://www.equilibrium.com for further details.

Another reason to point your browser to Equilibrium's home page is for updates. Equilibrium is constantly developing ProScripts for both software versions. ProScripts are scripts Equilibrium creates in order for you to simplify commonly used complex and repetitive operations. You can download scripts from Equilibrium's Web page and apply them as you would any script. Equilibrium also supplies a list of Frequently Asked Questions (FAQs) at their Web site, a good resource for finding the answers you need.

DeBabelizer Pro for Windows

DeBabelizer Pro for Windows

The efficiency and power that Macintosh users have long enjoyed is now available for PC users with the debut of DeBabelizer Pro for Windows. The first part of this book is devoted to DeBabelizer Pro for Windows. Each chapter in this section covers one of the basic DeBabelizer Pro functions.

The DeBabelizer Pro functions covered are creating and applying palettes, batch automations, scripting, and file conversions. Each function has its own individual chapter, explaining how the function works and how to use it.

DeBabelizer Pro sports an elegant interface in comparison to its Macintosh counterpart, and you will learn about the software's interface and how it works.

There are also chapters covering using DeBabelizer for Web graphics, animations and videos, and CD-ROM and multimedia.

Starting at the Beginning

How This Chapter Works...

In this chapter, you get an overview of DeBabelizer Pro's basic functions and tools. You'll see, at a high level, what the program can do. You will also get a good look at the program's interface. DeBabelizer Pro's functions are only briefly described because they are given greater attention throughout the remainder of the book. You will also see all the program's options broken down by task and functionality.

Because DeBabelizer Pro has gotten a facelift, its functionality is more organized. The new interface makes it easier for you to find what you need to get the job done. Some options may be listed in more than one place because they are multi-tasking, so to speak. The functionality can be used in several different ways. For example, you can Sort a palette to find out more information about the colors in the palette, and you can also Sort a palette to order the colors in a specific order. For the most part, the functionality will be explained under its most common use.

The areas this chapter covers are:

- **The Basics:** explains the program's interface and its tools

- **File Conversions:** explains the file conversion functionality DeBabelizer Pro

- **Color Depth:** explains how to create palettes and change a file's color depth

- **Image Manipulation:** explains the different ways you can change a file's appearance

- **Batching:** explains DeBabelizer Pro's automated processes

- **Scripting:** explains how to create your own user-defined scripts

DeBabelizer Interface

The user interface for DeBabelizer versions on the Macintosh (Toolbox and prior) was challenging, due to the enormous number of options available. For example, the Save As dialog box alone had 11 options and some of those options lead to even *more* options. Luckily, DeBabelizer Pro for Windows has a completely new and improved interface with streamlined functionality, resulting in making our jobs much easier. Thank you, Equilibrium.

The DeBabelizer Pro interface is far more graphical and intuitive and takes full advantage of the drag-and-drop capabilities of newer operating systems. It also offers streamlined functionality for greater user convenience. The trick to the interface is that a lot of the options are repeated throughout the program. So once you get used to the DeBabelizer Pro way of doing things, you're in business.

Helpful Help

In DeBabelizer Pro, Help is exactly that, *helpful*. It is always available to you and is very thorough.

If you are a person who never stops to ask for directions, you probably won't be using Help, but we recommend visiting there. DeBabelizer Pro has two forms of online Help. It makes use of the standard Windows online Help search facilities as shown in Figure 1.1. You can also access Help through the Help menu in the main program menu bar.

FIGURE 1.1

If you are the type who never asks for directions, you'll probably never see this Help window.

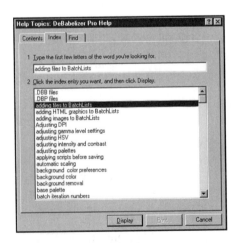

A useful thing about the Windows Help menu (WinHelp) is that you can add your own notes to it. After the main Help screen (shown in Figure 1.1) comes up, you can double-click a specific topic. After you click the topic, a screen comes up explaining the selected topic. You can then select the **Edit** menu and add your own notes by selecting Annotate from the submenu. This is great for keeping your own notes on how things work in DeBabelizer Pro. Figure 1.2 shows the pop-up menu with Annotate selected to add your own notes. You can also print the information in the Help window.

FIGURE 1.2

Adding your own info to make Help more personal.

For instance, say you have been using the cropping function. You have several ways by which you can crop, such as an Absolute method or a Relative method. You can add annotation to the Help that put these methods into your own words. You now have your own personalized notes within Help to refer to whenever you need them. You can use this as a way to keep notes for more complex functions such as scripting or batch automations. These notes can be referred to by coworkers as well.

DeBabelizer Pro also has an additional version of Help—Help text boxes. By either clicking the Help custom toolbar button, clicking the titlebar question mark icon when available, or pressing F1 on the keyboard, you can call up Help text boxes. These help text boxes, however, are only available for dialog boxes.

Internet Help

Another helpful source is Equilibrium's Web page (www.equilibrium.com), where you can find answers and information on their Frequently Asked Questions (FAQs) page. You can also find upgrade patches to your current software version.

If you aren't sure what an item or option is in a dialog box, you can place the cursor in the dialog box option and press F1. A Help text box immediately comes up for the option over which your cursor is placed. DeBabelizer Pro brings up a different help text box for whatever option you click in the window. Figure 1.3 is an example of a help text box.

11

FIGURE 1.3

DeBabelizer Pro's help text box gives extra information. Notice the Help icon at the top of the dialog box for quick access to help text boxes. Not all options have a help text box.

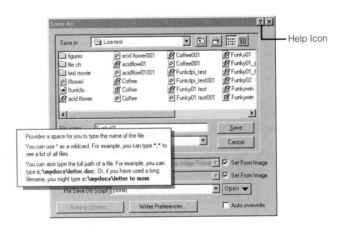

Help Icon

The Basics

A current trend in the computer industry is that application software is taking on a more cross-platform, hybrid look. New software is incorporating many Macintosh and PC interface elements, and the new DeBabelizer Pro is no exception to this trend. For instance, in the current interface you can customize your toolbar and access almost any program function from a toolbar icon—a definite Microsoftism. You can also make some of the tools free-floating palettes, a common Macintosh software attribute.

A handy new feature is the capability to customize your toolbars. You can have a button on your toolbar so that with just a click, you can rotate an image 90 degrees. Many functions within DeBabelizer Pro can be activated with a custom button. Each DeBabelizer Pro functionality is represented by a group of custom buttons. For example, you can display custom buttons for the Palette functions. The custom buttons available for the Palette functions are: Set Pixel Depth, Set Palette and Remap, Reduce Colors, Convert to Black and White/Grayscale, Remove Unused and/or Duplicates, Sort, Merge, Create Palette, and Equalize. All 16 of the Palette function custom buttons will appear; you cannot select individual buttons from within the group. You can display custom buttons on your toolbar by going to the **View** menu and selecting **Toolbars**, or by pressing the key combination specific to your computer platform.

TIP

Double-clicking a floating palette returns it to its docked position. This works on index palettes for images and on the toolbar icons.

Choosing **View** brings up the Custom Toolbar dialog box, which breaks down the actions DeBabelizer Pro does. Figure 1.4 displays the choices of the customized buttons you can have. By placing a check in the box next to the function you want,

12

the grouped icons available for that function get a toolbar button. This is convenient for functions you use often and provides an alternative to using key commands.

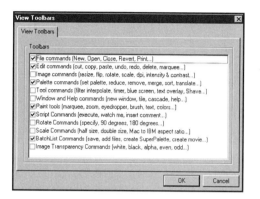

FIGURE 1.4

You can customize your toolbar according to functionality.

File Information Is Always Around

The bottom right-hand corner of the desktop displays important file information. In previous versions, this information is located on the toolbar. From left to right, the information is as follows: the X, Y coordinates for your cursor; the index color number for the cursor point and the values for the index color in Red, Green, and Blue (RGB) values, and the equivalent Hue, Saturation, and Value (HSV) values. This information is valuable when you are tweaking images and palettes. Figure 1.5 is an example of the toolbar's file information.

13

FIGURE 1.5

Information for the placement of the cursor helps when you need to tweak palettes or images.

Palette

A palette is a table of the colors used in an image.

If you have an image open with an alpha channel, this information will also be listed in the bottom-right corner. As you click across the image, the alpha will read 0 (Black) or 255 (White). From this you can figure out what part of the image is masked out.

The lower-right corner of the screen also houses the status bar. You need to toggle the preferences to see the status bar. You can set this preference by selecting the **View** menu and checking the Status Bar option. This a handy feature for supplying program information and can provide a visual clue if the system freezes.

TIP

You can make tools or customized toolbar buttons free-floating palettes by clicking and dragging them. You can also relocate them around the edge of the desktop to place them in the exact location for greater convenience.

The Tools

The Tools work the same way as they do in most imaging software. The Tools shown in Figure 1.6 are the standard tools that are available when launching the program.

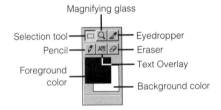

FIGURE 1.6

DeBabelizer Pro's tools you can use to manipulate files.

Selection Tool

By clicking and dragging with the Selection tool you get an outline of an area. You'll notice it no longer has the marching ants. The selection outline is a dotted box with eight handles, similar to the outline of a desktop publishing text box. Four of the eight nodes mark the corners of the selection and the remaining four are the midpoints of the sides. You can drag any of the handles to resize the selection. When you move the selection outline, it does just that. It moves *only* the selection outline; the image below is left intact until you combine the movement with a Control or Alt key. (This is a fundamental change from version 1.6.5 and earlier.) You can only move the image inside the selection outline when it is a floating selection. A floating selection is a floating copy of the image beneath it.

Key Combinations

You can affect a selection in several ways by combining the a key combination as you use the Selection tool. The following is a list of what each key combination does:

- **Shift Key:** Clicking a handle while holding down the Shift key constrains the selection's aspect ratio or the ratio to width to height. If you click the Shift key *before* you drag the selection tool, your selection is constrained to a square.

- **Control Key:** Holding down the Control key while clicking a selection handle makes a floating copy of the selection area. The floating selection can be moved around and skewed depending on how you resize the selection handle.

- **Alt Key:** Clicking a handle and holding down the Alt key moves the selection and rips it off the canvas leaving a hole filled in by your foreground color.

Selection Menu Options

The selection area can be further modified by accessing the **Edit** menu and choosing **Select: Specify**. Figure 1.7 illustrates the selection options available in the Select dialog box. Under this menu are terms such as *float* and *stamp*. A floating selection is a floating copy of the image beneath it. The image's integrity is intact; if you press the Delete key, it removes the floating selection and the image below is untouched.

Stamping a selection is when a floating selection is deactivated and the selection is stamped onto the image permanently. DeBabelizer Pro uses the standard Control-D to deactivate a selection, or you can click outside the selection area to deselect or stamp a floating selection.

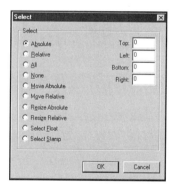

15

FIGURE 1.7

The different ways to affect the selection. You can move it in absolute numbers or by relative numbers.

Magnifying Glass

This tool enables you to zoom into a specific part of the image by clicking the mouse button. Holding the Alt key gives you the de-magnifying glass so that you can zoom out. Clicking the image will zoom in by 100 percent so the ratios will be 1:1, 2:1, 4:1. You can also access a submenu for this under the **View** menu if you have an image open.

Eyedropper

The Eyedropper tool enables you to select certain colors by clicking within an image. If you click an open file, the "captured" color becomes the Foreground color. The information associated with the cursor point is displayed to the bottom right of the toolbar as mentioned earlier. Holding down the Shift key while clicking selects the

Background color. You can click an image directly or on an image's palette, if it has one, to get colors. An image will only have a palette displayed if it is 8 bits or less. Clicking the Alt key switches the Eyedropper to a Pencil; holding down the Alt key enables you to select a new background color.

Pencil

The Pencil tool selects one pixel and replaces it with the Foreground color. The Pencil can write in as many pixels as you draw. You could clean up edges on an image if you needed to clean up an image. For example, if you have palletized an image and for some reason one stray pixel is converted to an awkward color, you could select a color and clean it up with the Pencil tool for a quick fix.

Paint Color

The Paint Color tool displays the selected color the paint tools will use. It includes two tiles, a foreground color, and a background color. If you double-click the color tile, a color dialog box pops up, enabling you to modify the color by entering RGB or HSV values, or by choosing a new color as shown in Figure 1.8. The Color dialog box offers a default set of basic set of colors and also enables you to add custom colors. This is convenient when working with custom palettes. You can also click and drag along the rainbow to select a desired color.

FIGURE 1.8

Choosing colors within DeBabelizer Pro.

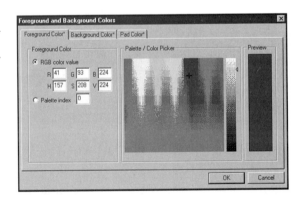

Eraser

The Eraser tool replaces the image with the background color. You can clear away the image with the Eraser tool.

Opening Files

The **Open** dialog box enables you to see a preview of the image if the preview box is checked. DeBabelizer Pro also displays information about the file, such as file type, bit depth, dimensions, file size, creation date, and date the file was last modified.

You can access the Reader Preferences, if available for this file format, directly from the **Open** dialog box. The Reader Preferences can be set before you open the file.

File Formats for Reader Preferences

The Reader Preferences tells DeBabelizer Pro how to read a file format. Reader Preferences are only available for four file formats: PhotoCD, Raw, SoftImage, and Wavefront. Chapter 2 goes into greater detail about this.

You can also specify which file types to look for (displaying only those file types) via the field labeled **Files of type**. In Figure 1.9, it is set to all Image Files, but you could be more specific. This option enables you to quickly access just the file format you need. Only the files fitting the file format selected are displayed in the window.

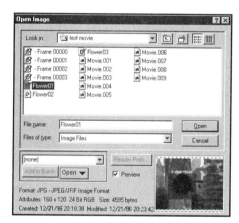

FIGURE 1.9

Quickly accessing the exact file format you are looking for is a convenient way to disregard files you do not need.

17

DeBabelizer Pro cannot only open more than one file at a time but can open as many files or images as memory allows. (In previous versions of DeBabelizer, you could only open one file at a time.) You can have an image, a movie, a script, and a BatchList all open at the same time in DeBabelizer Pro. If you open a file that is already in 256 colors, it will automatically pull up its palette. If the file is in millions of colors, no palette will be displayed; a file only has a palette if it in 8 bits or less. Image windows now have more information than they did in prior DeBabelizer versions, such as Image dimensions and pixel depth. Figure 1.10 is an example of an image window.

You can see each of the channels individually from the image window by pressing its respective button. If an image has an alpha or mask channel, you can see it from the image window as well.

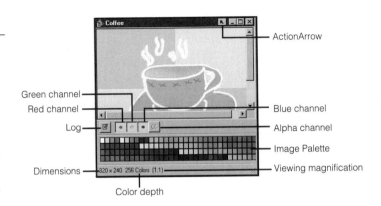

FIGURE 1.10

Image window information displays the dimensions of the file and its view size: 100%. This image has a palette, which you can remove from the image window to create a free-floating palette.

ActionArrows™

A feature new to DeBabelizer Pro is ActionArrows™. An ActionArrow™ is a tiny arrow found on the titlebar of a file. You can have an ActionArrow™ on an image, movie, script, palette, or BatchList. By dragging and dropping a file's ActionArrow™ onto another file you can quickly change a file's properties. For example, if you take an image's ActionArrow™ and drop it onto an open BatchList, the file will automatically be added to the BatchList. Another example is if you drop an ActionArrow™ onto an open script, the image will automatically undergo the changes set in the script. This is handy for quickly changing files.

TIP

In DeBabelizer Pro, most files have an ActionArrow™. This includes scripts, BatchLists, palettes, SuperPalettes, images, and movies. Only Logs do not have an ActionArrow™.

Logs

Another feature new to DeBabelizer Pro is the Log window. It keeps track of all the actions you apply to a file—from selection size to pixel changes. You then can drag and drop the specific action from the Log window, shown in Figure 1.11, into an open script file. You can also take Log actions and apply them to another open image or BatchList.

Most files generate a Log. Images and movies generate a Log as do BatchLists. Only scripts and SuperPalettes don't have Logs. You can access Logs by going under the **View** menu and selecting **Log**.

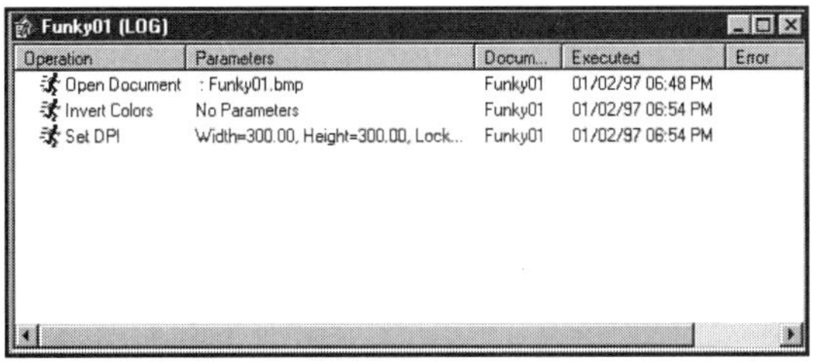

FIGURE 1.11

The Log window displays the size of your selection in pixels. It gives all the details of what you have done under the Parameters column.

Previous DeBabelizer Logs

In older versions of DeBabelizer you had a log, but it was not as integral a part of the program as it is now.

You can organize the Log window by clicking the column headings—Operation, Parameters, Document, Executed, and Error. You could, for instance, click the Operation header to sort the actions, and the Parameter column would then tell you the specifics of the action applied. For example, in Figure 1.11 the Log tells you that dpi was set to 300. The most important column in the Log is the Error column, which lets you know if something didn't work the way it should. This is especially handy for BatchList Logs. If you are running a script on a BatchList, knowing whether an action was carried out is an important proofing device.

19

Logs only record the changes that take place for each session. If you save the file and close it, when you reopen it, the Log will be clear. Only when you make changes will information register in the Log file. You can, however, save Logs as you work on a file. To do this, make the Log window active and choose **Save As** from the **File** menu. The default extension for a log file is .dbl and is automatically added to the filename. This is a excellent feature when you want to re-create the changes into the form of a script. You can also clear an active log file by right-clicking the mouse on the Log window.

Save As Access

By pressing the keyboard combination to Save while an active Log window is open, the Save As dialog box automatically comes up.

The Right Click

Right-clicking the mouse in DeBabelizer Pro for Windows gives you quick access to menus. A menu can change according to the files you have open. Figure 1.12 is an example of a right-click on an image window. You can also right-click movies, palettes, BatchLists, scripts, Logs, and SuperPalettes.

FIGURE 1.12

From this menu, you can quickly manipulate the image without using the main menus.

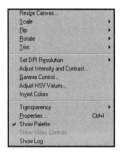

Opening Internal DeBabelizer Files

DeBabelizer Pro saves scripts, palettes, logs, and BatchLists as independent files, which can be opened up for tweaking. Because DeBabelizer Pro now saves the files individually, you have greater flexibility in storing them and using them again later. This is great for when you are moving from workstation to workstation or if you are working with other remote users.

Importing and Exporting

In addition to opening existing files or creating new files, DeBabelizer Pro can import and export files by using third-party Photoshop plug-ins. To do this, Adobe Photoshop must be installed on your computer. You also need to tell DeBabelizer Pro where the plug-ins are on your hard drive. You can tell DeBabelizer Pro where to find your Plug-ins folder by going into Preferences and choosing the Directories screen: **File/Preferences/Set Preferences/Directories**.

Exports and Imports

In DeBabelizer you can export palettes, scripts, catalog styles, and BatchLists and then import them back in at a later time or on a another machine.

Saving

DeBabelizer Pro enables you to save an image directly over itself. DeBabelizer Pro no longer assumes you are saving just to convert to another file format.

Saving Options

DeBabelizer Toolbox only lets you perform a Save As. You can, however, use Save As like a Save by not changing the file's name and it will replace the open file.

The **Save As** dialog box, shown in Figure 1.13, gives you the option to change a file's format as well as many other options.

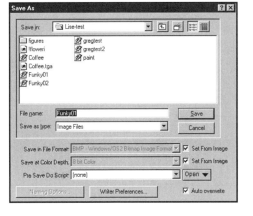

FIGURE 1.13

The Save As dialog box enables you to apply a script while saving.

From the **Save As** dialog box, you can change the filename of the image you are saving. The dialog box also tells you the current file format associated with the file. If you change the filename, you can tell it to keep the format and color depth it currently has by checking the "Set From Image" checkbox. If you want to change the format or color depth, you need to uncheck this box and then the pop-up menu becomes active.

DeBabelizer Pro lets you run scripts in a couple of different places. The **Save As** dialog box will let you run a script as you save the file. If you had a set script for a custom palette, you could apply it here.

Another option of the **Save As** dialog box is **Writer Preferences**. DeBabelizer Pro can modify the way certain file formats are written. Chapter 2 will explain writer preferences in more detail.

The Naming Options is grayed out in the **Save As** dialog because you are saving only one file. Later when you are batching lots of files, the Naming Options button is available to you. Both these options will be covered in more detail in Chapter 6, "Batch Automations."

TIP

If you save to a file format that requires fewer colors than the file format you are currently using, DeBabelizer Pro will automatically remap the image as you save. For example, if you are saving a Photoshop document to a GIF, it will convert it to 256 colors.

DeBabelizer Pro Preferences

Many of the option settings are automatically remembered by DeBabelizer Pro. If you quit and then relaunch the application, DeBabelizer Pro retains the settings from the previous session. Also, settings in one dialog box can affect the settings in another. Chapter 6 covers this in greater detail. To clear all settings, go to the **File** menu, select **Preferences**, and choose the **Factory Defaults** option. This automatically clears all personal settings you may have chosen and returns to the default program settings.

Figure 1.14 shows the **Preferences** dialog box. It has many options you can personalize to your own liking. Some of the options can be found elsewhere in the program as well.

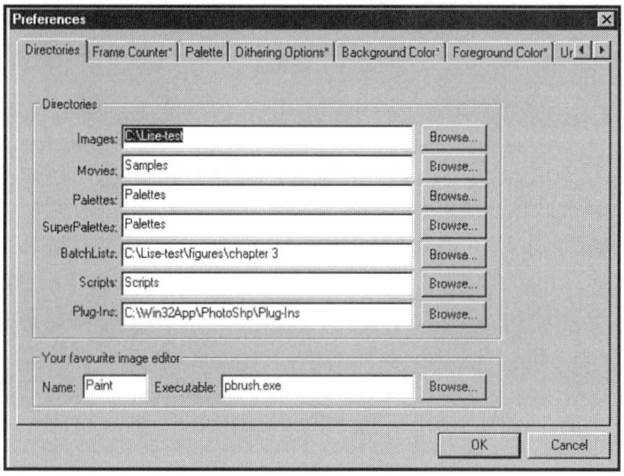

FIGURE 1.14

In the Preferences dialog box, the tabs with an asterisk are global settings.

22

The Preferences dialog box has 10 options you can change (certain options are covered in greater detail in later chapters). The 10 options under Preferences are:

- **Directories:** You can personalize the directories to which you save your files. DeBabelizer Pro automatically retains the name of the folder you last saved or opened by default until you specify a new destination. By clicking Browse, you can change the destination folder. This can be a handy tool if your company has a network directory structure it follows; you can have DeBabelizer Pro feed right into the directory structure. You can change the default folders for images, movies, palettes, SuperPalettes, BatchLists, and scripts. This is also where you tell DeBabelizer Pro to find your Photoshop plug-ins. Another important feature is designation of a default image editor, such as Photoshop. More will be explained about this in this chapter.

- **Frame Counter:** This is a global setting. When you are working with animations or movies you can designate the numbering of frames that make up the file. This is important when applying a filter to a series of images in a BatchList or several frames in a movie file. You can tell DeBabelizer Pro to count the frames and how to count the frames so that you get the results you want. Frame Counter is discussed further in Chapter 9, "Working with Digital Video and Animations."

- **Palette:** When creating Palettes the image is polled to find the most popular colors. You can adjust the bias DeBabelizer Pro will use to determine the most popular colors. Color selection is discussed further in Chapter 5, "Working with Palettes."

- **Dithering Options:** This is a global setting; once it is set here it affects other areas. You can tell DeBabelizer Pro how much dithering you want to apply to an image while it is being remapped to a palette. Dithering is a way to fake your eyes into believing a file has more colors in it than it does. You apply dithering to an image when you are reducing the number of colors it has. The default for DeBabelizer Pro for Windows is 87 percent. You can designate not to dither a background color, an important feature for images digitized on a blue screen. DeBabelizer offers two dithering methods or algorithms, *Albie* and *Diffusion*. Dithering Options is discussed further in Chapter 5.

- **Pad Color:** This is a global setting. The Pad color is the color that will be used when adding to your canvas size. For example, if you rotate an image and expand its bounds the Pad color will fill in the new canvas. You can designate a RGB, HSV, an index color, the background or foreground color, or the most popular color in a file as the Pad color. More on this Chapter 3.

- **Background Color:** This is a global setting. You can designate an index color or an RGB color as a background color. This is the color that will be used by the tools. More on this Chapter 3, "Working with Images."

- **Foreground Color:** This is a global setting. You can designate what will be used as a foreground color, which will be used by the tools. More on this Chapter 3.

- **Undo:** You can specify how many levels of undo are available. This is a great feature but requires a great deal of memory; the higher the number of undos you have, the higher the RAM must be to run the software. You have the choice of buffering the undos to virtual memory or to a local disk drive. You can also specify a directory path for the undo temp file. Having a large number of undos can slow your computer.

- **Palette Bar:** You can change the size of the Palette's color tiles. The size of the squares is measured in pixels. You can also choose to view the index numbers, but the box has to be big enough to see them. More on this in Chapter 5.

- **View Toolbars:** This is where you can decide which functions will have a custom toolbar button. You have a choice of having buttons for 12 different functions. You can't mix and match, unfortunately. This is discussed earlier in this chapter.

23

Launching Other Programs

As mentioned, you can launch your favorite image editing program directly from within DeBabelizer Pro. If you have Photoshop installed on your computer and have selected it as your favorite image editor under the Directories preference, you can

automatically launch Photoshop from **Tools** menu by selecting **Start Paint**. If you do
not have Photoshop, DeBabelizer defaults to standard Windows Paint program.

You can also directly access the Windows Explorer from within DeBabelizer Pro.
This enables you to access the directory structure and drag and drop the folders onto
an open BatchList or script. To do this, select **Start Explorer** from the **Tools** menu.
This is the quickest way to add an entire folder of images to your BatchList.

Printing

You can choose to print directly from DeBabelizer Pro, and the entire image or just a
selection can be printed. You can change the document's orientation by going into
Print Setup under the **File** menu.

Another handy feature is the capability to print a file's properties. You can do this for
images, movies, and palettes. Figure 1.15 is an example of an Image's Properties.
The filename and its DPI resolution, bit depth, and size are some of the included
options you can choose to print.

FIGURE **1.15**

*Keeping track of
an image's infor-
mation, especially
the version, is an
important part of
file management.*

If you were going to print a palette, the **Print Properties** dialog box would be full of
information regarding the Palette, such as its RGB or HSV values.

TIP

You can access the properties for images and palettes without printing them by
clicking the **View** menu and selecting **Properties**, or by using the keyboard
command Control-I.

Scripts and BatchLists have no properties. You can, however, print BatchLists.
Making prints of BatchLists can be a helpful tool for project management if you need
to have a paper trail to help in managing the project.

Attempting to print a script causes crashing problems at present, printing focus
should be limited to images, movies, logs, and palettes.

You can also print in a batch. DeBabelizer Pro renamed this a Batch Automation. From within the Batch Automation screen under the *Tools* menu, you can print images, BatchLists, and directories. Doing this kind of printing is discussed further in Chapter 6.

The final kind of printing you can do is printing a Log. You can print the Log of any file, palette, or BatchList. Figure 1.16 is an example of the print options available for printing a Log. Printing a Log is handy when you need to have an artist follow the steps you did to an image. It is also handy for figuring out how to get a script to do the work for you.

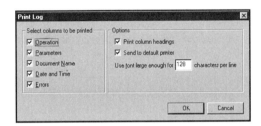

FIGURE 1.16

To double-check your work, you can print a Log, even if it's just to have a paper trail of its Document and Error entries.

25

Restoring a File

DeBabelizer Pro has two ways to restore a file after it has been manipulated. You can either use **File/Revert to Original** or use the Undo command. *Revert to Original* returns the document back to its previously saved status. Undo reverts the file to what it was before the last function was performed. How many levels of undos you set in your preferences determines how far back you can use undos.

I have found Revert to Original to be tricky. Unlike other program's reverts, DeBabelizer Pro's adds a twist. For example, suppose you save the image with a new name before making any changes to it. You then make some changes to the newly named file and decide you don't like them. If you select Revert to Original now, it reverts back to the Original image—not the image with the new name. You can tell by the name in the titlebar. This spin on Revert to Original only works if you do the renaming and image changes all in one session. Revert to Original is only available if you have made changes to an open file.

The second method of restoring a file is Undo. Undo works like any other program's undo function. DeBabelizer Pro also gives you the option to Redo your last change so that you can go back and forth between Undo and Redo for those non-committal types.

Cut, Copy, and Paste

DeBabelizer Pro handles copying and pasting like other programs. You can cut and paste an entire image or just a selection of it. If you copy a portion of an image and want to paste it into another, you can draw a selection in the destination image. The selection you are copying will line up to the upper-right corner of the selection marquee in the destination file. If what you are copying is larger than the selection, it doesn't matter. It will still line up to that upper-right corner and the entire copied selection will be pasted there.

Copying Selections & Color Depth

If you copy a selection from one file into another file, the selection will remap to the color depth of the image into which it is being copied.

To remove or cut a floating selection you can press Control-X to get rid of it. You can also press the Delete key or choose **Delete** from the **Edit** menu. If the selection is not floating, pressing the Delete key removes the active selection area without damaging the image below. If you use the Cut command, however, you will fill in the selection with your background color.

After a selection is pasted into the document, you can still manipulate it. As long as the selection is active, handles and all, you can skew or scale it by pulling on one of the handles. Once the outline is gone, it's part of the canvas and it's a permanent change. You can also affect the way it is pasted into by going to the **Transparency** submenu under the **Edit** menu.

File Conversions

As the computer industry continues to grow, the demands for true cross-platform compatibility also continue to grow. The digital world requires these different platforms to work together. With a program like DeBabelizer Pro, file formats from various platforms can be passed back and forth with much greater ease. It makes life much easier for anyone who has to get a project created on a Mac, with artwork created on an SGI, out the door in a PC-readable format.

DeBabelizer Pro can read and write in 90 or so file formats. These file formats include multiple platforms such as Macintosh, IBM, SGI, Unix, and Amiga. At this time, DeBabelizer Pro can only support RGB files. Support of CMYK files is anticipated in future versions.

Certain file formats that DeBabelizer Pro supports have extra dialog boxes of their own to offer additional options. For example, GIFs can be interlaced or non-interlaced, with or without background transparency. DeBabelizer Pro can open file formats that include still images, digital movies, and animations. DeBabelizer Pro is quite diverse in the formats it can process. Some file formats have specific requirements that need to be met in order to save a document into the format. Otherwise, you may not get the results you expect.

One of the most powerful functions of DeBabelizer Pro is that you can combine file conversions with a batch automation or a script. The power of DeBabelizer Pro lies in the grouping of these functions together.

Readers and Writers

DeBabelizer Pro gives certain file formats extra options for how they can be opened or read. You can tweak these files by going to the **File** menu and selecting **Preferences: Reader Preferences**. Figure 1.17 shows the dialog box for the Reader Preferences. For example, you could open up a PhotoCD file according to the resolution you want.

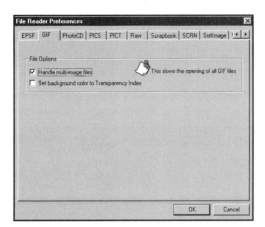

FIGURE 1.17

DeBabelizer Pro has a total of four different file types that you can tweak for reading.

27

DeBabelizer Pro enables you to modify the way certain files formats are written, in addition to the way the files are read. You can access this option via the **Save As** dialog box. It automatically brings up the preferences for the file format you are saving in. Not all file formats have a Writer Preference option. More information on Reader and Writer Preferences is in Chapter 2, "Working with File Formats."

Color Depth

DeBabelizer Pro offers many options for handling a file's color depth. Color depth basically refers to the colors and the number of colors used to create an image, movie, or animation. These colors are represented by a palette, as shown in Figure 1.10. Several standard palettes come with DeBabelizer Pro, including the Mac and Windows default color palettes, and the Netscape 216-color Web palette.

DeBabelizer Pro's color functions fall into two main categories with some crisscrossing. They are the color reduction of files and the creation or editing of palettes. The color reduction functions reduce the number of colors in the file. Creating or editing a palette enables you to create an index of the colors to be used. You can create a custom Palette or apply one of DeBabelizer's default Palettes to one or more files.

Color Reduction

Color reduction involves reducing the number of colors in a file or conforming an image or movie to a specific palette with fewer colors than the original file (remapping). Generally, you are taking a file that has a high number of colors (for example, a million colors) and converting it into fewer colors (256 colors). DeBabelizer Pro offers many ways to reduce the number of colors a file has. Figure 1.18 shows the different ways this can be accomplished. You can also convert RGB files into grayscale.

FIGURE 1.18

The top section of the menu is the different methods you can use to remove colors from an image. The bottom three sections are for creating or tweaking palettes.

28

Palette/Set Pixel Depth enables you to set a pre-defined bit depth automatically. For example, if you know you need to reduce the image to 8 bits you can select the 8 bits option under the submenu shown in Figure 1.19. These options enable you to apply dithering if you want.

FIGURE 1.19

A quick way to reduce a file's bit depth.

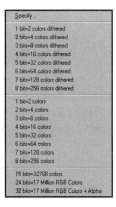

Using the **Set Pixel Depth** function does not enable you to apply a particular palette. It reduces the file based on the colors the file is already using. You can increase a file's bit depth, but it will not add color or information to your file. Choosing **Specify** enables you to fine-tune the Dithering Options and Background Color to be applied when changing the pixel depth and other options rather than going to the Preferences dialog box before selecting Set Pixel Depth.

To change the pixel depth and apply a defined palette, you should use the **Set Palette & Remap Pixels** option. You can visibly see the palette choices; any default and custom palette will be available to you. It will remap the colors in the file to the closest equivalent in the target palette.

Using the **Reduce Colors** function can reduce the number of colors in an image even further. Using it after setting your palette enables you to maintain the original base palette colors while reducing the actual number of colors in the file. This is useful when you are trying to reduce your file to smallest size it can be while maintaining color information. With Web graphics, for example, you want to have colors for interest but you want the file size to be small.

Grayscale and Black and White Images

You can also take files that are in RGB mode and convert them to grayscale. It works in the same way that changing a file's pixel depth did; you can convert the file according to a default value. Figure 1.20 shows the preset values you can choose under the **Convert to Grayscale** submenu of the **Palette** menu. Selecting the **Specify** option enables you to change the Dithering applied and Background Color.

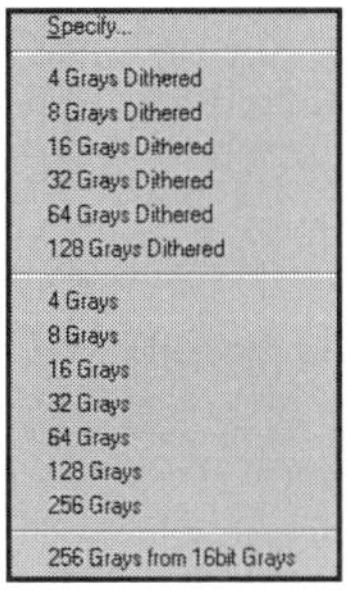

Specify...
4 Grays Dithered
8 Grays Dithered
16 Grays Dithered
32 Grays Dithered
64 Grays Dithered
128 Grays Dithered
4 Grays
8 Grays
16 Grays
32 Grays
64 Grays
128 Grays
256 Grays
256 Grays from 16bit Grays

FIGURE 1.20

A quick way of reducing a file to grayscale and applying a particular bit depth.

If you want to convert a 24-bit image to grayscale, you can adjust the Hue, Saturation, and Brightness values via **Image/Adjust HSV Values**. Using this function temporarily remaps the image to 8 bits so that you can see the adjustments you make in real-time. You can bring the Saturation level down to –255 to remove all the color. The file will be converted to grayscale. After applying this technique, the image is in 24-bit grayscale.

DeBabelizer Pro also gives you the option of converting files into Black and White in two methods: Black and White Dither or Threshold. Both options bring up an additional dialog box so you can apply the right levels of dithering for the desired effect.

What is great about these methods is that they are dynamic dialog boxes. As you apply the technique from its dialog box, you can see the changes happening to the open file simultaneously.

Faking Out Your Eyes

So you know DeBabelizer Pro can reduce colors and the word dithering has been thrown around a lot. Reducing a file's colors while making the file still look good is no easy feat. One of the ways to keep the image looking good is by dithering. Dithering is the ability to fake out your eyes. When you have an 8-bit image, which only has 256 colors to play with, dithering allows the image to look as if there are more colors than there really are. The program does this by placing adjacent colors next to each other in such a way that they actually look like there are more than just two adjacent colors. In other words, they blend to give the illusion of new colors. Dithering gives the appearance of shading and highlighting. You can notice dithering in a file if you zoom in really close or if you are working with a very low-resolution file.

The dithering options preference is available via **File/Preferences/Set Preferences/Dithering Options**. It controls the amount of dithering occurring in the palletizing or remapping of an image as well as the method of dithering used. After these options are set, whenever dithering is required, it will dither according to the preferences you have chosen. If you change the dithering options while creating a script, it will affect the dithering options globally. This is something that you always need to check because your preferences can mess up your scripts if you're not careful.

Creating Palettes

Creating palettes is one of the most impressive features of DeBabelizer Pro. A palette stores the colors used in creating an image. Some palettes include colors not used in the image because they are used in the computer's interface, which could be, for example, the first and last 10 colors in a Windows palette.

If you are going to be using a series of images to create a custom palette, you will want to consider *all* of the images to create the optimal custom palette; this kind of palette is known as a *SuperPalette*. You can create a custom palette for multiple images by using DeBabelizer Pro's SuperPalette function. DeBabelizer Pro can take a BatchList of images, analyze their color usage, and come up with the most common colors present in the series of images. You can decide how many colors are to be included in the palette, from 256 down. The custom palette is tweaked to perfection by using the many options DeBabelizer Pro has to manipulate palettes.

The method DeBabelizer Pro uses for constructing a palette is called polling. DeBabelizer Pro analyzes the image and takes a poll on the colors in the image and creates a palette based on the most popular "votes." If you are working with a series of files, these votes carry over from image to image. In the end, the votes are tabulated to find the most globally common colors used and those colors make their way into the custom palette.

Saving Palettes

In DeBabelizer Pro, you can save Palettes as independent files. They are like any other file and can be saved or reopened for later use. The extension used for palette files in DeBabelizer Pro is .pal. You cannot use palette files interchangeably with other programs.

To save a palette, you need to create one first. If you have an image open, which has a palette, you select **Create Palette** from the **Palette** menu. You automatically get a representation of the file's palette in the new palette window. You can save the palette and apply it later to other files. In DeBabelizer Toolbox, palettes are saved within the program interface. You can save palettes or stash them.

The hitch is that a file must already be indexed so that it has a palette associated with it. If, for example, you had a file that was in millions of colors, **Create Palette** would be grayed out.

31

Modifying Existing Palettes

Once a palette has been created, you can edit it or tweak it with the many options DeBabelizer Pro offers. You can apply a number of changes to a Palette. You can tweak the colors in the palette or just tweak the pixels attached to the palette color. Figure 1.18 is the menu options for working with palettes. Refer to the middle two sections of Figure 1.18, which offer ways to modify a palette's colors:

- **Remove Colors:** You can remove unused or repetitive colors from a palette. This is helpful when you are trying to optimize files for the Web.

- **Merge:** You can merge two existing palettes to create a new optimized palette. If you have two custom palettes that are ideal for two separate sections on a title, you can Merge them to create a hybrid palette.

- **Sort:** The Sort palette submenu has a number of options that you can apply to sorting a palette. It results in rearranging the tiles in the palette according to the type of sort you do. You can sort according to brightness or popularity, just to name a couple possibilities. This is a means of quickly Macintizing a Palette if need be. The Macintizing a palette will be explained further in Chapter 3.

You can also physically move a palette's colors around. If you right-click an image palette, you get the menu shown in Figure 1.21. You can manipulate the colors in the palette or the pixels in the image. These options can be toggled on and off by clicking the check mark next to them.

FIGURE 1.21

You can select colors in the palette to remap to its closest equivalent by selecting that option.

Image Manipulation

DeBabelizer Pro offers most of the basic tools that an image editing software package would include. These functions can be combined with batches or scripts to automate the manipulations. You can apply the editing functions to the entire file or to just a selection. These functions are available under the **Image** menu. For more information, see Chapter 3, "Working with Images."

Resizing the Canvas

Canvas size refers to the dimensions of the overall file. You can add to a file or cut from it, depending on the values you set in the Resize Canvas options window. A negative number will, in essence, crop the image. If you add to the image, you can tell it what color to use to pad the image. You can also decide where the padding will go.

Scaling Your Images

The Scale function enables you to resize an image. You can specify your own attributes or you can use a set of default proportions for quick changes. You can convert a file to have the Mac or PC aspect ratio, which can be handy for cross-platform projects. All of these options are convenient for adding to scripts.

Rotation

You can manipulate the image by rotating it. Rotation values in 90° increments are available, but you can set your own specified degree. You can rotate in a clockwise or counter-clockwise direction. You can also decide how the image boundaries react, either by cutting off at the image's boundaries or creating new boundaries to include the entire rotated image.

You can also use the **Flip** submenu to change your file. You can flip the image from left to right and from up to down. If you have text on an image, the left to right flip will make the text read backward.

Cropping and Using Trim

You can crop a file by using the Trim function, which crops the image according to the options you select. You can choose to trim to the active selection. Trim lets DeBabelizer Pro be more selective about how the image gets trimmed. The Trim function is more selective because it is based on the colors used in the file. For example, you can trim an image to its white edges. DeBabelizer Pro has several options for trimming an image. You will learn about the different ways of trimming in Chapter 3.

Selections and Transparency

You learned about selections earlier when the Selection tool was explained. DeBabelizer Pro uses the common commands for selecting all of the image (Ctrl-A) and deselecting (Ctrl-D), which is a nice carry over from other programs. Once you release the active selection, you're committed.

DeBabelizer Pro has a few options you can choose from when creating a selection. They are built around an absolute selection size and a relative selection size. You can also move the selection from within this dialog box.

You can further tweak the selection in various ways by using the Transparency options. The Transparency options affect the way a selection is pasted. DeBabelizer Pro offers a lot of options for how to affect the pasted selection. For example, you can make all pixels that are white become transparent in the selection. More on selections in Chapter 3.

Set Resolution

Resolution refers to the amount of dots or pixels in a file. For instance, if you choose 100 dpi, you get a file with 100 dots or pixels per inch. If you choose 300 dpi, it has 300 pixels per inch; the more pixels an image has the more detail available. DeBabelizer Pro handles resolution a bit differently than other image editing software. Only if the Lock Printing Size option is checked will the file's size increase when resolution is increased. If it is not checked then the file size will remain the same. Increasing the resolution increases the number of pixels in the file.

You can easily change the resolution of file within DeBabelizer Pro. As is usually the case, DeBabelizer Pro gives you a few popular choices, but you can still specify your own resolution if you need to. This is handy for writing scripts and doing Batch Printing. This function is useful to apply before you make print outs of your images. The image will not appear any different onscreen. DeBabelizer Pro handles resolution differently from other image editing software; only if Lock Printing Size is on will the pasting of the different resolution files be apparent. For example, if you were to paste an image at 100 dpi into another file that has been increased to 300 dpi, the pasted 100 dpi image would appear to be swimming in the 300 dpi image. Figure

1.22 is an example of this kind of paste. Once again, this only happens if the Lock Printing Size option is checked.

FIGURE 1.22

It is important to remember the dpi of an image when you are planning to execute a script involving images of different resolutions. Your pasting may have unexpected results if the Lock Printing Size option is enabled.

Tweaking Images Further

You can change other attributes an image has besides its size and dpi resolution. DeBabelizer Pro can adjust an image's brightness or levels.

The Adjust Intensity and Contrast function, for example, is similar to Photoshop's Levels Command, except you can also adjust the intensity (brightness), contrast, and the RGB values in one dialog box. It also shows you the adjusted palette for your image as you make the changes, which is a nice feature.

You can also Adjust the Hue, Saturation, and Value (brightness) values of an image. DeBabelizer Pro refers to Hue Saturation and Brightness (HSB) as HSV. Once again, you can see the adjusted palette as you make your changes.

Another way you can change your image's values is by choosing **Invert Colors**. This option works exactly the way it does in most image editing software. The opposite colors values of your original colors will be swapped with the image taking on the appearance of a negative.

Gamma

You can control the Gamma of your files, which is the amount of contrast found in the midtones of your image. Gamma affects the midtones without affecting the highlights or shadows. It gives the appearance of brightening an image. Often, when a movie has been created on a Mac and is seen on a PC, the files appear very dark. You can play with Gamma to help the movie look better. You can set DeBabelizer Pro to display according to a designated Gamma values and are given several options to choose from. Using positive numbers will brighten your image whereas negative numbers will darken an image. For those Gamma experts, you can even designate your own Gamma level by playing with the RGB graph.

Text Overlay

You can apply text to your images by using the *Text Overlay* function. Suppose you wanted to create a copyright with your name on the files you created. Text overlay enables you to place user-defined text over the image. You can specify where you would like to position the text, the color of the text, and the color of the background of the text box if you want one. If you don't want a background color, you can supply a transparency effect so that only the text shows. DeBabelizer Pro lets you choose the font and the font size according to what is loaded in your system. Figure 1.23 shows what the Text Overlay dialog box looks like so you can preview the text before committing to it.

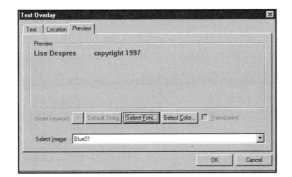

FIGURE 1.23

You can copyright your images with your name and the date.

35

Adding Third-Party Effects to Images

You can apply most third-party filters for Photoshop to images within DeBabelizer Pro. This is great for adding to scripts. It also enables you to add functionality that DeBabelizer Pro does not directly support, similar to the export and import functions.

What You Can Do to Channels

Every image displayed by DeBabelizer Pro contains three channels and is represented as red, green, or blue (RGB). Even grayscale images have RGB channels. All three channels combined gives us the image we see onscreen.

Each channel represents at the most 8 bits; that is how you come up with a 24-bit image (3 × 8 bits). A 32-bit image has four channels, the fourth channel being an alpha channel or mask. From the Image window, you can view each channel individually, including the alpha channel. You can also view the channels by selecting **Channels** under the **View** menu.

The **Channels** submenu enables you to manipulate the individual channels, RGB, or the alpha channel. You can also apply transparency options to specific channels to get different effects. You could load the alpha channel, or mask and then apply it to a batch of images. You could change the intensity and contrast of not only the image but apply all the different methods discussed to a particular channel.

Having Fun with Moving Images

All the image manipulations discussed here can be applied to multiple image files or animations, or AVI files. These file formats can be palettized and tweaked as well. They also have some things going for them that single-framed images don't.

Digital Video is represented by fields divided into even and odd lines. DeBabelizer Pro not only reads fields but gives you a chance to manipulate them. You can interpolate the fields if the digitized image comes in fuzzy. You can also swap out fields or apply changes to just the even or odd lines. (Still images also have fields.)

You can make sure that digital video going out to video has TV-safe colors by using the NTSC/PAL Hot Pixel Fixer function under the **Tools** menu. This prevents the image from running hot while playing on your TV screen by using the NTSC or PAL television standards.

You can remove images digitized against a blue screen by using the Blue Screen Removal function, also under the **Tools** menu. Blue screening is used mostly in special effects in which you want to composite one image over another. More on all of this is in Chapter Nine.

Batching

Batching has always been one of the most important features of DeBabelizer. The Batch processes enable you to automate certain functions, such as saving, to a series of images. Batching can be done while the computer is unattended.

DeBabelizer Pro comes with three categories of automated batch processes: SuperPalette, Save, and Print. There are variations of these as well. For example, you can create a SuperPalette and apply it to your images or just create the SuperPalette without applying. You also have a variation on the Save Batch Automation. You can just Save files or you can Save while a SuperPalette is applied. Doing an automated Save is a popular batch process; you can do file conversions into new file formats. You can also print out files in a batch run.

DeBabelizer pro offers other Batch Processes that are not offered under the Batch Automation menu. For example, **Create Movie** enables you to take a series of files and stuff them into one multiple frame file. DeBabelizer Pro also has the capability to set the compression and data rates. You can also export each frame of a movie file into a BatchList of the individual frames.

All of these batch processes require that a BatchList be created. A BatchList is a list of the files to be processed. BatchLists now are saved as independent files, so you can reopen them at later date to edit or reapply. The file extension for a saved BatchList is .dbb. Batch processes will be discussed in further detail in Chapter 6, "Batch Automations."

TIP

As you open a file you can automatically add it to an existing BatchList or create a new one, from the **Open** dialog box. Next to the **Add to Batch** button is the **Open** button. The **Add to Batch** button will be grayed out until you select a Batch List or create a new one.

In the Windows version, you can launch the Windows Explorer via the **Tools** menu. From the Windows Explorer, you can drag and drop entire folders of images to create your own BatchLists.

Scripting

Scripting is another powerful function of DeBabelizer Pro. It can be combined with a Batch Automation to automate several functions at a time, while being applied to a series of files. It has allowed us many a quick lunch when under a tight deadline.

Basically, a script is a customized list of tasks you tell DeBabelizer Pro to do automatically. Creating scripts is similar to creating a macro. You can create new scripts and edit existing scripts. You can also save them for future use. The best part is that like batch automations, scripts can be done unattended. For example, you could set the machine to run overnight.

Scripts can be created in three ways. You can go to the **File** menu and select **New Script** and start to create a script by using the dialog box shown in Figure 1.24. You could also select **Watch Me** under the **Script** menu (visible only when a script window is present and active—in other words, when its title bar is highlighted). **Watch Me** is a kind of tape recorder that records what you do as you physically pull down menus and click options and dialog boxes. DeBabelizer Pro records your actions and logs them into the script window. You can also create a script by dragging items from a file's or BatchList's Log. You see line by line the tasks the script is set to do. You can then tweak the script and save it for future use.

TIP

Remember you need to have either a BatchList or a script active (its titlebar must be highlighted) in order to see the **Batch** menu or **Script** menu.

FIGURE 1.24

Creating a script from scratch by inserting the commands available.

You don't need to overlap script functions with Batch Automations. For example, if you are going to dither a group of images, set the script to do that portion only. The Batch Save will handle opening and saving the files.

Scripts can include anything that you can think of that is a pull-down menu option. For example a script can include Photoshop filters, Readers or Writers—the list is endless. To run a script, select **Execute** under the **Script** menu and choose one of the Scripts listed. You can also drag and drop a script's ActionArrow™ onto an image and it will automatically execute it. You can also do this with a BatchList and it will remember how to save the file with a correct path name!

CHAPTER 2

Working with File Formats

DeBabelizer Pro can read and write over 90 different file formats including many image, animation, and digital video formats. Supported file formats include those used by various computer platforms such as Amiga, PC, Mac, Unix, and others, as well as proprietary file formats from companies such as Avid, Digital F/X, and Electric Image. (For a complete list of supported formats, see Appendix A, "File Formats Supported by DeBabelizer Pro and DeBabelizer Toolbox.")

DeBabelizer Pro is an indispensable tool for multimedia work. Often, artwork is created on one platform for manipulation in another, or created for viewing on a different platform. This cross-platform accessibility is one of DeBabelizer Pro's strengths. Even if a file format is not directly supported by DeBabelizer Pro, you can use third-party Photoshop Plug-ins to extend DeBabelizer Pro's capabilities.

Types of File Formats

Before discussing the files DeBabelizer Pro supports directly, a few words need to be said about file types. There are two types of graphic file formats: vector and bitmap. DeBabelizer Pro handles bitmapped file formats only; at the present time it does *not* support vector file formats. A Windows program that does support vector formats is Hijaak Pro by Quarterdeck.

Bitmaps

So what is a bitmapped file? A bitmap is a file containing a map or grid of bits that are represented by pixels. The pixels are arranged in such a way that as a group they give the illusion of form. Even though collectively the pixels give the illusion of form, you can still isolate and manipulate the pixels individually. Bitmapped files include information about the dimensions of the file, its resolution, bit depth, the color model it is using, and the type. Bitmaps are also known as raster files.

Most multimedia programs can only handle bitmapped graphics, so vector graphics need to be converted into bitmapped images before they can be manipulated in DeBabelizer Pro. Converting a vector file into a bitmap is called rasterizing a file. When you rasterize a file, it converts the vector file information into pixels. An example of rasterizing a file is when you open an Illustrator EPS file in Photoshop.

Vectors

Vector files, also known as object-oriented files, consist of lines, curves, and geometric shapes. You can combine these elements in layers. A vector file contains information about the attributes of these objects. An object, for example, can have a stroke or fill. Adobe Illustrator is an example of a vector file program. Basically, these objects have end points associated with them. DeBabelizer Pro can't read vector files.

Hybrids

Sometimes it is possible to have a hybrid of a vector and bitmap file format. An example of a hybrid file is an EPS (Encapsulated PostScript) file; EPS files include both vector and bitmap information. PostScript is a page description language telling the printer what to print, what the image will look like, and its attributes. An EPS file contains the vector or PostScript information *and* an embedded low-resolution bitmap of the vector image. DeBabelizer Pro supports bitmapped EPS files—but not vector EPS—created by programs such as Adobe Illustrator.

Compression

You can reduce the size of a file by compressing it. Different file formats use different compression algorithms and DeBabelizer Pro can read and write most of these algorithms. The file format you choose depends on the type of image you want to compress. Compression methods are usually categorized in two ways, Lossy or Lossless.

Lossless Compression

The Lossless method does as its name implies. Lossless compression enables you to compress a file in such a way that no information is lost. When the file is decompressed, it looks exactly like the original. Compression is an important factor to keep in mind. Often, limited storage space and quick access to files are required in different aspects of multimedia.

Two widely used forms of Lossless compression methods that DeBabelizer Pro can read and write are RLE (Run Length Encoding) and LZW (Lempel-Ziv-Welch). RLE breaks a bitmap down by colors. It clumps the colors in rows according to its grid. For example, a file using RLE compression would read 16 White, five Black to describe one row of a file's grid. LZW, on the other hand, scans the image and discovers trends occurring in the image and compresses it according to those trends.

A GIF file is an example of a Lossless compression format, as is a compressed TIFF. These formats lend themselves well to computer-generated and 3-D–rendered artwork.

Lossy Compression

Lossy compression throws out file information as it compresses it. An example of this is JPEG, or Joint Photographic Experts Group, the group that created the standard. Although it sounds scary to throw out information, JPEGs are used often and if used correctly, do a great job. By using JPEGs, you can choose the degree of compression, as shown in Figure 2.1. This helps you get the best image for the smallest size file and manually tailor the final results to your particular needs. JPEG is a compression method as well as a file format.

41

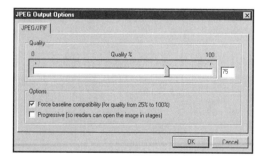

FIGURE 2.1

You can tell DeBabelizer Pro how much compression to use when saving in the JPEG format.

All of these compression formats are used in different circumstances. For instance, JPEG is used mostly for photographic, continuous tone images. It can also be applied to QuickTime movies. It is not as well suited for computer-generated images, such as animations. Figures 2.2 to 2.4 show what a computer-generated image looks like when saved using JPEG compression.

FIGURE 2.2

Computer-generated artwork.

FIGURE 2.3

The image is zoomed in to see what it looks like without compression.

42

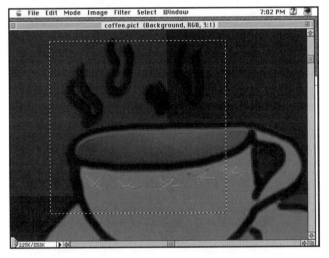

You will want to use a different compression method for different file types. File types often apply the compression that is best suited for them internally. For example, the GIF format uses a LZW compression method; as you are saving the file you are not made aware of this, it does it automatically.

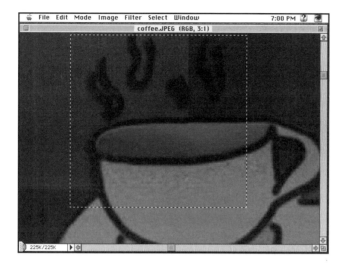

FIGURE 2.4

The image is saved using JPEG compression and you can see the image beginning to break up.

Pixel Packing

Another term you should be familiar with when discussing file formats is Pixel Packing, which is an efficient way to store bitmaps. It stores pixels into the free space of a byte and stored byte information may only take up half of the byte space. By using pixel packing, you can stuff more information into the remaining unused space. Pixel Packing is an efficient way of storing your file's information and is done seamlessly as you save your files. Pixel Packing is not connected to a particular compression algorithm—it is a form of data compression your computer uses to store the file's information.

Pixel packing is handled differently by PCs and Macs; the order of the pixels varies. The Mac reads pixel data from the left (highest order bit) to the right, meaning it reads the channels in the following order red, green, and blue. The PC, however, reads pixel data in the reverse. Knowing how your pixels are read is only pertinent to the Raw Reader Preference.

If, for instance, you have a file that cannot be opened by the conventional DeBabelizer Pro methods, you can try to open it as a Raw file. Playing with the setting in the Raw Reader Preference may help to open the file in the unknown format. Knowing which way the unknown file format stores its pixels is important when you try to retrieve the data.

NOTE

DeBabelizer Toolbox refers to Pixel Packing as PackBits.

43

File Format Constraints

It is good to know the requirements of the various file formats you will work with. File formats can require a certain color depth and can apply their own compression. For example, GIFs need to be in 8-bit or less color depth and use the LZW Lossless compression method. JPEGs can only be in 24-bit color or 8-bit grayscale and apply a Lossy compression. So if you have a photographic image you want to use on the Web, saving it as a JPEG would be best. Knowing what each file format can handle helps your format conversions run smoothly.

DeBabelizer Pro also automatically adds a default extension at the end of the file name according to the file format chosen (see Appendix A for a list of default file formats). Unfortunately, some of the default extensions have changed since DeBabelizer Toolbox. Figure 2.5 shows the **Save As** dialog box with the **Save in File Format** highlighted. Notice that the bit depth changes automatically as well. Figure 2.6 shows the scrolling list for bit depth for the GIF file format. For example, if the Set From Image option is checked in the Save As dialog box, the pull-down menu for Save in File Format is grayed out. DeBabelizer Pro automatically thinks you are going to maintain the same file format. Once you unmark the Set From Image checkbox, you can change the file format to GIF and DeBabelizer Pro defaults to 8-bit in the Save at Color Depth field.

44

FIGURE 2.5

If the Set From Image option is checked in the Save As dialog box, the Save in File Format, which here is highlighted, is grayed out.

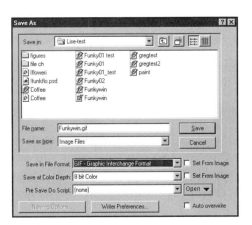

TIP

A complete list of the file formats supported by DeBabelizer Pro and DeBabelizer Toolbox can be found in Appendix A.

FIGURE 2.6

If another file format is chosen, the bit depth scrolling list would be different. Choosing to save as a Photoshop file format, for example, would display 24-bit color in the Save at Color Depth field.

Reader Preferences

DeBabelizer Pro can read and write many file types, but some formats DeBabelizer Pro can *only* read. The list of files that DeBabelizer Pro can read is in the Open File Type in the Open dialog box. The list of file formats DeBabelizer Pro can write to are under the Save as type submenu in the Save As dialog box. For a complete list of the files DeBabelizer Pro can read and write, see Appendix A.

DeBabelizer Pro enables you to tweak the way it can read and write certain file formats. You can change the way DeBabelizer Pro reads file formats by going to the File menu and selecting **Preferences/Reader Preferences**. You can only tweak the Reader Preferences for four supported file formats: Photo CD, Raw, SoftImage, and Wavefront files. Figure 2.7 shows the File Reader Preferences dialog box.

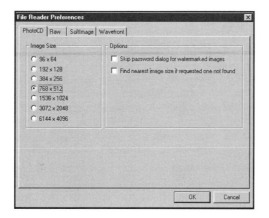

FIGURE 2.7

You can modify the Reader Preferences to open file formats to give you extra flexibility.

Reader Preferences adjust the way you can open a file. You can use the Reader Preferences to ensure that your images are read the way they should be. You can also use it to open files requiring more flexibility as in the example of PhotoCD images. Changing the settings of the Readers Preferences gives you added flexibility in opening these file formats. The following is a list of the Reader preferences available in DeBabelizer Pro.

- **PhotoCD:** PhotoCD is a proprietary file format created by Kodak to save images on a CD. PhotoCD images come in different sizes and resolutions. You can automatically set DeBabelizer Pro to open a particular size, ranging from 96 × 64, 192 × 128, 384 × 256, 768 × 512, 1536 × 1024, 3072 × 2048, and 6144 × 4096. If you are not sure what size and resolution your PhotoCD images are, you can have DeBabelizer Pro pick the closest size equivalent. Using this option is handy when batching involves PhotoCD images. You can also set the option to skip over the Password dialog box for watermarked images. Watermarked images require a password be given to remove the watermark.

- **Raw:** This is the simplest form in which an RGB image can be saved. The file contains the dimensions of the image and an uncompressed image. You need to tell DeBabelizer Pro the file's bit depth, bytes/pixel, image size, Palette info, channel order, and if the channels are interleaved. This file typically has an ASCII text header telling you the type of file and its dimensions. You can designate the file you want to open by opening it in the Raw Filename (see Figure 2.8). The file's size automatically appears next to its name. You can hit the Guess buttons for DeBabelizer Pro to guess the file's dimensions.

FIGURE 2.8

The File Reader Preferences for the Raw file format.

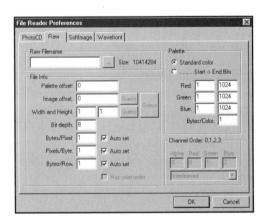

Pixel Packing was discussed earlier and comes into play in the File Reader Preferences dialog box. If you are dealing with a file that has more than one pixel per byte, you can enter in that information. This is a useful way to open files whose file format is uncertain. Playing with the different settings in this dialog box can assist you in opening the unknown file.

- **SoftImage:** SoftImage is a three-dimensional rendering program for SGI and Windows NT platforms. When SoftImage files are copied over a network, they can get corrupted by converting the file to text instead of staying in a binary mode. If your file has been corrupted, the carriage returns (CR) are swapped out for line feeds (LF). Your image will come in partially but will be coupled with garbage. DeBabelizer Pro enables you to protect the file from swapping out the CRs and LFs to prevent this. If the file has not been corrupted, you can check the Do not swap CR/LFs option.

- **Wavefront:** Wavefront is a three-dimensional software for SGI. Animation files can store multiple frames in one file. The way the frames are stored varies as well. Each frame can be saved in its entirety, or you can save only the portion that changes. Using this Reader Preference ensures the entire frame is loaded and not just the difference between each frame.

Using Reader Preferences gives you additional flexibility for specific file formats. For example, if you have a series of images that are on a PhotoCD, you may want to open up all the images at one particular resolution. You could write a script to open the files and convert them to another file format.

If you are having difficulty getting your Wavefront and SoftImage files to open up correctly, the Reader Preferences are good place to check. Changing the settings here can help you to open the file correctly. You can also use the Raw Reader Preferences to open up foreign files whose file format is unknown. You can play with the settings to see what will work. Using the Guess options in the Raw dialog box makes DeBabelizer Pro analyze the file to figure out what is in it.

TIP

You can also find the Reader Preferences directly in the Open dialog box.

Writer Preferences

DeBabelizer Pro enables you to modify the way certain file formats are written, but not all file formats have Writer Preferences. Most of the file formats offering Writer Preferences do so because the file format offers the option of compression. You will want to use the compression version of the file format when size is an issue. Other file formats give you more options. The following is a list of the Writer Preferences available to you and how you can set them:

- **BMP:** BMP file format offers you the option to compress the file using RLE compression or to leave it uncompressed. The color depth available for the file varies depending on whether you apply compression or not. As a compressed file, the color depth available is 4-bit or 8-bit.

- **EPSF:** You can save an EPS file as a grayscale or color file *without* previews. Saving without previews reduces the file size.

- **Digital Fx:** This file format supports being saved as either a TitleMan or VideoFx file.

- **FLI/FLC:** This animation file format can be saved with different frame rate options. You can also have the file loop. You can choose to save it either as a FLI or a FLC file format.

- **GEM:** You can save this file format either as grayscale or with fixed colors. If you save the file as a grayscale, it uses the GEM format. If you save the file with a fixed color palette, it uses the IMG format. The IMG format has a palette of only 16 colors, which are based on the file's colors.

- **GIF:** The GIF format can be written in a couple of different ways. The GIF file format can have just one image per file or many images per file as in an animation (GIF89). DeBabelizer Pro can write both formats.

  You can also give a GIF file a transparency setting. With the GIF Writer Preferences, you can assign the transparent color to be the background color, an index color, or the ULC—the color in the 0 position of a palette. Applying a transparency setting to GIFs enables you to create files with the appearance of an irregular shape. DeBabelizer Pro can also interlace the GIF format. Interlacing gives you the impression of the image coming into focus as it is opened or downloaded. It has a step-by-step, blocky appearance.

  In a GIF that has multiple images, you can specify the frame rate/seconds or seconds/frame. You are basically telling DeBabelizer Pro how quickly you want the animation to display the frames in the file. You can also set the Disposal Method. The Disposal Method is what happens to the frames as they play according to their frame rate. You can add Comments to each frame as well. Figure 2.9 is the dialog box for the GIF Writer Preferences.

- **IFF:** You can save an IFF file in various CD-I file formats (see Figure 2.10). You have several choices for CD-I formats, each depending on the CD-I player involved. You can also specify your own YUV settings. YUV is the native signal format of video compressed with MPEG or Indeo codecs. It takes up less space than RGB color space.

- **JPEG:** You were introduced to JPEG earlier in this chapter. Figure 2.11 is the dialog box for the JPEG Writer Preferences. You can indicate how much compression you would like to apply to the image by using the slide rule or entering in the value. The more compression you apply, the smaller the file, and the more information is thrown out. DeBabelizer Pro can also make the JPEG file progressive, similar to an interlaced GIF in appearance, so the image comes up in stages.

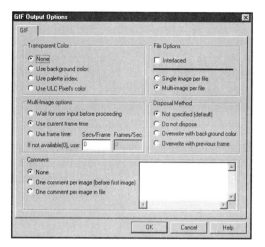

FIGURE 2.9

The Writer Preferences for the GIF format. You can create multi-image GIFs as well as the standard single image GIF.

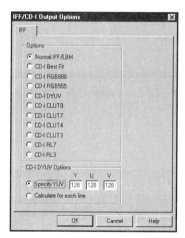

FIGURE 2.10

The different options for saving an IFF file.

49

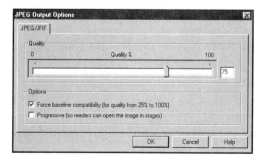

FIGURE 2.11

When saving in JPEG format, you can alter the amount of compression you want to apply.

- **PIC:** You can choose to save the SoftImage files as compressed or uncompressed.

- **Raw:** The simplest of image files. This file format can have an ASCII header that contains the image's dimensions and information. You can choose to write the image with or without this header.

- **SGI:** You can choose to save SGI file formats as compressed or uncompressed.

- **Targa:** You can choose to save Targa files as compressed or uncompressed.

- **TIFF:** The TIFF file format was first introduced as a scanning format by Aldus. TIFF is also a common file format for faxes. For this reason, you can choose to save TIFF files with CCITT (Comité Consultatif International Téléphonique et Télégraphique), the committee responsible for setting the standards for data communications.

Figure 2.12 shows the options you can choose from to write a document in the TIFF file format. The TIFF format can save in the Group 3 protocol, which is used for sending fax images over phone lines. DeBabelizer Pro can also write Group 4, which is the protocol for fax files sent over ISDN networks.

The CCITT, Group 3, and Group 4 versions of TIFF files are all 1-bit images. The standard TIFF format can be saved as a grayscale or color image. Whether you save the TIFF as a grayscale or color image, you have the options of saving it with no compression, lossless compression, or with Pixel Packing (PackBits). Depending on whether the file is for the Mac or the PC, if you select PackBits, you need to select the appropriate byte order.

FIGURE **2.12**

Numerous TIFF file formats are available in the Writers Preferences.

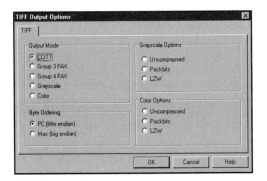

The Writer Preferences are good for allowing flexibility in saving files. You can change the Writer Preferences as you go and incorporate them into BatchLists and scripts.

File Extensions for Internal Files

Not only does DeBabelizer Pro support file formats for images, movies, and animations, DeBabelizer Pro can create its own files as well. You can create scripts, BatchLists, logs, palettes, and SuperPalettes and each of these file types has its own file extension. Unfortunately, these are not backward-compatible with DeBabelizer Toolbox. The list for DeBabelizer Pro files is as follows:

.pal   Palette
.dbp   SuperPalette
.dbs   Script
.dbb   BatchList
.dbl   Log

3

Working with Images

Before you can begin to fully utilize the graphics processing power of DeBabelizer Pro, you should familiarize yourself with some of the basic functions and image manipulation facilities of the program. Besides the concepts of opening, saving, cutting, and pasting, this chapter covers editing tasks such as cropping, rotating, resizing, and setting dpi resolution—functions that can be found grouped together under the **Image** menu. These functions provide some of the basic capabilities of DeBabelizer for image editing but will nonetheless become highly useful to you. You might be able to effectively execute the same operations in other image editing programs, but DeBabelizer Pro offers some unique and productivity-enhancing capabilities, making it an excellent tool even for the more basic image editing functions you need to perform.

The areas this chapter covers include the following:

- Different methods of opening an image

- The Open Image dialog

- Setting reader preferences

- Selecting, cutting, copying, and pasting

- Flipping and rotating an image

- Scaling an image

- Resizing the canvas and trimming (cropping) an image

- Adjusting image resolution

- Adjusting image colors

- Adjusting gamma and gun controls

- Working with channels, masks, and overlays

- Image fields

- Saving an image

- Setting writer preferences

Opening an Image

One of the most basic functions in DeBabelizer Pro is opening an image, which is naturally a precursor to working with one. The easiest way to open an image is by using the **File:Open** command to bring up the **Open Image** dialog box (see Figure 3.1). This dialog box gives you a number of options to facilitate opening and working with images in addition to allowing you to preview the image before opening it. The first option is file filtering, which enables you to scan only for files of a particular type in the dialog box's listing of available files. You can, for example, choose to display only GIF files in the file list area, making it much easier to select a specific file type in a very large directory with numerous different kinds of available files. File filtering is accessible via the field labeled Files of type: in the Open Image dialog box. Simply choose the desired file type by pulling down the menu and scrolling the list to select the desired format.

FIGURE 3.1

The Open Image dialog box set to filter for GIF files.

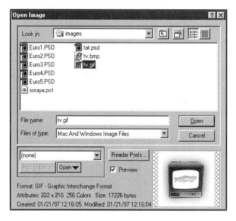

A second option is the capability to add the file to a BatchList directly from the Open Image dialog box. BatchLists are one of the most important and powerful components of DeBabelizer. A BatchList is a list of files, which you can treat as a single file by automatically applying the same operation(s) to every file in that list. The batch field displays a scrollable list of all currently open BatchLists; if none are open, the window will indicate (none). You can create a BatchList by selecting New from the pulldown menu. Then to add files, simply select the file and click the Add to Batch button to add to the BatchList. For more about BatchLists, refer to Chapter 12, "Batch Processes."

As with most functions in DeBabelizer Pro, there are numerous ways of accomplishing the same action. You will encounter this continually as you familiarize yourself with the program. Opening images is an excellent example—there are four basic methods of opening a file. The method you choose depends on which you find most convenient and best suits your needs. The following is a list of ways you can open images in DeBabelizer Pro:

- Using the Open Image dialog box

- Dragging and dropping an image from the Windows Explorer

- Opening an image from a BatchList window by double-clicking the image name

- Opening an image via a script command

Dragging and Dropping an Image from the Windows Explorer

The Windows Explorer in Windows 95/NT is directly accessible in DeBabelizer Pro under the **Tools** menu by choosing **Start Explorer**, or you can launch it from the operating system via the Windows Start button. DeBabelizer Pro fully supports drag and drop to and from the Explorer window. To open a file from the Explorer, simply drag it anywhere on top of a DeBabelizer Pro window and the file automatically opens in a new window. DeBabelizer Pro also directly supports adding images and image folders to BatchList windows via drag and drop from the Explorer.

Opening from a BatchList

To open an image directly from a BatchList window, double-click the file name in the BatchList window.

Opening an Image via a Script Command

Images can also be opened via script commands. Scripts allow further automation of DeBabelizer functions and are fully customizable. Dragging an Image Open command from a log window to a script window, for example, creates a Script command to open the image. You'll learn more about scripts in Chapter 7, "Scripting."

Setting Reader Preferences

Setting the Reader Preferences enables you to determine how DeBabelizer Pro reads certain file types. Currently, Reader Preferences are available for four types of file formats: PhotoCD, Raw, SoftImage, and Wavefront. You can access the **Reader Preferences** directly in the Open Image dialog or by opening the Preferences window under **File:Preferences:Reader Preferences**. Click the appropriate tab to access the Reader Preferences for that file. The dialog boxes provide you with numerous custom options for reading each file type listed.

Selecting, Cutting, Copying, and Pasting Images

Selecting, cutting, copying, and pasting images and image areas are basic functions with which you may be familiar. DeBabelizer Pro, however, allows some special capabilities that make for greater precision and helps facilitate these operations further.

Making Selections

Most of the image manipulation operations in DeBabelizer Pro are applicable to both an entire image or to portions of it. To apply an operation to a portion or area of an image, you must first select the area. This section covers the methods of making and defining selection, and the various additional options that facilitate creating and working with selections.

The easiest way to select an area of an image is with the Selection Marquee tool, which is the default tool in the Paint Tools toolbar and looks like a tiny marquee. By activating this tool (clicking it), you can make rectangular selections in the image window the same way you do in many other programs, by dragging the Selection Marquee to the desired size and shape. Square selections can be made by holding the Shift key down just before you make your selection, and keeping it down until you are done.

After you have created your selection, you'll notice that the Selection Marquee in the image now has eight black "handles" along the perimeter of the marquee (see Figure 3.2). These handles are used to resize the selection. Resizing selection areas is covered in the next section.

Figure 3.2

A selection has been applied to an image using the Selection Marquee tool. Drag one of the black handles to resize the marquee.

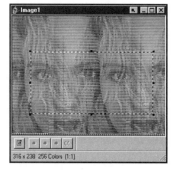

Another way to define a selection is by using the Select option (accessible under the **Edit** menu). This calls up the Select dialog box, shown in Figure 3.3, where you can enter precise numeric values to define your selection. This can be extremely useful if you have to make the same pixel selection over and over to a series of images. In the Select dialog box, numeric values are entered either as Absolute or Relative. Absolute values enable you to define the selection boundaries as the distance in pixels from the top, left, bottom, and right sides of the image. Relative values enable you to define the distance of each boundary relative to the *current* selection.

FIGURE 3.3

The Select dialog box showing options for entering precise numeric values for a selection.

57

The Select dialog box also enables you to select All or None of an image, or you can use the keyboard commands Ctrl+A for All and Ctrl+D for None. These functions are particularly useful when constructing scripts. You can also perform a select None by clicking the mouse outside of the Selection Marquee, pressing the Delete key, or choosing Delete from the **Edit** menu.

Moving and Resizing the Selection

There are several ways of moving and resizing a selection marquee. The easiest way to resize the selection is to move the cross-hair over one of the handles, at which point it becomes a two-pointed arrow. Click and drag the handle to resize the selection as desired. To maintain the same aspect ratio, hold the Shift key down while dragging. The same is true for moving the selection. Hold the cursor over the selection until it becomes a four pointed arrow, then click and drag the selection to the desired location. The Selection Marquee moves while retaining its size. Of course, you can use the Select dialog box to accomplish both of these tasks with even greater precision.

The Resize Absolute and Relative options work the same way as the Select Absolute and Relative options, presenting input values for top, left, bottom, and right (refer to Figure 3.3). The Move Absolute and Relative options differ only in that they prompt for Up/Down and Left/Right values. Selecting Move Absolute moves the selection to the absolute pixel positions you set; a negative number moves the selection beyond the boundaries of the image. Selecting Move Relative uses positive values to move down or to the right, and negative values to move up or to the left.

The last two options in the Select dialog box are Select Float and Select Stamp, which are similar to cut, copy, and paste. The Select Float option generates what is called a floater from the selected pixels. A *floater* is basically a pasted selection that "floats" above the current image without affecting the underlying pixels. A floater can be moved anywhere in the image and the pixels underneath the floater remain untouched until the area is deselected or the Select Stamp option is invoked. You can also create a floater by holding the Control key down when you move a selection marquee using the mouse.

Cutting, Copying, and Pasting

Cut, copy, and paste in DeBabelizer Pro work much like they do in many other image editing programs. The standard cut, copy, and paste keyboard commands work in DeBabelizer Pro: Ctrl+X (cut), Ctrl+C (copy), and Ctrl+V (paste). In addition, you can use the corresponding buttons in the Edit Commands toolbar to perform these same functions; just look for the group of three icons starting with a scissors (Cut).

By cutting an area out of the image, you fill the selected area with the current background color and copy the contents to the Clipboard. You can accomplish the same thing without copying the contents to the Clipboard by selecting Clear from the **Edit** menu. Cut permanently removes the pixels in your selection.

Pasting an image essentially creates a floater, and whether you have a selection active at the time you paste can affect pasting behavior. Performing a paste operation while there is an active selection places the contents of the paste in the same location as the selection, creating a floater that preserves the underlying pixels. If there is no active Selection Marquee, the pasted item is positioned at the most recently selected pixel in the image. If there is no recently selected pixel, the pasted image is positioned in the center of the image window.

Flipping and Rotating an Image

DeBabelizer Pro enables you to easily flip and rotate images. Flipping an image provides a mirror of the image on an either vertical or horizontal axis, as show in Figure 3.4. You can flip an image using the **Flip** submenu under the **Image** menu; or you can use the corresponding icons in the Image commands toolbar, if you have it turned on in your toolbars preferences. DeBabelizer Pro enables you to flip an image or selection area in either a left to right or top to bottom direction.

FIGURE 3.4

This figure illustrates three images. The first is the original, the second has been flipped top to bottom, and the third flipped left to right.

The Image Commands toolbar also provides icons for rotating your image by calling up the Rotate dialog box. Choosing Rotate directly from the **Image** menu enables you to rotate the image in 90°, 180°, or 270° clockwise increments bypassing the dialog box; you can also choose Specify to choose another angle, which also brings you to the Rotate dialog box.

After you open the Rotate dialog box, you are presented with four tabbed options, as shown in Figure 3.5. The main option is General, where you dictate the degree of rotation and whether it is to occur in a clockwise or counter-clockwise direction. You also determine how the bounds of the image are affected. Selecting Expand rotates the image without cropping it. Selecting Same Size retains the image size and thus crops the image as it changes its position in the image window. Both options are illustrated in Figure 3.6.

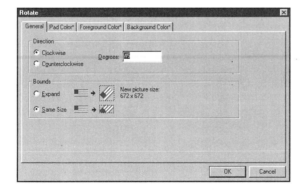

FIGURE **3.5**

The Rotate dialog box.

FIGURE 3.6

The original image and the results of applying the Expand bounds option and the Same Size option from the Rotate dialog box.

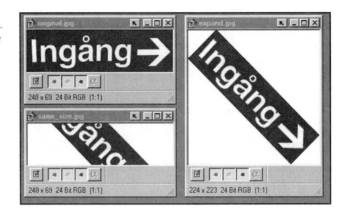

When you rotate an image enough degrees, you often create empty areas in the image as the selection is rotated; the empty areas have to be filled with a single color, which DeBabelizer Pro refers to as a pad color. Figure 3.7 shows the Pad Color* tab for the Rotate dialog box. Remember that the asterisk means that this is a global option.

To define a pad color, choose one of the available options, all of which provide previews in the box to the far right. The first option enables you to input your own RGB color using RGB or HSV values, or by picking up a color from Color Picker rainbow. After you pick a color, you can lighten or darken it using the slider to the right of the rainbow picker. The Palette index brings up the current image's palette, enabling you to choose any of the colors in the current palette as a pad color. To choose the current foreground or background colors, choose one of the next two options. If you don't like the current foreground or background colors, you can change them without exiting this dialog box by selecting the Foreground or Background Color* tabs and modifying them. To choose the color most commonly used in the image for your pad color, select the Most popular color option.

FIGURE 3.7

Defining a pad color when rotating an image.

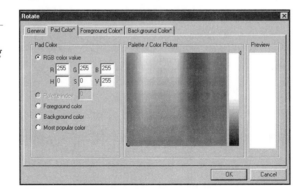

Scaling an Image

DeBabelizer Pro's scaling functions enable you to reduce or enlarge an image by a specified amount. Unlike many image editing programs however, DeBabelizer Pro gives you a comprehensive list of options beyond simple reduction and enlargement, making it one of the best tools available for image scaling.

Scaling is accomplished through the Scale dialog box accessible under the **Image** menu or by clicking the scale icon in the Image Commands toolbar. All scaling operations can be performed on the entire image or only to a selected area of an image. Choosing Scale from the **Image** menu provides eight submenus with the preset automatic scaling values described below.

Preset Scaling Options

DeBabelizer Pro provides several common predefined scaling values built into the **Scale** menu for quick and easy access:

- **Half Size:** This command automatically reduces the height and width of the image by 50 percent, maintaining the current aspect ratio.

- **Double Size:** This command automatically increases the height and width of the image by 200 percent, maintaining the current aspect ratio.

61

- **Half Horizontal:** This command will reduce the width of the image by 50 percent while leaving the height the same. It does not maintain the image's aspect ratio and produces an image that appears to be stretched vertically.

- **Half Vertical:** This command reduces the height of the image by 50 percent while leaving the width the same. It does not maintain the image's aspect ratio and produces an image that appears to be stretched horizontally.

- **Double Horizontal:** This command increases the width of the image by 200 percent while leaving the height the same. It does not maintain the image's aspect ratio and produces an image that appears to be stretched horizontally.

- **Double Vertical:** This command increases the height of the image by 200 percent while leaving the width the same. It does not maintain the image's aspect ratio and produces an image that appears to be stretched vertically.

- **PC to Mac Aspect Ratio:** Pixels on Windows monitors are sometimes taller than they are wide, whereas Macintosh pixels tend to be square. This inconsistency sometimes results in images that look distorted when transferring between the two platforms. Images created on a PC that look distorted on a Mac benefit from this command by converting from the PC aspect ratio to the Mac aspect ratio by reducing the width of the image by 83 percent.

- **Mac to PC Aspect Ratio:** Images created on a Mac that look distorted on a PC benefit from this command by converting from the Mac aspect ratio to the PC aspect ratio by reducing the height of the image by 83 percent.

If none of the preset scaling options fit your needs, you can select **Specify** from the **Image:Scale** submenu or simply go straight to the Scale dialog box by clicking the scale icon in the toolbar to bring up the dialog box shown in Figure 3.8.

FIGURE 3.8

The Scale dialog box offers a comprehensive list of scaling options.

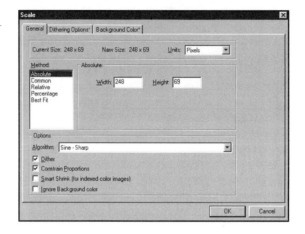

Scaling Methods

The Scale dialog box enables you to define custom parameters for your scaling operations. The first option is your choice of measurement units, offering pixels, inches, centimeters, millimeters, picas, or points as units of measurement. Notice that changing the measurement units affects the values of the Current Size and New Size directly to the left of the Units pull-down menu.

The next option is the Scaling Method. There are five choices:

- **Absolute:** This method enables you to specify the new height and width of the image or selection using absolute values. If you want to constrain the image's proportions (maintain the same aspect ratio), be sure to check the option marked Constrain Proportions in the Options area of this dialog box. This applies to all of the other method options as well.

- **Common:** This method presents a drop-down list of common image sizes (8 × 10, 4 × 5, 8.5 × 11, and so on) as predefined values.

- **Relative:** This method enables you to increase or decrease the width and height by relative amounts. For example, choosing a width of 1 and a height of 1 would increase a 4 × 5 image to a new size of 5 × 6. You can use negative numbers to reduce the dimensions.

- **Percentage:** This method enables you to specify a percentage value for scaling your image.

- **Best Fit:** This method automatically determines the best size, based on the size of the image's canvas, while maintaining the current aspect ratio.

Scaling Options

The Scale dialog box provides a number of options for determining how DeBabelizer Pro scales an image in the area of the window labeled Options. The first option enables you to choose a scaling algorithm from the Algorithm pull-down menu. You can experiment to find which of the seven algorithms produces the best results, or you can use the default setting. For most operations, the differences between running the different algorithms are quite subtle, but experimentation and your own subjective analysis are the best ways to judge.

- **Sine-Sharp:** This setting is the default. It produces the sharpest image but can create ringing around enlarged images. It is recommended for helping to retain thin lines in an image when reducing.

- **Cubic-Smooth:** This algorithm is a compromise between the Sine-Sharp and B-Spline methods. It is better suited for reducing images.

- **B-Spline-Smooth+Blur:** This option produces a smoother image with a noticeable degree of blur.

- **Bell-Smoother:** This option also produces a smooth image; it can cause some blurring, though less than the B-Spline method.

- **Box-Jaggy:** This option avoids the blurring caused by smoothing but produces a jaggy result. It is better suited for high detail images.

- **Averaging for Shrink, Simple Sample for Grow:** This method is the fastest for scaling and provides decent scaling results, though not as sharp as the default method.

- **Simple Sample-Jaggy:** This option is similar to the Box-Jaggy method but processes more quickly.

After selecting the appropriate algorithm, you have four more options, which you can check or uncheck to apply:

- **Dither:** This option instructs DeBabelizer Pro to automatically apply dithering during the scaling operation, using the current dithering settings. You can modify the dithering setting by clicking the Dithering Options* tab in the Scale dialog box.

- **Constrain Proportions:** This choice maintains the aspect ratio of the image when turned on. Changing the value of the width or height individually automatically changes the other value to maintain the aspect ratio.

- **Smart Shrink (for indexed color image):** This option is best for reducing images with 256 colors or less.

- **Ignore Background color:** This option is best used when scaling an image with a solid background color and results in a sharper image. Turning on the option avoids anti-aliasing the edges of the image against the background color

63

resulting in color blurring between the object and its background. Make sure that your background color tile is defined as the same background color in your image for this option to work properly. You can change the background color by clicking the Background Color* tab in Scale dialog box.

More Options

Dithering options for scaled images are accessible by clicking the Dithering Options* tab in the Scale dialog box. Normally, turning the dithering on utilizes the current dithering settings. To modify the current setting without leaving the Scale dialog box, click the Dithering Options* tab. You can specify the amount of dithering in percentages, toggle between Albie and Diffusion methods, and avoid dithering background colors.

You can also change the background color without leaving the Scale dialog box by clicking the Background Color* tab. You can choose an RGB color or specify a color from the current palette for your background color.

Resizing the Canvas and Trimming (Cropping) Images

You increase the size of the image canvas by adding space around the current image without actually scaling it up. This is the opposite of trimming or cropping, where you decrease the image dimensions without scaling the image. If the new size of the image is specified as larger than the current image, DeBabelizer Pro increases the canvas by padding the image. If the new size is smaller, DeBabelizer Pro crops the edges of the image.

Figure 3.9 shows the Resize Canvas dialog box, accessible under the **Image** menu or from the Image Commands toolbar. This dialog box is similar to the Scale and Rotate dialog boxes discussed previously. In addition to the General options tab, this dialog box offers settings for Pad Color*, Foreground Color*, and Background Color*. These tab settings work exactly as they do in the Scale and Rotate dialog boxes. The only differences are in the General tabbed options.

In the Resize Canvas dialog box General options, there are five methods for resizing the canvas. Notice, though, the inclusion of placement grids and left, top, right, and bottom input windows. Also, make note that despite the name of the command, this function only resizes the canvas if no part of the image has been selected with the Selection Marquee. If there is an active Selection Marquee before choosing this operation, only the area within the marquee is resized.

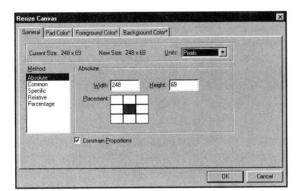

FIGURE 3.9

The Resize Canvas dialog box.

Resizing Methods

You have the option of maintaining the current aspect ratio of the image or selection with the following methods by checking the Constrain Proportions checkbox:

- **Absolute:** This method enables you to specify the dimensions of the entire canvas or selected image area. The placement grid functions exactly as it does in Adobe Photoshop. The dark square in the grid represents the location of the original image in relation to the padding or cropping after the canvas is resized. You can change the placement by clicking in any of the nine squares (refer to Figure 3.9).

65

- **Common:** This method enables you to choose a number of predefined sizes from a drop-down menu. It also utilizes a placement grid for determining image padding/cropping.

- **Specific:** This method enables you to specify numerically the amount to pad or crop from each of the Left, Right, Top, and Bottom edges. The numbers in the inside of the box represent the height and width of the image, based on the values you provide in the four windows (see Figure 3.10).

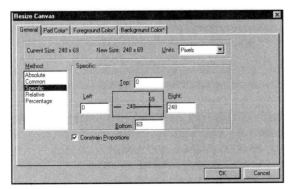

FIGURE 3.10

The Resize Canvas dialog box with the Specific method chosen.

- **Relative:** This method enables you to specify relative numerical values by which DeBabelizer Pro expands or contracts the image. Positive values increase the canvas size; negative values trim the canvas size (see Figure 3.11).

FIGURE 3.11

The Resize Canvas dialog box with the Relative method chosen.

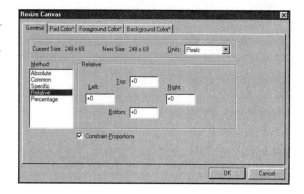

- **Percentage:** This method enables you to specify percentage values for resizing the canvas. Values in excess of 100 percent expand the canvas, while values of 99 percent or less trim the canvas. A placement grid is provided for determining the relation of the original image to the new canvas boundaries (see Figure 3.12).

FIGURE 3.12

The Resize Canvas dialog box with the Percentage method chosen.

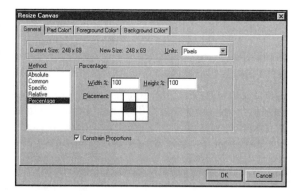

Trimming Commands

Trimming operations are available by choosing Trim from the **Image** menu and are essentially the same thing as cropping. Trimming an image is a form of resizing the canvas except that it involves cutting away portions of the image rather than adding to it. You can apply the trim operation to a selected portion of an image or to the entire image itself. There are six trim commands available from the **Trim** submenu (see Figure 3.13).

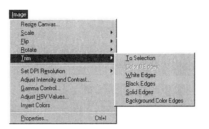

FIGURE 3.13

The six trimming options available from the Trim submenu of the Image menu.

- **To Selection:** Use this command to remove all parts of the image outside the Selection Marquee. This command is only available when there is a currently active selection.

- **Color 0 Edges:** This command only works with indexed color images (256 colors or less). Selecting this command trims the image to the smallest bounding rectangle that doesn't include the color at palette index 0.

- **White Edges:** This command crops the image to the smallest bounding rectangle that doesn't include white. It can be used to remove unused white space from around an image.

- **Black Edges:** This command crops the image to the smallest bounding rectangle that doesn't include black. It can be used to remove unused black space from around an image.

- **Solid Edges:** This command crops the image to the smallest bounding rectangle where every edge remains the same color.

- **Background Color Edges:** This command crops the image to the smallest bounding rectangle that doesn't include the background color. It can be used to remove unused background color space around the image.

67

Adjusting Image Resolution

Adjusting image resolution is an important component of image editing. Image resolution refers to the spacing of image pixels or dots, generally described in terms of dpi (dots per inch) or ppi (pixels per inch). Image resolution is distinct from image size, which refers to the physical dimensions (width and height) of an image. Together, image resolution and image size determine the file size of the image or the amount of memory it occupies. Because image resolution, image size, and file size all maintain a direct relationship, raising or lowering any one of these affects one or both of the others. Unlike vector images, raster images are resolution dependent. Consequently, the higher the resolution of the image, the greater the detail and the apparent quality of the image.

It is important to understand the differences between monitor resolution and image resolution. Regardless of the actual resolution of your image, you can alter the resolution that your computer monitor uses to display the image, because it also uses a grid of dots for display. Changing the resolution setting affects how large or small the image displays on your screen but does not effect the actual resolution of the image. A monitor with a high resolution setting displays images smaller than a monitor with a lower resolution setting.

You can set or change the resolution of your image via the Set DPI Resolution submenu under the **Image** menu or the Set DPI Resolution dialog box, accessible from this same submenu. You can also click the appropriate icon in the Image Commands toolbar. If you are not sure of the current resolution of your image, you can always check the image properties by calling up the Image Info window (see Figure 3.14). There are several ways to call up the Image info window: selecting Properties from the **View** menu, pressing Ctrl+I on the keyboard, or right-clicking the image and selecting Properties from the pop-up menu; this is the easiest way.

The quickest way to change your image resolution is from the **Set DPI Resolution** submenu in the **Image** menu. Here you have several common predefined image resolutions ranging from 72 to 300 dpi that can be quickly applied by selecting them in the menu.

FIGURE 3.14

The Image Info window gives you information about the current image parameters.

The first six settings in the submenu affect the final printed dimensions of your image, while the next six include scaling, which automatically scales the image to maintain the current print size and applies dithering based on the current dithering options settings. You can choose your own custom settings by either choosing Specify in the Set DPI Resolution submenu or by directly entering values into the Set DPI Resolution dialog box (see Figure 3.15). This dialog box displays the current dpi setting and enables you to manually enter the new settings.

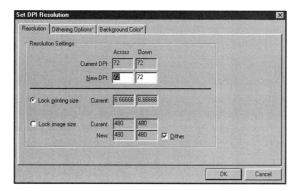

FIGURE 3.15

The Set DPI Resolution dialog box enables you to change the image resolution.

When changing these settings you have the option to lock the printing size or the image size. Remember that these values all have direct relationships. Locking the printed size requires you to change the image size settings to alter the dpi, while locking the image size requires you to change the printed size of the image to change the dpi. The dialog box also provides the option to change the dithering options via the Dithering Options* tab. The image resolution that you choose ultimately depends on how you intend to use your image. Generally, images that are meant strictly for screen display work best at around 72 dpi. Images intended for professional printing applications usually require a much higher resolution.

69

Adjusting Image Colors

DeBabelizer Pro enables you to modify the color parameters of an image by altering the HSV values of the image pixels or by adjusting the overall intensity and contrast of the image or individual image channels. These adjustments can be made to either the entire image or to only a selected area by using the selection marquee.

Adjusting HSV Values

You can modify image color by manipulating the HSV (hue, saturation, and brightness) values through the Adjust HSV Values dialog box accessible under the Image menu or by clicking the appropriate icon in the Image Commands toolbar. Either of these commands brings up the dialog box illustrated in Figure 3.16.

Figure 3.16

The Adjust HSV Values dialog box enables you to alter the hue, saturation, and brightness of an image or selected area.

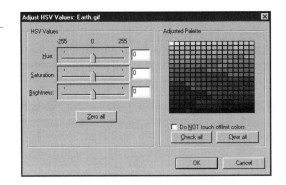

The Adjust HSV Values dialog box displays three sliders for controlling the amount of hue, saturation, or brightness in the image. If the image is indexed, you also see the image's palette displayed in the Adjusted Palette area of the dialog box. The image being modified also updates dynamically as you adjust these values. The Adjusted Palette area also enables you to designate off-limit colors, or colors that can be protected from modification when you change the HSV values. This option is useful if you only want to modify a specific color or range of colors in the palette and is only available for indexed color images. You'll learn more about indexed palettes in Chapters Four and Five.

Designating Off-limit Colors (Indexed Color Images Only)

If you want to protect some of the colors in your indexed image from shifting, you can designate them as off-limits. To designate a color or range of colors as off-limits, check the option labeled Do NOT touch off-limit colors, and select the colors you would like to remain off-limits. Click a color in the palette to select it; notice that the color now has a white triangle knocked out of it. To select multiple colors, you can hold the Control key down while you click additional colors until you select all the ones you want off-limits. To select a range of colors, you can Shift-click additional colors until you select all the colors you wish to remain off-limits (as long as the colors are contiguous in the palette).

Alternately, you can select colors using the Selection Marquee to select an area of the image. Doing so selects the corresponding colors in the Adjusted Palette window that fall within the selection you choose. If you prefer to pick the colors in the image you want to alter rather than leave afflicts, click the Check all button to select all the colors. Then, while holding the Ctrl key down, select the colors in the image using the Selection Marquee. This operation unmarks the colors that fall within your selection. You can also use Clear all to unmark all the colors and start over.

Making the Adjustments

After you designate the colors you want to modify, you are ready to make your adjustments. Hue, saturation, and brightness are measured using 256 values, ranging from 0 to 255. The sliders enable you to quickly make adjustments to the values, or you can simply type a number from –255 to 255 in the value's adjacent window to raise or lower the setting. A higher number increases the setting, while a negative number decreases it. The Zero all button simply sets all the current values to zero, which is particularly useful because the window always opens using the settings from the most recent session. You should always set your values to zero before making your adjustments, unless you want to use the settings from the last adjustment.

- **Hue** refers to the actual colors in the image, and moving the hue slider is the equivalent of moving the cursor around a color wheel to select a color.

- **Saturation** refers to the purity and intensity of the color. A higher value means a deeper, more intense color; a lower value makes for a paler image, to the point that the image drops all color at –255. Removing all the saturation is another way of converting a color image to grayscale.

- **Brightness** refers to the amount of light reflected by an image. A higher value makes for a brighter image; a lower one makes for a darker image.

With all these values, you need to experiment with different settings to obtain the optimal results. It is best to use small adjustments because larger adjustments often have drastic and unpredictable effects on the overall image color balance.

71

Adjusting Intensity and Contrast

You can also modify image color by manipulating the Intensity and Contrast of the image or selected pixels through the Adjust Intensity/Contrast dialog box accessible under the Image menu or by clicking the appropriate icon in the Image Commands toolbar. Either of these commands brings up the dialog box illustrated in Figure 3.17.

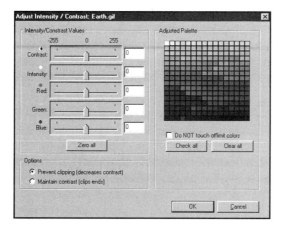

FIGURE 3.17

The Adjust Intensity / Contrast dialog box enables you to alter the intensity and contrast of an image or selected area.

Designating Off-limit Colors

You designate off-limit colors in exactly the same fashion as you do with the Adjust HSV Values dialog box. Similarly, this option is only available with indexed color images containing 256 colors or less.

Making the Adjustments

Like hue, saturation, and brightness, intensity and contrast are measured using 256 values ranging from 0 to 255. Use the sliders to increase or decrease the values of the intensity and contrast of the image or selected area. Intensity refers to the degree of shade in an image. Increasing the value removes shade, or makes the image lighter; decreasing the value adds shade, or makes it darker. See the following section for setting the options for calculating intensity levels.

Contrast refers to the gradations between the lightest, middle, and darkest tones in the image. Increasing the contrast value increases the gradation between these tones making the image darker and snappier; lowering the contrast value decreases it, making it lighter and more dull. Be sure to click the Zero all button to reset the sliders from the previous session before making your adjustments.

Better-Looking Images Cross-Platform

PC computers generally display the same images darker than Macintosh computers due to their lower display gamma. If you create artwork on one platform for use on the other, you can compensate for this difference by adjusting the intensity of the image. If your image was created on a Macintosh, you can create a lighter, more gamma-balanced image for better display on a PC by increasing the intensity. Type a value of between +10 and +15 next to the intensity slider to get a nice cross-platform gamma-balanced image. Do the opposite when going from PC to Mac.

The Red, Green, and Blue channel sliders enable you to offset each of the color channels from the master intensity/contrast setting. After you set the intensity and contrast level, you can increase/decrease the levels in any channel by raising or lowering its value. The three different channels of an RGB image often contain distinct information that you might want to isolate in addition to increasing or decreasing the amounts of these primary colors in the image. For instance, the green channel of an RGB image usually contains most of the image detail. Increasing the contrast in this channel could be more effective than increasing the contrast of the entire image. You could also affect the red channel, which generally has the highest amount of contrast of the three channels. The blue channel usually contains most of the "garbage" and image imperfections, so you would generally not want to increase the contrast in this channel. Remember though, that these adjustments can have unexpected results on the hue and saturation of your image. You should only make these adjustments in small increments and use trial and error to find the ideal adjustment levels.

The two options at the lower left of the Adjust Intensity/Contrast dialog box enable you to select between different methods of calculating intensity. Choosing the Prevent clipping method calculates values proportionately using your input values as a percentage to increase or decrease the original value. Thus, a value of 255 increases the intensity by 100 percent; a value of 128 increases it by 50 percent. Choosing the Maintain contrast method calculates values additively. Thus, a value of 0 becomes 128 if you choose 128 as a value; an original value of 128 becomes 256 with 128 as the input value. Values above 256 become "clipped" to 256 so that inputting a value of 128 for an original value of 200 would clip to 256 rather than adding to 328.

The NTSC/PAL Hot Pixel Fixer

DeBabelizer Pro's NTSC/PAL Hot Pixel Fixer provides a way of ensuring that your images will display properly on an NTSC or PAL device—such as a television screen—through the use of a special built-in filter. The composite video signal used on television devices utilizes the YIQ color space rather than the RGB color space used to display on your computer monitor. When images created on an RGB device are converted to YIQ and then to a composite signal, certain colors, especially highly saturated ones with high intensity levels, will fall beyond the display capabilities of the television screen. This results in a potential for these colors becoming distorted or shifting drastically in the color spectrum. The potentially "dangerous" pixels are referred to as Hot Pixels. Running the NTSC/PAL Hot Pixel Fixer will determine which pixels could cause potential problems and automatically adjust their intensity and saturation to fall within the safe zone for a composite video signal.

The NTSC/PAL Hot Pixel Fixer is accessible under the Tools menu or by clicking the appropriate icon in the Tool Commands toolbar. Doing so calls up the dialog box displayed in Figure 3.18.

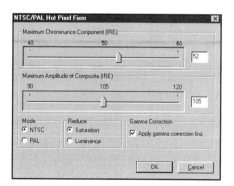

FIGURE 3.18

The NTSC/PAL Hot Pixel fixer enables you to adjust the saturation and intensity of image pixels to make them safe for display on video devices using a composite signal.

DeBabelizer Pro provides recommended default values for the filter, but you can specify your own. You can adjust the Maximum Chrominance Component and Maximum Amplitude of Composite by adjusting the sliders or manually entering a number. The maximum chrominance has a default value of 52, where the value is the upper limit of the Maximum Chrominance Component of the IRE signal. You can set this to any value between 40 and 60.

The Maximum Amplitude of Composite has a default value of 112, which represents the upper limit of the amplitude of the composite signal. You can set this to any value between 90 and 120.

After you have determined the values, you can select the appropriate mode by clicking NTSC (American standard) or PAL (European standard) and choosing the method of reduction. Choosing the reduction method determines how DeBabelizer Pro corrects problem pixels, by either reducing saturation or reducing luminance. Checking the Gamma Correction option causes DeBabelizer Pro to perform gamma correction prior to adjusting the pixels. DeBabelizer Pro applies a gamma value of 2.2 for NTSC and 2.8 for PAL to the RGB pixels prior to conversion when this option is checked.

Adjusting Gamma and Gun Controls

Gamma refers to the amount of contrast present in the midtones of the image and has the effect of brightening or darkening the image as the gamma value changes. A lower gamma results in a darker image, while a higher one results in a brighter image. Gamma also comes into play when displaying graphics and movies on different display devices as gamma levels vary from device to device. Adjusting Gamma levels allows you to compensate for these differences.

DeBabelizer Pro enables you to alter an image's gamma setting by changing the color value of each gun via the Gamma Control dialog box. Why would you be concerned with gun control in an image editing program? Actually, the term gun refers to the color guns used in electronic displays that shoot beams of light at the back of the screen. Each red, green, and blue color in an RGB monitor has a total of 256 levels, each of which is plotted as a dot by DeBabelizer Pro on the RGB settings graph in the Gamma Control dialog box (see Figure 3.19).

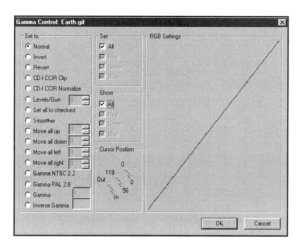

FIGURE 3.19

The Gamma Control dialog box provides powerful, if somewhat daunting, image adjustment capabilities.

The diagonal line in the window represents a graphical map of each color gun that you can edit by drawing with your mouse or by directly entering a value. In the graph, the X axis represents the current image level values, and the Y axis represents the new values. Although the graph line may appear black at first, it actually represents the three red, green, and blue lines overlapping each other. You can see the lines separate if you choose to set or show any of the individual color levels independently of the others.

You can apply gamma correction to an entire image or just to the area in your selection marquee. The automatic settings under Set to provide numerous pre-set gamma values for you to choose from, some of which enable you to enter additional values in the adjacent fields. You can also manually edit the gamma curve in the Gamma Control dialog box by performing the following steps:

1. Specify the color values you want to set in the area marked Set. You can choose any or all the channels. Uncheck the All box (default) in order to select the red, green, or blue channels individually.

2. Specify the color values you want to show in the area marked Show. Again, you can choose any or all of the color values. Notice that changing the Show colors affects the color of the graph line in the RGB settings.

3. Set the desired gamma levels in the graph manually or by using the automatic settings. To set the graph manually, you can drag your mouse to draw a new curve. Use the Cursor Position display to act as a guide for setting the values. The In value (X) corresponds to the current level, and the Out value (Y) corresponds to the new level.

> **TIP**
>
> Different display devices use different gamma settings. If you know the gamma value of the monitor or display device your images or movies are targeted for, you can manually insert the value in the Gamma Control dialog by selecting Gamma under "Set to" and typing in the value.

Working with Channels, Masks, and Overlays

If you have worked with a program like Adobe Photoshop before, you're probably familiar with channels, masks, and overlays. DeBabelizer Toolbox supports channel operations but not masks and overlays; these functions are new to DeBabelizer Pro. Together they allow for some powerful image editing capabilities.

A channel in an image editing program is similar to a printing plate used in offset printing. Every DeBabelizer image contains at least one channel and as many as four. RGB images have three channels, one for red, green, and blue. Together they combine, like printing plates, to create new colors. The fourth channel is the alpha channel, which is usually used for masking. Masking enables you to define areas of an image that will be protected from image edits to the rest of the image. Overlays enable you to add text or graphics over an image and control the transparency of the overlaid image in order to blend it with the underlying pixels.

Working with Channels

The first step in working with channels is learning how to turn on and off channel displays. Like Photoshop, you can choose to display only red, green, blue, alpha, or all the channels at once, although by default an image has all its RGB channels turned on when you open it. The easiest way to turn on and off individual channels is to click the channel display buttons underneath the image. The channel display can also be set from the View menu by choosing Channels and toggling each individual channel on or off by checking or unchecking it.

Images up to 24-bits usually have a red, green, and blue channel, and 32-bit images also have an alpha channel. You can also use the channel buttons directly on the bottom right of your image window (see Figure 3.20) to turn on and off channels. Note that you can dock or undock the channel buttons toolbar from the image window. Any changes or adjustments you make to an image only affect the displayed channel(s) for most operations. With a 32-bit image, turning on the alpha channel automatically hides the other channels.

FIGURE 3.20

The four channel display buttons are located at the bottom of the image window and represent red, green, blue, and alpha.

Swapping Image Channels

Swapping channels enables you to create certain image effects. Swapping involves taking the color usage information from one channel and switching it with another. With non-indexed RGB images, the channels for each pixel are swapped; with indexed images, the channels of the palette are swapped and the pixels remapped to the resulting palette. There are three commands for swapping channels that are accessible by selecting Channels from the Tools menu.

Swap R <-> G: This command swaps the red and green channels
Swap G <-> B: This command swaps the green and blue channels
Swap B <-> R: This command swaps the blue and red channels

Rotating Image Channels

Rotating image channels is like swapping channels, except that it involves swapping the information of three or more channels instead of two. You can choose the following commands by selecting Channels from the **Tools** menu.

Rotate R -> G -> B -> R: This command shifts each value to the right so that the current red moves to green, green moves to blue, and blue moves to red.
Rotate R -> G -> B -> A -> R: This command is only available with images containing an alpha channel and shifts each value to the right, as in the above example.

Converting Channels to Grayscale

DeBabelizer Pro provides an easy method of converting any image channel to grayscale. This operation strips the color information from the channel without affecting the image brightness. You can do this for any of the red, green, blue, or alpha channels by selecting one of the following commands from the Channels submenu of the **Tools** menu. Performing this operation on all the channels effectively converts the entire image to grayscale.

Convert R -> Grayscale: converts the red channel to grayscale

Convert G -> Grayscale: converts the green channel to grayscale

Convert B -> Grayscale: converts the blue channel to grayscale

Convert A -> Grayscale: converts the alpha channel to grayscale

Inverting Image Channels

Inverting image channels enables you to take the current channel's color value and invert it. For example, a value of 0 inverts to 255; a value of 128 inverts to 129. This function creates a "negative" of the channel, and performing it on all the channels creates a negative of the entire image, useful in creating special image effects. The invert command is accessible by selecting Invert Colors under the Image menu. Use the channel on/off buttons in the image window to turn channels on or off to invert individual channel colors. Use the image's channel buttons to turn off channels before performing the command to affect individual channels.

FIGURE 3.21

The Invert command can be performed on an entire image, selection area, or to any channel. The image on the left is the original image and the image on the right has had its red channel inverted.

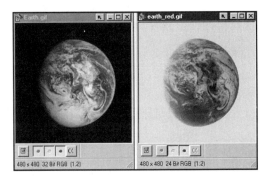

Creating an Alpha Channel (Mask)

A mask is essentially an alpha channel, comprised of a silhouette used to isolate certain parts of the image to facilitate the editing of select areas of the image. You can, for example, create a mask using type, then apply an effect to the image that will only effect areas inside or outside of the type mask, making for various type special effects. Because it is an alpha channel, a mask can only contain grayscale or black and white pixel data. You can paste pixels directly into the alpha channel from another image or from the same image. Because the mask is an 8-bit channel, any image data you paste into an alpha channel is automatically stripped of color data. The resulting image pixels retain the intensity values of the pasted image but are stripped of all color/hue information.

To create an alpha channel, you must first be working with an image that is 15, 24, or 32 bits in color-depth. You cannot create an alpha channel for an indexed color image (8-bit or less) without converting it to a higher bit-depth first. Use the Create Alpha Channel command in the Channels submenu of the **Tools** menu to bring up the Create Alpha Channel dialog box pictured in Figure 3.22.

FIGURE 3.22

The Create Alpha Channel dialog box.

In an alpha channel mask, pure white is opaque, while pure black is transparent. In-between shades gradually become transparent the closer they are to black. When pasting an image (with an alpha channel) onto another image, black in the alpha channel becomes transparent in the pasted selection; the white areas in the alpha allow that portion of the image to paste in opaque and overwrite the underlying image. This allows for some very nice compositing capabilities.

79

When you create a new alpha channel, the first step is to select the appropriate transparency factors. This choice determines how the image pixels are copied into the new alpha channel. You can choose any or all the following options:

- **Background Color:** This setting takes all the pixels in the image using the current background color and makes them transparent (white). Only non-background color pixels are copied into the alpha channel.

- **Foreground Color:** This setting takes all the pixels in the image using the current foreground color and makes them transparent (white). Only non-foreground color pixels are copied into the alpha channel.

- **White:** This setting takes all the white pixels in the image and makes them transparent (white). Only non-white pixels get copied into the alpha channel.

- **Black:** This setting takes all the black pixels in the image and makes them transparent (white). Only non-black pixels get copied into the alpha channel.

After you select the appropriate transparency factors, you need to set the Non-Transparent Pixels option to determine the type of mask you create, a grayscale or a black and white mask.

- **Use Luminance:** This option creates a grayscale mask from your image using the brightness values of the non-transparent pixels. In this case, a pixel that is 50 percent black (gray) will be 50 percent transparent.

- **Fully Opaque:** This option creates a black and white mask from the image using only the non-transparent pixels. In this case, pixels will be either 100 percent transparent or 100 percent opaque with no in-between values.

Working with Overlays

Overlays enable you to add text or images on top of an image and control the way they blend with the underlying pixels.

Image Overlays

The easiest way to create an image overlay is to paste a floater onto the image (see the section "Copying, Cutting, and Pasting" earlier in this chapter) and modify its transparency settings. Using the copy and paste commands, you can take any image and paste it on top of the current image. As long as the image retains the selection marquee around it, it continues to be a floater, floating on top of the underlying pixels regardless of where you move it. The selection ceases to be a floater when you deselect it or stamp it onto the underlying pixels. Normally, stamping the floater erases the underlying pixels completely; this section, however, describes how you can modify the transparency of the floater as it gets stamped by modifying the transparency settings (see Figure 3.23).

FIGURE 3.23

An image overlay with the transparency settings checked for black. The black areas of Earth.gif become transparent when pasted over Euro2.PSD.

The transparency settings can be set by selecting Transparency from the **Edit** menu or by clicking the appropriate icon in the Transparency toolbar. In the **Transparency** submenu, you can turn a transparency command on or off by checking it. You can check as many options as you like or none of them; the same is true for the icons in the Transparency toolbar. All the options affect the transparency of the floating image and the results are viewable before the image is stamped. The following transparency options are available:

- **Clear Transparency Settings:** This option unchecks all the transparency settings, turning them all off.

- **White:** This setting makes all the white pixels in the floating selection transparent.

- **Black:** This setting makes all the black pixels in the floating selection transparent.

- **Alpha Channel:** This setting uses the alpha channel pixels as a transparency mask. A pure black pixel in the alpha channel replaces the floater's underlying pixel with the floating pixel. A pure white pixel in the alpha channel makes the floating pixel transparent so that the underlying pixel shows through. Intermediate gray pixels create a blending between the floating and underlying pixel, depending on how light or dark they are.

- **Background Color:** This setting makes all the pixels using the current background color in the floating selection transparent.

- **Even/Odd Lines:** These settings make alternating horizontal lines of pixels transparent—a useful option when working with digitized images.

Text Overlays

Text overlays enable you to place text into your images and control the way the text blends with the underlying image pixels. Adding a text overlay is accomplished by choosing Text Overlay from the **Tools** menu or by selecting the Text tool in the Paint Tools toolbar. The current transparency options are applied to the overlaid pixels when you create your text overlay.

The Text Overlay dialog box enables you to type in your desired text as well as specify the font, location, and color of the overlay (see Figure 3.24). In addition, DeBabelizer Pro enables you to automatically include general information about the file. The following steps explain how to create a text, overlay via the Text Overlay dialog box. When you are finished specifying your text, you can click the preview tab to preview the overlay before applying it.

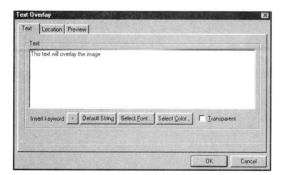

FIGURE **3.24**

The Text Overlay dialog box enables you to place text into an image.

1. Enter the desired text in the text entry area. You can insert specific keywords for such things as file info, image info, timer data (useful in batch processing), drive data, current time and date, and so on. The Default String option enables you to automatically enter a string of pre-defined data including file name, date, size, number of colors, dpi resolution, and current cell number.

81

2. Specify the font type and size by clicking the Select Font button and choosing the appropriate options.

3. Select the font color by clicking the Select Color button.

4. Specify the text transparency by checking or unchecking the Transparent box. With this option checked, the text is placed over the image without a background box.

5. Set the location of the text overlay by clicking the location tab and specifying the location in the image.

TIP

DeBabelizer Pro's Text Overlay function enables you to automatically insert a large variety of keywords into your images. These include such useful items as file name, size, data path, image size, resolution, current time, date, and so on. A timer function also enables you to set and insert a time entry, especially useful during large batch processes.

Image Fields

Digital images are divided into two horizontal rows of image pixels with each odd and even set of lines classified as a separate field. The Even field is the set of even numbered lines beginning with the first, which is numbered 0. The Odd field is the set of odd numbered lines beginning with the second, which is numbered one. You can hold your cursor over any portion of your image and look at the Y coordinate in the status bar to tell which field the cursor is located at, depending on whether the number is odd or even. Dividing an image into fields enables you to perform certain operations to the odd or even fields individually, which can, among other things, help to correct for distortions in digitized images.

NOTE

Image fields are discussed in this section only as they pertain to still images. They are discussed in further detail in Chapter 9, "Working with Digital Video and Animations," as they pertain to digital video.

Saving an Image

Naturally, after you begin editing and working with an image, you will need to save it. You have two options when you save an image: Save or Save As. If you have multiple images open, a third option is available, Save All, which saves all currently open files. If you choose Save As, you can access several more options when you save your images. The Save As dialog box is shown in Figure 3.25.

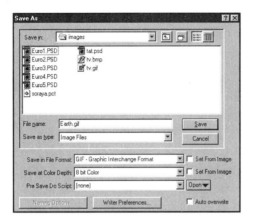

FIGURE 3.25

The Save As dialog box.

In the Save As dialog box, you provide a name for your image and determine where it will be saved, using the standard Windows directory controls. The Save in File Format drop-down menu enables you to choose a file format to save your image.

83

The drop-down menu presents a list of all the file formats that DeBabelizer Pro is capable of writing. Clicking the Set From Image box chooses the format the file is currently in as the default format. The same is true for color depth. You can choose a color depth from the drop-down menu or click the Set From Image option to use the current bit depth. The Pre-Save Do Script drop down menu presents a list of all currently open scripts that you can choose to perform by selecting from the list. The script is performed prior to saving. You can also access an existing script file, if it's not currently open, by clicking the Open box to the right and using the standard Windows directory structure to find the script file to use.

Setting Writer Preferences

Because many writeable file formats have numerous options associated with them, DeBabelizer Pro enables these options to be set by clicking the Writer Preferences button in the Save As dialog box. Depending on the file format selected for the image, clicking on the Writer Preferences button calls up the writer preferences for that image. If clicking the button doesn't bring up any writer preferences, then no preferences are available for that particular file format. The following is a simplified list of writer options for file formats supported by DeBabelizer Pro. For more information on specific file formats, see Appendix A.

Available file format writer preferences by file extension:

BMP: compressed or uncompressed
BOB: none

CUT: none
EPSF: grayscale no preview or color no preview
EIDI (Electronic Image): none
FITS: none
FLI/FLC: FLI or FLC, frame rate, loop mode
GIF: You can specify numerous settings for the following options—transparent color, multi-image options, interlacing, comments, disposal method (for gif animations)
ICO: none
IFF: numerous options for CD-I file type
IMG/GEM: grayscale or fixed colors
JPG: quality setting (1–100), baseline compatibility, progressive format
MAC: none
MSP: none
NEO: none
PICT: none
PCS: none
PIC: compressed or uncompressed
PIX: none
PLN: none
PNG: none
PSD: none
PXR: none
QDV: none
RAS: none
RGB: header or no header
RLA: (WaveFront) none
RLE: none
SCN: none
SGI: compressed or uncompressed
TDIM/GRAF: Titleman of VideoFX
TGA: compressed or uncompressed
TIF: fax, grayscale, or color modes; Mac or PC byte ordering; compression options—uncompressed, packbits, or LZW
TIM: none
XWD: none
YUV: none

You now are familiar with the basic image editing functions of DeBabelizer Pro and have a good foundation to begin exploring the rest of the program. You should also familiarize yourself with the various toolbars that let you access most of the functions mentioned in this chapter by merely clicking an icon. These are added or removed under File:Preferences:Set Preferences:View Toolbars. After you decide upon your favorite/most needed editing functions, you can easily customize your toolbars so that those functions are always only a click away.

CHAPTER 4

How Color Works— A Palette Primer

What is a palette? And why is it so important? The answers to these questions make the life of anyone involved in multimedia much easier. A palette is a table of the possible colors that can be used to display your project's graphics. The bottom line for why palettes are so important is appearance and size.

Computer monitors display colors through RGB (Red, Green, and Blue) color space. A big problem for people working in print, which relies on CMYK (Cyan, Magenta, Yellow, and blacK) values is getting your computer monitor (RGB) to display what the colors really look like in print (CMYK). Luckily, in multimedia, you are designing your project to be played on someone else's computer monitor whether it is a CD-ROM title or a Web page; so you are designing for the RGB colorspace. When working in a visual medium, color plays an important part of the equation. You want your graphics to look good.

Color is invariably linked to file size. File size is an important issue in any multimedia project. If you are designing a Web page, you want small graphics that look good so that users don't wait for images to download. If you are designing a CD-ROM, you have 650 MB of room on a disc to hold images, sound, video, animations, and so on. It can fill up pretty quickly. So, color is important for not only the appearance of a graphic but for performance as well. The more colors an image has, the more space it takes up. The file sizes of artwork at 256 colors take up considerably less room than artwork at 24-bits. Artwork created for multimedia is reduced to, at the most, 8 bits.

Once you have cleared the hurdles of appearance and size, figuring out the best way to display the artwork in just 256 colors or less becomes an important part of any multimedia project. This is the art of creating a custom palette. Coming up with the ideal colors to be used over a series of images is an arduous task, but with DeBabelizer Pro's assistance it is very easy.

What Is a Bit?

Before learning how to create a palette we need to understand more about bits. The term bit has been cavalierly thrown about when talking about color. A bit is the smallest amount of information you can have on a computer. Technically speaking, it is represented by a 1 or a 0, or an Off or an On state. The higher the bit depth—the number of bits used to represent a color in an image—the more color depth you can have. For example, an image in 32-bit color has millions of colors available to display it. The key is to think of it as a range of possible colors, and this range depends directly upon the number of bits you can have. The more bits you have the bigger the range of possible colors to be displayed.

Because a bit can only be a 1 or 0, all bit depths are based on the equation of 2^x; the numbers are exponential. This is how you come up with the final numbers of colors you can have according to its bit depth. For example, an 8-bit image contains up to 2^8 power or 256 colors. The number of bits tells you the bit depth of an image. For your convenience, you can look it up in the table below. (Notice that all these options are available from the Set Pixel Depth dialog box in the Palette menu.)

TABLE 4.1

The Most Common Bit Depths

Bit Depth	Number of Colors/Grays
1-bit	2
2-bit	4
4-bit	16
8-bit	256
15-bit	32768
16-bit	65536
24-bit	16 million
32-bit	16 million + 8-bit alpha

You are not locked into these numbers. As Web designers know, it is possible to have a 7-bit image. In Web graphics you want to include as few colors as possible to reduce the file size, but you want to be careful not to degrade the image. The more colors a file has, the larger file's size. As bit depth increases, the range of colors available also increases and so does its file size—a delicate balance between size and appearance.

86

Using different bit depths gives you different results. An image saved at 7 bits looks very different from an image saved at 24 bits. Figures 4.1 through 4.3 are examples of the same image saved at different bit depths (please refer to the CD to view the figures in this chapter in color).

Figure **4.1**

An image at 24-bit depth.

87

Figure **4.2**

The same image at 8-bit depth.

FIGURE 4.3

The same image's 4-bit depth.

Going from Bits to Palettes

If you are designing graphics for a CD-ROM title, your goal is to run the project at 8 bits. Using 8-bit color depth gives you a palette of a maximum 256 colors. You hear terms like Index Table or Custom LookUp Table (CLUT) used interchangeably with the term palette. Figure 4.4 is an example of a palette.

FIGURE 4.4

A typical palette.

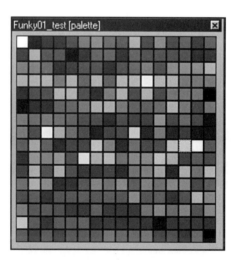

NOTE

The terms bit depth and color depth are used interchangeably.

The next step after deciding the number of colors you want your palette to have is determining what colors are going to be included in the palette. Only the colors included in the palette will be used to display the graphics in your project. Deciding what colors will be included in a palette is where DeBabelizer Pro comes in. DeBabelizer Pro can analyze images and determine their most common colors and create a palette based on this information. This procedure will be explained in more detail in Chapter 5, "Working with Palettes."

NOTE

Palettes can belong to browsers or software programs and even platforms: Netscape's Palette, an Indeo Palette, or the Window's Palette, for example.

An important consideration for developing a palette is knowing the final platform your project will be displayed on. You may need to include the platform colors as a base palette. A base palette is the core colors to be included in the custom palette. For example, if you are designing a kiosk to run under Windows, you need to include the Windows base palette and the kiosk palette must include the Windows interface colors, known as the Windows Default 20 Palette. Including the Windows base palette ensures your images will display correctly when played on a PC. Including the Windows base palette will take 20 slots of the available 256, leaving 236 positions open for custom colors. DeBabelizer Pro can help you to identify the most popular colors in your images and create a palette based on this information.

How Palettes Are Set Up

A palette is used in 8-bit or less color depth, because a palette can only hold up to 256 colors at maximum. You do not have to have a palette that has 256 colors; palettes can have anywhere between 2 and 256 colors. For example, you could have a palette that only has 16 colors. The colors in a palette are organized by their index numbers.

NOTE

Conforming a file to 8 bits or less is also called indexing.

Each of the color tiles in the palette in Figure 4.4 has an index number associated with it. The program doesn't know the image by its color; the program references the color by its index number.

Index numbers begin at 0 and end at 255. Some platforms require palettes to number colors in a certain fashion. For example, a Macintosh Palette requires white to be at the 0 position and black to be at 255; the rest of the colors can be placed randomly. The Windows Palette requires the opposite, having black at the 0 position and white at 255. As mentioned earlier, the Windows Palette also requires that the first 10 and last 10 positions in the palette be standard set colors for Windows interface colors.

> **TIP**
>
> In an indexed image, you can find out what a color's index number is by clicking either the Palette or the image with the Eyedropper tool. The index number is shown in the bottom right corner of the desktop.

Index numbers are useful information to know in case you modify or tweak your custom palette. You may have to modify a palette to ensure your graphics are displayed in the optimum way. Some images may not be as attractive after they are indexed to a custom palette. The images may have banding or artifacts added to them during remapping. When this happens, you may have to modify your palette. More information on how to modify palettes is in the next chapter. For now, the next step is to find out what colors are included in the possible 256 available positions.

Working with Custom Palettes

With a tool like DeBabelizer Pro, you can create your own custom palette instead of using a standard palette like the Macintosh Palette or Windows Palette. Using a custom palette has an advantage of using colors that are based on your artwork as opposed to conforming the artwork to a standard set of colors like the Macintosh palette. Customizing a palette is good for a series of images that are going to be used throughout a CD-ROM title, for instance. Sometimes remapping the pixels to match a standard palette creates havoc within the image, causing unattractive banding or noise. Figure 4.5 illustrates this fact.

FIGURE **4.5**

Image dithered to the standard Windows Palette.

In Figure 4.5, using its own custom palette, the background of the image is smooth and without artifacts. In Figure 4.6, the background has noise in it; while indexing the image to the Windows Palette, noise or artifacts were added to the otherwise solid background. Working with Custom Palettes help to make your artwork look its best because the palette uses colors already in use in the graphic. The trick is finding a custom palette that works for the entire series of images used in your CD-ROM title, especially if the images are very different from one another colorwise.

FIGURE **4.6**

Image dithered to its own custom Palette.

In creating custom palettes, DeBabelizer Pro uses an adaptive palette to arrive at its Custom Palettes. As DeBabelizer Pro analyzes the color information in each of the graphics in a BatchList, colors are then added or adapted to the custom palette. DeBabelizer Pro does the difficult work for you, polling the color information and coming up with the optimum color palettes based on the series of images.

An added benefit of working with custom palettes is that they significantly reduce the size of your files. A 24-bit image takes up significantly more space than a 8-bit or indexed image (see Figure 4.7). Custom Palettes help to keep the numbers in check.

FIGURE **4.7**

Saving a file in 8-bit saves half the space of a 24-bit image. These numbers add up when you are dealing with space constraints.

Another added benefit of working with custom palettes is that they help to prevent palette flashing. In authoring tools, storing the Palette information takes up memory, and the load up time of switching from one palette to another can cause the screen to flash as the system tries to juggle the available number of display colors. If you can come up with a custom palette for the entire project, palette flash can be avoided.

Applying the Palette

After DeBabelizer Pro has polled the images and figured out what colors to include in the palette, you now have to apply the palette to the artwork. The pixels in the image are remapped to the new palette. Remapping assigns the pixels a new color from the new palette that best matches the old color. One of the ways to remap the pixels is called dithering.

Dithering plays a trick on the eye. It creates the illusion that there are more colors involved in an image than are really present. It does this by remapping colors next to one another in such a way as to give the appearance of shading. Figures 4.8 through 4.10 illustrate the difference between dithering and no dithering.

FIGURE **4.8**

A 24-bit image before it is remapped.

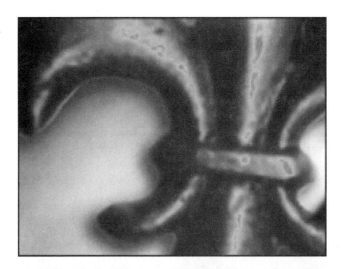

92

FIGURE **4.9**

Image is remapped to 256 colors and no dithering.

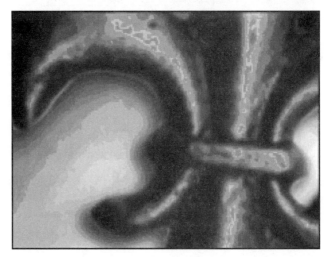

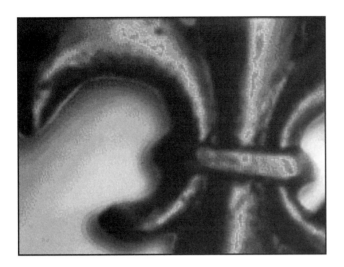

FIGURE 4.10

Image is remapped and dithering set to 88%.

As you can see in Figure 4.9, which was not dithered, the image has pools of colors in it, which have a flat perspective because they are just one contiguous color. The pools are surrounded by other pools, giving an undesirable and unattractive banding effect. The image in Figure 4.10, however, has more subtleties and no pools. The effect is that the image has some definition or shading. The dithering gives the illusion of these subtleties. No colors were added to the palette to create this effect; the pixels were given different palette colors.

You can determine how much dithering to apply to a file within DeBabelizer Pro when remapping files to a palette. The amount of dithering used in an image depends on how much the image can handle. The litmus test is what looks good to your eye. Dithering can sometimes soften an image. If you see an image breaking up, then you have dithered it too far. Too much dithering can create weird artifacts that resemble noise. DeBabelizer Pro uses two different methods of dithering. A full description of DeBabelizer Pro's dithering methods is in Chapter 5.

When indexing or remapping an image to a palette, you are essentially throwing out color information. You are taking an image that has millions of colors and conforming it to only 256 colors or less. Colors are switched and the closest representative in the palette is chosen; this is why you need to test your palette to make sure it makes all the images in your BatchList look good. Some images may be more problematic than others because of the range of colors used to initially create them in 24-bit color. You may have to modify the custom palette or may need to change the actual colors used in the original image.

After an image is indexed, the original color information is gone. If you want to change the bit depth back to 24-bit, DeBabelizer Pro lets you, but it cannot re-create the colors that were once there. It is always a good idea to have your originals saved somewhere else. If you convert an indexed image to 24-bit DeBabelizer Pro converts it to millions of colors, but the image still looks like the indexed image.

Palettes to Choose

Standard palettes already exist—you can use the Macintosh or Windows standard, for instance. There are also palettes that are set up for video, like NTSC or Indeo.

Using different palettes achieves different effects, as illustrated in Figures 4.4 and 4.5. The Windows Palette generally has more contrast than the Macintosh Palette and tends to darken an image—something to consider when deciding on a palette. One way around some of these differences is to create a hybrid palette. For instance, Web designers have been talking about using a hybrid of the Windows and Macintosh Palettes, with a palette of 216 common colors.

Because the industry is truly cross-platform these days, creating art on the Macintosh and having your final project running on the PC is a common occurrence. Using the standard palettes makes indexing images effortless and painless. The only drawback is that your graphics may not be as attractive as they would be when using a custom palette.

Now that you have whet your appetite on color depth and palettes, you are ready to learn the rest of DeBabelizer Pro's palette capabilities in the next chapter.

CHAPTER 5

Working with Palettes

In the previous chapter, you learned the basic concepts behind indexing images and palettes. In this chapter, the focus is on how DeBabelizer Pro handles palettes and what you can do with palettes. DeBabelizer Pro offers many options, both in applying the palette and in manipulating the palette itself.

A Plethora of Palettes

You can create palettes in a few different ways, but first you need to understand the different types of palettes within DeBabelizer Pro; understanding the palettes is essential to using them effectively. There are three different types of palettes: image palettes, stand-alone palettes, and SuperPalettes.

Palette Definition

A *palette* is a the color table displaying all of the colors used in a indexed image.

Image Palettes

An image palette is a palette associated with an indexed image. An indexed image is an image that has been reduced to 8-bit color depth or less. The image palette automatically comes up when you open an indexed file and displays all the colors used in the file. If no palette comes up when the image is opened, you have an image greater than 8 bits in depth. You can pull image palettes out of the image window; DeBabelizer Pro refers to this as undocking the palette.

Indexing & Palettizing

Indexing an image and palettizing an image are the same thing. The terms refer to the process of reducing the number of colors in a file to at the most 256 colors.

The titlebar of an undocked image palette has the same name of the image it came from with "[palette]" next to it. There is no file extension for an image palette because you cannot save it independent of the associated image. The image palette is part of the image file.

You can use the image palette to find out what colors an image is using to display itself. You can change the colors in the image palette to new colors, which can affect the image as well. Working with an image's palette can make subtle changes to the image. For example, if your image requires a palette color to be transparent, you can go into the image's palette to set a color as transparent. More about setting the transparency attribute and others later in this chapter.

Stand-Alone Palettes

The second type of palette in DeBabelizer Pro is a stand-alone palette. It can be one of the 22 default palettes that DeBabelizer Pro comes with, such as the Windows or Netscape palettes, or it can be a palette that you create either from an image palette or a SuperPalette.

To create your own stand-alone palette, you need to have an indexed image or SuperPalette open and active. While the indexed image or SuperPalette is active, choose **Create Palette** from the **Palette** menu. The image palette or SuperPalette automatically appears as a stand-alone palette that can be saved as an independent file. DeBabelizer Pro adds the default extension of .pal to stand-alone palettes. The new stand-alone palette can be applied to other images or BatchLists.

To create a stand-alone palette from a 24-bit image, you first have to reduce the number of colors in the file to 8-bit. You can do this by applying the additional step of **Set Pixel Depth** under the **Palette** menu (see Figure 5.1). At the maximum, the palette can have 256 colors. After you reduce the bit depth, you can then select **Create Palette**. (Please refer to the CD to view the figures in this chapter in color.)

The difference between an image palette and a stand-alone palette is that an image palette is associated with a file. Sometimes image palettes and stand-alone palettes work hand-in-hand, such as applying a stand-alone palette to an image. In this example, the image palette is identical to the stand-alone palette. The major difference between an image palette and a stand-alone palette is that a stand-alone palette is independent of an image. Unlike an image palette or a SuperPalette, it is not associated with any files.

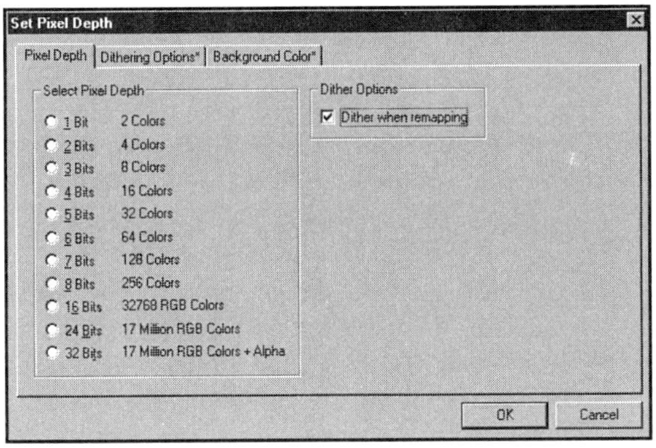

FIGURE 5.1

Set Pixel Depth
*is the first step in
creating custom
palettes for files
over 8-bit.*

TIP

You can tell the difference between a stand-alone palette and an undocked image
palette visually. The stand-alone palette has an ActionArrow on the titlebar and an
image palette does not. The image palette contains "[palette]" in the titlebar.

Stand-alone palettes can be applied to one file or multiple files. Generally, you will
use one of the default stand-alone palettes DeBabelizer Pro offers, such as the
Netscape palette, but you can create your own. The stand-alone palettes can be
included into a script or used in one of DeBabelizer Pro's Batch Automations.

SuperPalettes

The final type of DeBabelizer Pro palette is the SuperPalette. The SuperPalette is
the ultimate palette, containing more information than any other palette. It is an
independent file that can be saved and applied to other images or BatchLists. When
SuperPalettes are saved, DeBabelizer Pro adds the default extension of .dbp.

The SuperPalette is based on information compiled from polling the colors in a series
of files. The most common colors are then selected for the SuperPalette. This color
information is attached to the SuperPalette and never lost. Even if you add another
file to the SuperPalette after it has been created, the new color information is added
to the previous color information polled. Because the information is retained in the
SuperPalette, the new adapted SuperPalette is still an accurate representation of
the colors in all the files. If you create a stand-alone palette from a SuperPalette, the
stand-alone palette does not retain the polling information; the polling information
stays with the SuperPalette.

SuperPalettes are used to create a custom palette for a series of files. For example,
you can include all the files going into a project, such as still-images, animations, and
AVIs, to create the optimum palette for the project. The SuperPalette is a swatch of

the most common colors found in these files and should ideally display all your files beautifully.

Creating SuperPalettes is a common practice in multimedia work. Instead of being constrained to the colors used in a standard palette such as the Windows palette, you can create your own custom SuperPalette. Using a SuperPalette gives you greater flexibility in the colors you can use because it is based on the actual artwork going into the project.

The Palette Window

No matter what type of palette you are viewing, the palette window is a swatch of the colors available for the files to use. The palette represents the colors available for use in your files. You can modify the colors themselves as well as their positions within the palette.

In an Image Palette window, a relationship exists between the index colors and pixels. The pixels in the image are associated with a particular index color. If you click an image with the Eyedropper tool and "capture" an index color, the index color is highlighted in the image palette. Figure 5.2 is an example of the highlighted palette color.

FIGURE 5.2

Clicking the image highlights the palette color in the image palette.

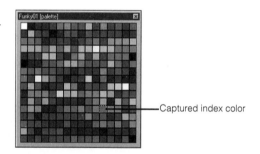

—Captured index color

You can also use the Eyedropper tool to "capture" an index color in the image to find out the color's index number within the image palette. The color's index number is listed in the bottom right corner of the desktop, along with the color's RGB and HSV values. You can only display the index number and color values for image palettes. SuperPalettes and stand-alone palette's index color information are not displayed at the bottom right by clicking the index colors.

TIP

If you have an index image open, the captured colors will appear in the foreground and background color tiles with the index number are in parentheses.

From the palette window, you can double-click any index color to see its RGB or HSV color formula. You can sort the palette window by using one of the **Sort** commands on the **Palette** menu. By sorting a palette window, you can compare it with another palette to see their similarities and their differences. When you are trying to troubleshoot a palette, sorting the palette can be useful to see the ranges of colors of the palette uses.

The Quick Access of the Right-Click

On the Windows platform, you have the right-clicking capabilities with a mouse. In DeBabelizer Pro if you right-click a palette window, you have quick access to additional options, depending on which kind of palette is clicked.

The Right-Click and the Image Palette

Figure 5.3 shows the options available to you when you right-click an image palette.

FIGURE 5.3

You can manipulate the pixels or the palette colors.

These options can be broken down into two categories: manipulating the pixels or palette and viewing the palette. All the options can be toggled on or off by placing a check mark next to them.

- **Remap Pixels:** If you make changes to the palette, only the file's pixels get changed, not the palette. Use this option if you just want to manipulate the image but keep the image's palette intact. Sometimes a few images will have difficulty translating to the project's custom palette, so you can use this method to fix the images without disrupting the project palette.

- **Rearrange Palette:** If you make changes, only the palette is affected and not the file's pixels. The image will not be affected.

- **Rearrange Palette and Remap Pixels:** If you make changes to either the palette or the pixels, both the palette and the pixels are affected. This option is useful for troubleshooting a problematic image. You can try to fix the image and, by default, its palette. You can then save the image palette as a stand-alone palette by using the **Create Palette** command on the **Palette** menu.

- **Replace with Closest:** If you select an index color from the palette, DeBabelizer Pro replaces the selected color with the next closest palette color. This is an effective way to reduce the colors in your palette. If the Rearrange Palette and Remap Pixels is checked, you can see how the image will break up as you combine colors with each other. You can also combine **Replace with Closest** with **Remove Colors: Used and Duplicate** under the **Palette** menu, for optimizing graphics for the Web.

- **Show Indexes:** The color's index numbers display on the palette when the Show Indexes option is checked.

- **Set Palette Size:** You can change how big or small the palette color tiles are viewed. You can make them big enough so that you can actually read the index numbers if the Show Indexes option is checked.

- **Create Palette:** You can take the image palette and convert it to a .pal file. You can then save the stand-alone palette and use it in other dialog boxes. As an image palette, the palette cannot be accessed in other dialog boxes like **Merge or Set Pixels** and **Remap** unless you save it as a stand-alone palette.

- **Docking View:** If this option is on, the image palette will be embedded into the image window border. If Docking View is off, the image palette is its own free-floating palette on the desktop. Double-clicking the titlebar of the undocked palette will embed it into the image window.

Right-Clicking a Stand-Alone Palette

You have fewer options to use when you right-click a stand-alone palette as shown in Figure 5.4. Right-clicking a stand-alone palette offers a few of the same options that an image palette menu does with the addition of the new option to view the palette's Properties. The **Properties** option brings up a dialog box titled **Palette Info**. This dialog box enables you to view the colors in the palette by their index numbers and their RGB or HSV values.

FIGURE **5.4**

Right-clicking a palette enables you to choose to view the palette's Properties.

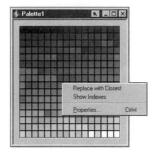

The Right-Click and the SuperPalette

Right-clicking a SuperPalette gives you quick access to the **SuperPalette** menu items as shown in Figure 5.5. The right-click menu offers several choices, a few you have seen from the other palette's right-click menus. A new option, however, that only SuperPalettes offer is the Factor in File option.

This feature adds a file to be included into the polling of the current SuperPalette. Choosing this option brings up a dialog box where you are prompted to find the file you want to add. This feature is useful when a file has been accidentally omitted from the SuperPalette batch process, or you can use it to add newly created artwork to the SuperPalette.

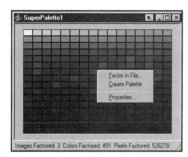

FIGURE 5.5

You can quickly create a stand-alone palette from the right-click submenu.

101

Modifying Index Colors

You can modify each color within a palette window by double-clicking it. Figure 5.6 is the **Palette Properties** dialog box that appears when you do so. It displays the chosen index color in its RGB and HSV values. It also enables you to apply additional Properties to the color.

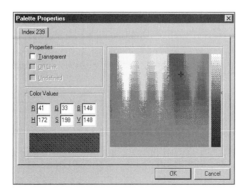

FIGURE 5.6

Palette Properties for index color 239. You can tweak this index color to whatever you need.

Properties Clarification

DeBabelizer Pro's use of the term "properties" can be confusing. When selecting Properties from the **View** menu, you get the **Palette Info** dialog box, which is information on the entire palette. If you double-click an index color, you get the Palette Properties for that particular index color.

You can change the color's values by either entering a specific value or doing it by eye using the color slider. Entering in the values for RGB or HSV is useful when you know a color's exact RGB or HSV formula. For example, when you know the exact RGB formula for a client's logo color, you can enter the RGB values for that color.

The Properties that DeBabelizer Pro enables you to assign to an index color are: Transparent, Off Limit, or Undefined. Each of these properties allows the index color to have extra functionality when it is applied to an image:

- **Transparent:** Using this option applies a transparency to the index color in the image. When you create a floating selection of the transparent color, anywhere the transparent color is in the floater will be transparent; even when the selection is stamped onto the image, the color is whited out.

TIP

If you have indexed images that are on a solid color background, you can give the solid background color a Transparency attribute from within the **Palette Properties** dialog box. When the image is pasted into another file with the same exact palette, the background is masked. This is a way to composite images.

- **Off Limit:** Setting a color to Off Limit protects it from color manipulations. If you manipulate the palette, this color will be protected. If the palette with the Off Limit color is applied to an image, the image will not remap to this color. This option appears in many of DeBabelizer Pro's palette functions.

- **Undefined:** Setting a color as Undefined reserves a space in the palette. No color will be associated with the position. Undefined acts as a placeholder in the palette.

An example of using one of these properties is Figure 5.7. In the image's palette, an index color was given a Transparent property. The sections of the image where the transparent color shows appear whited out.

You could use the Off Limit option when a blue screening process has been applied to an image. The blue color used in the background needs to be protected from manipulation and to prevent other images from using this color. Capture the index color being used as the blue background and your foreground color will have the index number in parentheses. In your palette, find the index number and set it to Off

Limit. You will see the Off Limit setting for index colors in other dialog boxes such as the Set Palette and Remap and the Reduce Colors dialog boxes.

FIGURE 5.7

The pixels appear in white wherever the Transparent index color appears in this image.

The Off Limit and Undefined options are not available through the image's Palette Properties; they are only available for stand-alone palettes. If you use the **Create Palette** from the **Palette** menu to an indexed image, the newly created stand-alone palette will enable you to designate index colors as Off Limit and Undefined.

The reason the image palette does not enable you to use these options is because the index colors only pertain to that specific image and pixels. The index colors in a stand-alone palette can then be applied to other files globally so the colors can be set to Off Limit or Undefined.

103

Figure 5.8 shows the icons DeBabelizer Pro uses to flag the index colors for a visible sign that the colors have been modified. The icons DeBabelizer Pro uses are: a red letter "T" for a Transparency setting, a color tile cut in half diagonally filled in white is used for the Off Limits setting, and a gray box with a white dot in the middle is used for the Undefined setting.

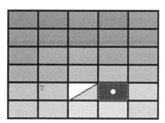

FIGURE 5.8

The icons placed on your palette for you to see that index colors have been given additional attributes.

NOTE

If you have added Properties to an index color within an image palette when you use the **Create Palette** from the **Palette** menu, the new stand-alone palette retains the Properties settings. For example, if you set a color to be Transparent in the image palette, it will be Transparent in the stand-alone palette as well.

Palette Info

Just as you can see an index color's Properties, you can also view a palette's Properties. Selecting Properties from the **View** menu displays a palette's Properties. A **Palette Info** dialog box appears, and the index colors are displayed according to their index number, RGB, or HSV values, depending on which is checked.

You can only use the Palette Properties option for image and stand-alone palettes. SuperPalettes have their own SuperPalette Properties (and the options in the SuperPalette Properties dialog box will be explained later in this chapter).

Figure 5.9 shows the Properties for a stand-alone palette (you can also view the properties of an image palette). Selecting the Properties option for an image palette brings up the Image Info and the Palette Info dialog boxes. You can Tab to the Palette Info. The difference between the Palette Info for a stand-alone palette and an image palette is that the Used option is grayed out. A stand-alone palette has no pixels attached to it so no colors are deemed as Used.

FIGURE 5.9

The Palette Info window for a stand-alone palette. Notice Used is grayed.

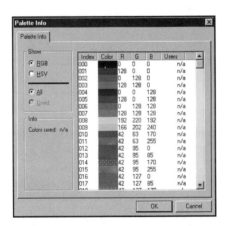

The only addition to a image palette's Properties from Figure 5.9 is that you can display all the index colors or just the index colors used in by the file. In Figure 5.9, the stand-alone palette's Properties has the Used option grayed out because no pixels are using the colors. DeBabelizer Pro lists the number of colors used in the file, which is a useful feature when you may need to merge palettes later.

Palette Logs

You can use the Palette Log to document changes you make to a palette. You can use this information to create scripts, or for a "paper trail" of the changes you have made. You can access the Palette Log by going under the **View** menu and selecting Log.

A new feature for DeBabelizer Pro is the ability to have logs for more than just a Batch Process and palettes are no exception to this. Only a stand-alone palette can have a log. An image palette's manipulations are recorded in the Image Log, yet SuperPalettes, however, do not have any sort of log.

Printing Palettes

You can print palettes directly from DeBabelizer Pro using **Print** under the **File** menu. For stand-alone palettes, you can also print the **Print Properties** under the **File: Print** menus. Selecting to print the Print Properties brings up the **Print Palette Info Options** dialog box.

The Print Palette Info Options is the same information found in the Palette Info window. The Print Palette Info Options dialog box gives you the choice to print out the RGB or HSV formulas for the index colors. You can also choose to print all the colors in the palette or just the colors used. The last option you can choose is whether the colors themselves will be printed out or not. Figure 5.10 shows the Print Palette Info Options dialog box.

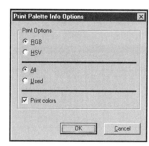

FIGURE 5.10

Having a printout of the Palette Info is useful when you need RGB values so that graphics can have text or logos created with an exact palette color.

105

DeBabelizer Pro lets you keep the print job open, which enables you to append other information onto the current print job. Using the keep print job open not only saves paper but helps you keep your information organized.

Having Fun with Palettes

Once you have created a palette, you can manipulate it in various ways. You can, for example, find the exact color information you need to know in order to manipulate the palette colors to get the results you want.

As mentioned earlier, if you modify an image palette, you can affect the pixels and/or the palette colors. You can also modify the index colors in stand-alone palettes. You can modify palettes in two ways: changing the index color's values and rearranging the order of the index colors. In the next section, you learn to do both.

Affecting the Palette Colors

Any of the image manipulation tools discussed in Chapter 3, "Working with Images," can be used on an indexed image, and from there you can use the **Create Palette** option to get a new palette. The new stand-alone palette reflects any adjustments you made to the image. You can also affect the index colors in an image palette with the **Equalize** option under the **Palette** menu.

The image manipulation options cannot be applied directly to stand-alone palettes. The only option for affecting the index colors in a stand-alone palette directly is **Invert Colors** under the **Image** menu.

Equalize

DeBabelizer Pro enables you to even out the range of colors in an image palette according to their brightness or saturation. You can even out the range by using the Equalize option under the **Palette** menu and can only apply this to an image palette.

Under the Equalize option you have three choices: Brightness, Saturation, or Brightness and Saturation.

- **Brightness:** This option evens out the brightness levels across the image and its palette so that the brightness of the palette's colors are more evenly distributed. The contrast of the colors may also increase. You can play with the brightness of a file when you are creating artwork on the Mac to be used on the PC. The PC tends to darken images when it displays them.

- **Saturation:** This option evens out the saturation levels across the image and its palette. Manipulating the image and palette by saturation can have some drastic results depending on how saturated the palette was to begin with. You may have to play with the saturation of a palette when you are outputting digital files to video.

- **Brightness and Saturation:** This option evens out an image and its palette by both the Saturation and Brightness.

> **NOTE**
>
> Applying some of the image manipulation tools to an indexed image and then creating a stand-alone palette is a tricky way to change the palette using DeBabelizer Pro's tools.

Invert Colors

The Invert option creates a negative of the original image. Invert Colors can be applied to image and stand-alone palettes so that when you invert palette colors, you get the opposite color value. For example, red would yield cyan, blue would yield yellow, and green would yield magenta. You may want to use this option for special effects.

Reorganizing the Palette

After you have tweaked your palette's index colors to perfection, you can rearrange the index colors positions within the palette. If you are organizing an image palette, you can do so without affecting the image's pixels and just rearrange the palette. You can use DeBabelizer Pro to organize the image palette for optimizing graphics and reducing their file size. You can rearrange a stand-alone palette as well as an image palette.

Sorting the Palette

DeBabelizer Pro gives you a number of ways to sort a palette. The **Sort Pallete** dialog box in Figure 5.11 can be found under the **Palette** menu. Using the **Sort** option can be applied to both image and stand-alone palettes. The Sort option is not available for SuperPalettes.

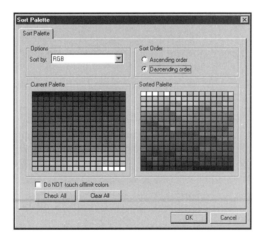

FIGURE 5.11

Sorting your palette can Macintize a palette. A Macintosh palette needs to have white at the 0 position and black at the 255 position.

You can sort the colors in the palette according to their RGB values, Brightness, HSB, HBS, YUV Saturation, or Popularity. You can do all these sorts in Ascending or Descending order. For example, sorting by Ascending order means the index colors go from 0 to 255 in RGB or HSV values. The index color in the first position would have 0 Red, 0 Blue, and 0 Green, if RGB is the color space you are using. The opposite is true if you sort the palette by Descending order; you are going from 255 down to 0.

The Sort option is useful to determine the color range a palette is covering to be certain it is the optimum palette for your project. The Sort function has an additional option of protecting index colors that are set to Off Limits. The Off Limits color would be protected from the Sort. The following is a list of the different sorts you can apply to a palette.

- **RGB:** Sorting by the RGB values means you go from 0 Red, 0 Green, 0 Blue levels to 255 Red, 255 Green, 255 Blue levels, or vise versa depending on whether you have Ascending or Descending checked. This is a quick way to Macintize a palette if you choose Descending order.

Using the Sort Command

You can set your **Sort** command to use Ascending or Descending order to rearrange the index colors. You can do this in the Specify dialog box; whatever setting you choose will be used by the **Sort** pull-down menu.

- **Brightness:** Brightness refers to a color's percentage of black. The less the percentage of black the brighter the color is. The palette will be sorted by this characteristic.

- **HSB:** Sorting by the color's values for Hue, Saturation, and Brightness. Saturation is the color's percentage of white. The less white applied to a color the more saturated the color is.

- **HBS:** Sorting by the color's values for Hue, Brightness, and Saturation. This differs from the preceding method because the color's percentage of black weighs heavier than its percentage of white.

- **YUV Saturation:** The color model used for digital video. The compressed video is stored in YUV color space because it takes up less space than RGB.

- **Popularity:** This sort option is only available for image palettes. In order to find out the popularity of a color, you need to have pixels attached to it, so an attached file using the colors is needed.

Sorting the palette with any of these options only manipulates the palette, the image is still intact. The index numbers associated with the colors will change, but the colors themselves do not.

NOTE

You cannot do any of the Sort functions to SuperPalettes. You can apply all the Sort options except Popularity to stand-alone palettes.

Rearranging Colors

Within DeBabelizer Pro, you can click and drag index colors to new positions within image and stand-alone palettes. You can use the Shift and Control keys to add to your selection of index colors to move. Once you drag an index color from one position within the palette to another, the color being dragged moves to the new position. All the other colors shift position to accommodate the switch.

You can also swap two color positions. To do this, hold down the Alt key while you drag an index color to its new position. This is another fast way to make a palette go from being a Macintosh palette (white first) to a Windows palette (black first). You can click the white and black colors to swap them.

Although you can't copy and paste from one palette to another palette, you can double-click the index color to get its Palette Properties dialog box. From the Palette Properties dialog box you can find the index color's RGB or HSV color formula. You can then go into the Palette Properties dialog box for another index color and enter in the formula for the RGB or HSV values. It isn't copying and pasting, but you can add colors this way. If you have left an Undefined position in your palette, this is a good way to add a color to your palette without replacing an index color that may be important. Hopefully in future versions, drag and dropping index colors from one palette to another will be available.

Another useful option is creating a gradient within the palette colors. You can do this by holding down the Shift key as you double-click the selected index colors. The dialog box shown in Figure 5.12 comes up for you to create your gradient.

109

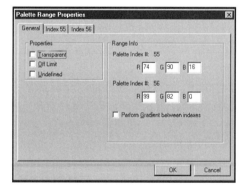

FIGURE 5.12

You can create index colors with gradients. You can even vary the colors by entering different values for the beginning and ending colors.

This is a useful option for images where banding occurs. Sometimes when you apply a palette, images can get a banding effect. Using the gradient option for index colors can help in removing this effect. After you create the gradient, you can apply the usual Properties of Transparent, Off Limit, and Undefined to it.

The Rearranging options are only available for image palettes and stand-alone palettes; you cannot use these to manipulate a SuperPalette directly. You can convert the SuperPalette to a stand-alone by using the Create Palette function from under the **Palette** menu first. After the SuperPalette is converted, you can apply the rearranging techniques to it.

Cleaning Up Palettes

You can clean up a palette by removing the unused and duplicate index colors in it. Those of you familiar with GifBuilder™ will recognize this process. Under the **Palette** menu, you can apply the **Remove Colors** function to streamline your palette by removing unused and/or duplicate index colors. This is a useful way to optimize your palette for the most efficient use of color and file space. Index color slots will open up for additional colors to be added to the palette. If reducing file size is your goal, then you are going to want to keep as few index colors as possible.

Modifying the Colors in a Palette

Now that you know how to physically move colors within the palette and how to manipulate the index colors, you can learn how to change the number of colors in a palette either by adding new colors or removing colors. DeBabelizer Pro gives you several options to modify the number of colors in a palette.

Using Merge Palettes

You can combine several palettes together in order for your graphics to display beautifully. You may have a set number of colors you know you need to include, such as the Windows base palette or exact logo colors. You can use the Merge function to combine several palettes together, which is done by selecting the **Merge** function from the **Palette** menu.

In the Merge function, you have three palettes to work with: the merge palette, your current palette, and the final palette. You can use Merge only on image and stand-alone palettes. All three types of palettes, however, can be used as the Merge palette, which is where the colors will be copied from.

In the Merge function, you can specifically choose the colors you need to be included in a palette. Say, for instance, you have a custom stand-alone palette you want to merge with the Windows default palette; the Merge option can be used to do this. Figure 5.13 is the dialog box for the Merge option.

You can use one of the 22 default palettes or create your own custom stand-alone palettes to use in the Merge option. The default palettes can be used as the Merge palette (see Figure 5.13 for position). The Merge palette is the palette you are copying from into your Current palette. You can also use any stand-alone palette or SuperPalette that is open on the desktop as a Merge palette. You can get to the additional palettes by clicking this triangle to the right of the **Merge Palette** pull-down menu in the Merge Palette dialog box. Clicking this triangle will show the available palettes on the desktop.

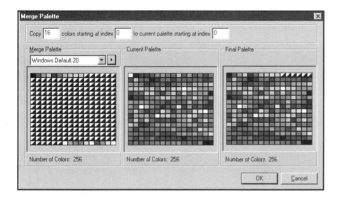

FIGURE 5.13

You can merge two palettes to get the optimum palette for your images or movie.

You can also save the SuperPalette as a stand-alone palette into DeBabelizer Pro's default Palettes folder inside the Equilibrium Folder in order for it to appear in the pull-down list.

111

TIP

You can designate both image and stand-alone palettes as your Current palette. You cannot use a SuperPalette as a Current palette.

You can select the number of colors you want to copy from the Merge Palette by entering the number in the Copy box. The first Starting at Index box is for specifying at what index position you want to copy from the Merge Palette. If you enter in a value of 16, for example, index color 16 would then be the first color to be coped into the Current palette. You can designate a number from 0 to 255, depending on the number of colors in your Merge Palette.

The next Starting at Index box is for placing the index colors into the final palette. For example, if you enter in a value of 36, the colors from the Merge Palette enter into the Final palette at index color 36. If you have a palette with open spaces at index color 216, you could start copying index colors into the final palette at that index number. Below each of the palettes is the number of colors it contains. In Figure 5.13, you will overwrite colors already in the palette because the final palette already has 256 colors.

A useful feature in the Merge option is that you can click an index color in the Merge Palette and the index number for the selected color will automatically appear in the first Starting at index number box. You can also click the index colors in the Current Palette to enter in the index number for the Final Palette's Starting at index number box. You can have DeBabelizer Pro count the index colors for you.

Reducing Colors

Another way of modifying a palette is to reduce the palette's colors. You can make an image palette have fewer colors by using the Reduce Colors function. This is a useful tool for optimizing Web graphics. The **Reduce Colors** can be found under the **Palette** menu. The Reduce Colors option can *only* be applied to image palettes directly. Figure 5.14 shows the dialog box for the Reduce Colors option.

FIGURE **5.14**

You can use a Base Palette to reduce the colors in a palette.

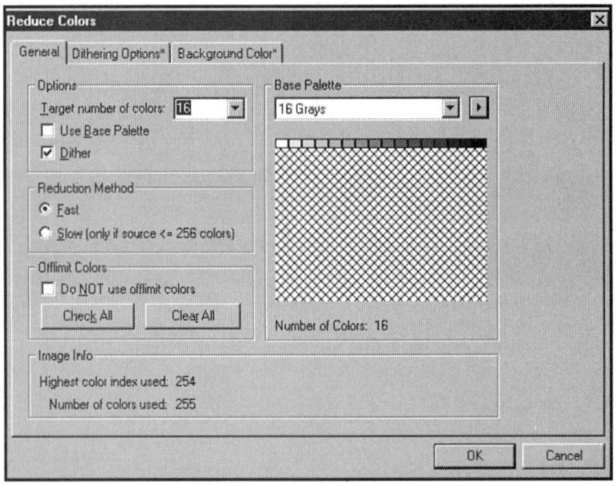

112

The Reduce Colors dialog box displays the image's color information. In the Image Info area, DeBabelizer Pro also tells you the highest color index the image uses and the number of colors used in the file. In Figure 5.14, you can see that the highest index number used in the image is 254.

You can determine the Target number of colors you want in the revised palette. If you wanted a 256-color palette to be reduced to 128, this is where you would choose to do so. The pull-down menu choices you have are: 2, 4, 8, 16, 32, 64, 128, and 256, which should be familiar numbers for now. You are not limited to these options, you could create a palette with 60 colors just by typing "60" in the Target number of colors field.

TIP

Notice the triangle right of the pull-down menu for Base Palette. This triangle enables you to access any stand-alone palettes or SuperPalettes open on the desktop.

DeBabelizer Pro can also reduce the palette by applying a Base Palette. A Base Palette makes up the first colors used in a palette; it is the core of the palette. All palettes have a Base Palette. By clicking the triangle right of the **Base Palette** pull-down menu, you can access any open stand-alone palettes or SuperPalettes to be used as a Base Palette. You also have the choice of applying any of the 22 default palettes as a Base Palette.

Reducing a palette with the Base Palette option checked is dependent on your target number and the Base Palette. For example, if you reduce to 32 colors using the Netscape palette, you are going to get the first two rows of the Netscape palette as your new reduced palette, if Use Base Palette is checked. If you choose the Windows Default 20 as the Base Palette, the first 10 colors are considered the Base Palette.

You can apply Reduce Colors to custom palettes as well. If the Use Base Palette is checked, the final reduced palettes tend to be monochromatic. You can get a fuller range of colors for a custom palette if the Use Base Palette option isn't checked.

From within the Reduce Colors dialog box, you can choose whether or not you want to dither while remapping. You can set how much dithering DeBabelizer Pro will apply by clicking the Dithering Options* tab. As the new reduced palette is created, the pixels are dithered to their new colors. Remember Dithering Options is a global setting; anything set here affects dithering everywhere else it is applied. You can also designate the settings for the Background Color from this dialog box, also a global setting.

113

You have a choice of two options to reduce the palette: Fast or Slow. Both options give identical results, but Slow just takes longer because it processes all the colors more precisely. Also, the Slow method can only be applied to files in 8-bit depth.

You can set index colors as Off Limits while reducing the palette to its new color depth. You can mark index colors as "safe" or you can clear index colors from being protected.

TIP

Remember the Reduce Colors option can only be applied to image palettes directly and not stand-alone palettes or SuperPalettes.

Combining Palettes After the Fact

It is often possible to have a custom stand-alone palette before discovering you need to add the Windows Default 20 to your perfect custom palette. You can use the Reduce Colors function to solve this. The ideal way to add the new colors is to redo your SuperPalette with the Windows Default 20 palette selected as the Base Palette.

The longer method is to open one of the images with the custom palette. Select the Reduce Colors option from under the **Palette** menu and reduce the image palette to

256 colors using the Windows Default 20 selected as the Base Palette. Make sure you have the Use Base Palette option checked. You now have a custom palette with the Windows Default 20 palette added.

Palettizing Files

Once you have created a custom stand-alone palette or know the standard palette you want to use, DeBabelizer Pro can apply it to your images. As you apply the palette, the images get remapped to the new colors. As the image is remapped, you can choose to have dithering applied as well. Applying dithering helps to fake your eyes into believing there are more colors present than there really are.

Dithering Options

DeBabelizer Pro gives you several options in dithering files to a palette. There are several ways you can get to the **Dithering Options*** dialog box and any remapping function will have the Dithering Options* available. The quickest way to get the Dithering Options* is to go to **Preferences: Set Preferences** under the **File** menu. Figure 5.15 shows the dialog box for Dithering Options*.

114

FIGURE 5.15

Don't always believe what you see; dithering tricks your eyes into thinking you have more colors than you do.

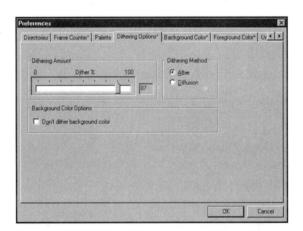

You can control the amount of dithering DeBabelizer Pro applies while palettizing files. The default setting is 87 percent. DeBabelizer Pro has two algorithms it uses to apply the dithering; they are: *Albie and Diffusion.*

These two methods apply different algorithms to arrive at dithering. Using the Diffusion algorithm gives the appearance of more than one level of brightness in dithering. Using the Albie algorithm gives results with slightly more contrast.

Whenever dithering is required, it will dither according to the preferences set in the **Dithering Options*** dialog box. If you have the **Dithering Options*** as part of a script, remember to go back and change it should you need a new dithering amount.

It is generally a good idea to check the **Set Preferences: Dithering Options*** to make sure DeBabelizer Pro is set up the way you need it.

When dithering in batches, some images may not handle the dithering as well as others. Sometimes certain ranges of colors will give you banding due to the range of palette colors and your reducing the image's bit depth. Finding out the optimal dithering amount is something you need to play with. Your eye is going to be the best judge when comes to dithering. As mentioned earlier, if you dither too much, images have the appearance of being colored in with pools of flat color with no shading or highlights.

TIP

A good source of help with banding is to open your file in Photoshop and apply the Noise filter. Use a low amount, like three or less, and select a Gaussian Distribution and a Monochromatic setting. After applying the Noise filter in Photoshop, re-palettize the file in DeBabelizer Pro; it should be without the banding effect. Basically, adding Noise to the files creates a fake dithering for you. You are changing a few of the pixels to break up the banding continuity.

115

Background Color and Dithering

The **Dithering Options*** and **Background Color*** options go hand-in-hand. Generally, everywhere you can change the Dithering Options* you can also change the background color. The Background Color* options can be important in images that have had a blue screen process done to them. A blue screen process means the files were shot in front of a blue screen so that they could be superimposed on another image. The Background Color* options are also important for images that have a color designated as a mask to be applied during programming. You can get to the Background Color* option quickly by going to **Preferences: Set Preferences** under the **File** menu.

The **Don't dither background color** checkbox in the **Dithering Options*** dialog box enables you to protect the background color of a file. (Refer to Figure 5.15 for an example of the **Dithering Options*** dialog box.) Protecting your background color is useful, as mentioned, when working with images digitized against a blue screen or for an image with a solid color (a mask) for the background. When solid colors are dithered, the dithering process can create artifacts or noise. The artifact defeats the purpose of having a solid background. To protect the background color, check the Don't dither background color checkbox in the Dithering Options* dialog box.

The background color can be chosen in several ways, as shown in Figure 5.16. You can enter in a known RGB or HSV color or use the color wheel slider for images higher than 8-bit color depth. For indexed images, you can select a background color by entering in the color's index number. After you select the Palette index number, the palette is displayed. You can click the actual palette to find the color as well; the corresponding index number automatically is given.

FIGURE 5.16

*Selecting new
background colors.*

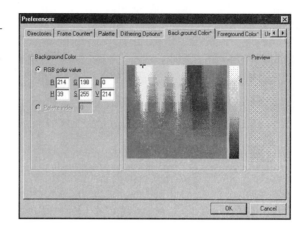

Changing Bit Depth

DeBabelizer Pro offers you several ways to change a file's bit depth. You can apply a palette to change the bit depth of the file or you can just change bit depth without applying any particular palette.

Setting the Pixel Depth

The quickest way to change a file's bit depth is to use the **Set Pixel Depth** option under the **Palette** menu. The Set Pixel Depth submenu gives you a choice of several ways of changing the pixel depth or bit depth of a file. You have a choice of the standard bit depths or you can use Specify from under the Set Pixel Depth submenu for more choices. Using Set Pixel Depth to an image creates an instant custom palette based on the colors already in the file. Figure 5.17 shows the Set Pixel Depth dialog box.

FIGURE 5.17

*Specifying the
Pixel Depth to
apply to your
images.*

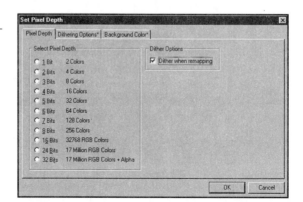

When you change an image to a new bit depth, an image palette appears in the image window. You can use **Create Palette** under the **Palette** menu on the image palette to save a stand-alone palette of your new image palette. After you have created the image or stand-alone palette, you can then use it to remap other files.

You can increase a file's pixel depth, but no new color information will be added to the image. It will look exactly the same because DeBabelizer Pro can't create color information. From within the Set Pixel Depth dialog box, you can change the dithering applied and the background color to be used.

You can use this method to create a fast custom palette for an image. If you are working on a project that does not need a consistent custom palette for all the images, you can use this method just to reduce its bit depth.

Creating Grayscale and Monochromatic Palettes

Palettes do not only have to be palettes of color; you can also create palettes out of black and white or shades of gray. DeBabelizer Pro can also create black and white or grayscale palettes.

Similar to your choices in Set Pixel Depth is the Convert to Grayscale option from under the **Palette** menu. You can change an image from color into grayscale applying this option and create a grayscale palette. Figure 5.18 is the dialog box for Convert to Grayscale option.

117

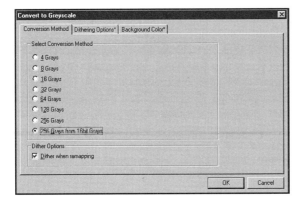

FIGURE 5.18

You can specify what color depth the grayscale file will have.

You can also make a 24-bit image grayscale, but by using a different method. You can use the Adjust the Hue, Saturation, and Brightness values via Image-Adjust HSV Values. Using this function automatically remaps the image to 15-bit to base the color adjustments on. You can bring the Saturation level down to –255 to remove all color from the image. The file will also be converted to grayscale and you will not be able to access its palette because it is 24-bit color.

Two options can change your files into black and white and create a monochromatic palette: Black and White Dither or Threshold. Using the Black and White Dither option brings up an additional dialog box so you can apply just the right level of dithering for the desired effect. What is convenient about the Black and White Dither and Threshold dialog boxes is they are dynamic; you can see the changes happen to the open file as you apply them.

Applying the Black and White Dither option uses a dithering technique to create a black and white image. If the pixel in the image is above a certain level, it is designated white or black accordingly. The result is an image that looks dotted or dithered. Figure 5.19 is a color image before Black and White Dither is applied. Figure 5.20 is the same image after the Black and White Dither option is applied. Depending on which dithering method you use, Albie or Diffusion, the end result varies slightly. You can use Black and White Dither to prepare images for the print world. Both the color and black and white versions of this figure are included on the CD-ROM.

FIGURE 5.19

The original image.

118

FIGURE 5.20

Applying a black and white palette to an image.

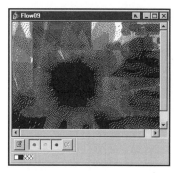

 Using the Threshold option to apply a black and white palette is a quick way to create a mask for a file. Within the Black and White Threshold dialog box, you have two ways to change the file to black and white. You can change the image by black percentage values or threshold values. You can enter in values for each method or use the slider to affect the image. Figure 5.21 is the dialog box for the Black and White Threshold option.

You can enter in a percentage for the amount of the image to be converted to black by using the black percentage. For example, entering in 75 percent means 75 percent of the image will be converted to black. The number you set in the threshold value box is used as a cut off point; anything below this value is changed to black. For example, you could enter in 128, and then any color level below 128 will change to black.

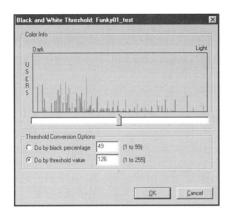

FIGURE 5.21

You can use the slider to change the image as you watch.

Using Set Palette and Remap Pixels

Another way of changing a file's bit depth is by using the **Set Palette and Remap** option from the **Palette** menu. Not only does this change your file's bit depth, but you can also apply a specific palette, an option Set Pixel Depth didn't offer. Figure 5.22 is the dialog box for the Set Palette and Remap option.

119

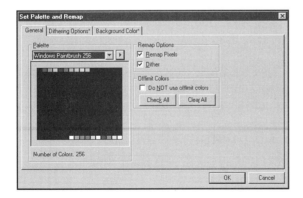

FIGURE 5.22

The Set Palette and Remap dialog box.

From within this dialog box, you can choose the palette to apply to the file. It can be a custom palette you just created from Set Pixel Depth or it could be one of the standard palettes that comes with DeBabelizer Pro. You can pull down the Palette submenu and all the stand-alone palettes saved into DeBabelizer Pro's Palette folder will be available to you. If you click the triangle to the right of the pull-down Palette menu, you can access any open stand-alone palette or SuperPalette.

You can choose to remap the pixels to the palette's closest color as the palette is applied. Remapping replaces the original colors with the closest color equivalent in the new palette. When this option is checked, it ensures the image will get the best color changes to the new palette. You can choose to apply dithering as you remap or not; sometimes dithering can lend a hand to the remapping process. Our familiar friends, Dithering Options* and Background Color* appear again.

You can also set Off Limit colors to the palette. The Off Limit color becomes a "safe" color. You can set the Off Limit color by clicking the color in the palette and the index color will be cut diagonally with half the box whited out. The color in the palette is protected from modification. It also prevents a palettized image from remapping to the safe color.

Set Palette and Remap is a quick way to palettize a file. If you have only one or two files and don't want to create a BatchList, you can use this option instead, as long as the palette is accessible. It is also good for testing images and palettes. Custom Palettes don't always work on all the files in a BatchList; you will have a few tricky files needing extra attention. Using the Set Palette and Remap option, you can test drive the palette on the tricky images, ensuring it works.

Reducing Colors to Create a Palette

The **Reduce Colors** option under the **Palette** menu has already been discussed, but it bears mentioning again. You can use Reduce Colors to create a custom palette as well. You can apply Reduce Colors to an open 24-bit image and designating 256 colors as your Target palette. It will create a palette based on whatever choices you make in the Base Palette pull-down menu.

You can also Reduce Colors to quickly create a hybrid custom palette. For example, you could open an image select 256 for the Target palette and select the Windows Default 20 as the Base Palette. The result would be a custom palette with the Windows Default 20 included. The new palette would not have all the information a SuperPalette would. It would only be representative of the file whose bit depth you changed, but it is another quick way to create or apply a palette.

The Granddaddy of All Custom Palettes

Creating a custom palette by using the SuperPalette function is the granddaddy of all custom palettes. DeBabelizer Pro can take a series of images and build a custom palette based on the color information on a series of files. SuperPalettes can be saved as independent files with the default extension of .dbp.

In most multimedia titles, you will want to come up with one palette to be used in the project. For example, if you are creating a CD-ROM title, you are going to want one custom palette for all your graphics. Creating a SuperPalette in DeBabelizer Pro is the way to do it.

Arriving at the SuperPalette

DeBabelizer Pro uses the metaphor of polling for constructing a SuperPalette. It takes a vote to find the most common colors in all the files included in the series. The files are analyzed and the colors are polled to create a palette based on the poll's results.

As DeBabelizer Pro goes through the series of files, including stills, animations, and movies, the SuperPalette adapts the colors. You can see this onscreen as DeBabelizer Pro opens the files and colors are added to the SuperPalette before your eyes. You can set the amount of polling DeBabelizer Pro will do in the Set Preferences settings under **File: Preferences** and select the Palette tab shown in Figure 5.23.

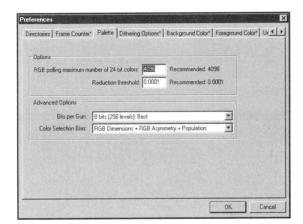

FIGURE 5.23

Setting the color polling of your files to get the results you want.

121

The default number DeBabelizer Pro uses for polling is 4096. You can go up to 35 thousand or as low as 256. Using higher numbers is a hit on speed and time. DeBabelizer Pro recommends 4096 because it seems to cover the bases for creating well-balanced palettes, colorwise.

The Reduction threshold number has to do with figuring out the cutoff for what colors get into the SuperPalette and what don't; it is the dividing line. The default fractional number is .0001. This number is multiplied by the total number of pixels in an image. The sum gives you the cutoff number for the number of pixels a color can have to make it into the SuperPalette.

If a color has fewer pixels represented than this sum, the color is ignored and doesn't make the SuperPalette. You can turn this option off by setting the Reduction threshold value to 0. Doing this would result in unnecessary colors making it into your SuperPalette.

The Bits per Gun option has to do with how many colors you can display. A monitor has three guns, one for Red, one for Green, and one for Blue. The lower the Bits per Gun, the less colors you can have represented, so fewer colors to choose from. You want to have 8 bits here so that you get the most colors for your palette.

Choosing the Color Selection Bias gives DeBabelizer Pro the criteria for deciding on what colors will be included in the SuperPalette and for any manipulation of a palette's colors. The Color Selection Bias gives you a pull-down menu of five choices. When the RGB color space is broken down and analyzed to be put into the SuperPalette, it gets divided into smaller boxes of color, depending on the criteria applied to the box and its color. The goal is to have a box that is a cube shape because it has the most accurate color representation. The following is a list of the Color Selection Biases you can choose from:

- **RGB Dimensions + RGB Asymmetry + Population:** This is the method DeBabelizer Pro recommends. It is the sum of the RGB dimensions of the box plus how close the box is to being a cube and the number of pixels in the box.

- **RGB Dimensions + Population:** The sum of the RGB dimensions of the box plus the pixels in the box.

- **RGB Volume * Population:** The product of the RGB dimensions of the box multiplied by the number of pixels in the box.

- **RGB Volume:** The product of the RGB dimensions of the box.

- **Population:** The number of pixels in the smallest box of color.

After you have created the perfect SuperPalette, you can view its Properties by either right-clicking a SuperPalette with the mouse or by going to the **SuperPalette** menu to select **Properties**. The SuperPalette menu only becomes available when a SuperPalette is open and active on the desktop.

The **SuperPalette Properties** is similar to the dialog box you saw when you first created a SuperPalette. The only addition is that under the Statistics section, there are no longer "0s" next to the information. The Properties displays the number of images used and the pixel count while the Statistics information is saved with the SuperPalette. You can also view the Statistics information on the SuperPalette window itself (see Figure 5.24).

Going into the SuperPalette Properties, you can at a later date reduce the number of colors you want the SuperPalette to be. It recreates a new SuperPalette based on all the color information polled from the original SuperPalette. This is amazingly convenient when you want to remap images to the same SuperPalette but with fewer colors.

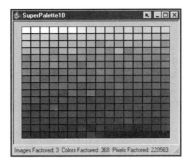

FIGURE 5.24

The Statistics are written at the bottom of the SuperPalette for easy access.

Creating SuperPalettes

You can create SuperPalettes from two different menus, **Batch** and **Tools: Batch Automations**. Using these two different methods gives you access to different options. The Batch menu is only available when a BatchList or Batch Log is active. For now, we will be discussing creating a SuperPalette from the Batch menu. In the next chapter, you will learn about creating a SuperPalette from the Tools: Batch Automations menu.

The only difference between the two SuperPalette functions is a Batch menu SuperPalette can only be created from an open BatchList. A SuperPalette from the Tools: Batch Automations menu can be created from several sources. All other features of the SuperPalette are the same. Figure 5.25 is the dialog box for creating a new SuperPalette.

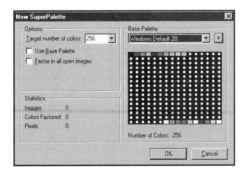

FIGURE 5.25

Creating new SuperPalettes for optimum display of your files.

DeBabelizer Pro can create a SuperPalette with as many as 256 colors and as few as one. You can type in how many colors you want in the SuperPalette to have or you can use a pull-down menu for the standard numbers.

A useful feature is assigning a Base Palette to be incorporated into the creation of the SuperPalette. Including a Base Palette can help you avoid doing unnecessary merging of palettes later on. You can create a SuperPalette with all the colors you know you need. By clicking the triangle next to the Base Palette pull-down menu, you have access to any stand-alone palettes or SuperPalettes open on the desktop.

If you are creating a SuperPalette from images that are already open on the desktop, you can check the Factor in all open images checkbox in the New SuperPalette dialog box. This feature is useful for when you need to add just one more picture to an already existing SuperPalette.

The Statistics section of the New SuperPalette dialog box is useful for checking the color information DeBabelizer Pro bases the SuperPalette on. All color information is retained in the SuperPalette for perpetuity. So if you need to add in another file as previously mentioned you will see the Statistics section change.

The Statistics section tells you the number of images polled, the number of colors factored, and the number of pixels polled. This information is useful for proofing. If you based a SuperPalette from a BatchList of 12 files and your Statistics section reflected only 11 images, then you know something is amiss.

Once you have perfected your SuperPalette, you can save it as a stand-alone palette file. To recreate the palette as a stand-alone, you can use the Create Palette from the **SuperPalette** right-click submenu or go under the **Palette** menu. None of the polling information will stay with the stand-alone palette; only the SuperPalette will have this information.

Stacking the Deck

The SuperPalette option is for creating the best possible custom palette based on a group of files. It bases the choice of colors for the SuperPalette by how much a color is used and by how much of it is in a file. You can, however, tamper with the election process by deliberately including images heavy in the colors you want. You can tip your cards by purposefully picking images that contain colors you want to be included in the palette, or by including the image more than once in the BatchList, if you are using a BatchList to create it.

TIP

One way to tip your hand is to cut up actual artwork containing the most vibrant colors into smaller pieces. The reason for this is if there is a constant unchanging background, such as a repetitive background image, or if the background is one color, these predominant colors will be given too much weight. By cutting into smaller pieces, it prevents DeBabelizer Pro from using too many of these same shades of colors and creates a more dynamic range of colors for the SuperPalette.

SuperPalette Menu

Once you have created your SuperPalette and it is active on the desktop, you have access to the **SuperPalette** menu, which is available only when a SuperPalette is active on the desktop. Figure 5.26 shows the choices available from the SuperPalette menu.

FIGURE 5.26

From this menu, you have quick access to adding a file to a SuperPalette.

Factor in File...
Create Palette
Properties...

The options from this menu are similar to the options you have when you right-click on a SuperPalette. You can Factor In a File if a file was inadvertently left out of the BatchList or you can create a stand-alone palette using the Create Palette option. You can also see the Properties for the SuperPalette.

CHAPTER 6

Batch Automations

Batch Automations enable you to automate a series of events. One of the reasons why DeBabelizer Pro is so popular is that after you set up the process, DeBabelizer Pro does the work for you. Five standard Batch Automations come with DeBabelizer Pro: Create SuperPalette, Create SuperPalette and Remap, Save, Save with SuperPalette, and Print. The Batch Automations can be found under the **Tools** menu.

DeBabelizer Pro Updates

DeBabelizer Pro for Windows offers a slimmed down version of the Batch Processes offered in the Toolbox version for the Macintosh. The Batch Processes of DeBabelizer Toolbox have also been renamed Batch Automations in DeBabelizer Pro. Popular scripts used in DeBabelizer Toolbox have also been built into Batch Automations in the new DeBabelizer Pro. For example, in the Toolbox version you had to write a script to remap your files to a SuperPalette. You no longer need the step of writing a script; you can simply run the Create SuperPalette and Remap Batch Automation.

All the Batch Automations are used to make your life a lot easier. You can set the process to run while you are off working at another computer or taking a lunch break. Batch Automations are at the heart of DeBabelizer Pro. Being able to save a *series* of files to a specific palette or in a different file format is much more efficient than having to open up each file one at a time and applying the same manipulations.

A brief description of each of the DeBabelizer Pro Batch Automations follows:

- **Create SuperPalette:** This process creates a SuperPalette—an optimized custom palette—based on a BatchList, directory of files, or images. You can create a SuperPalette from a few files or hundreds. The SuperPalette is the optimum custom palette for your project.

- **Create SuperPalette and Remap:** This Batch Automation creates the SuperPalette and then remaps the files in the BatchList to it. Instead of having to do the two separate processes of creating a SuperPalette and then applying the SuperPalette, you can do both in one process.

- **Save:** The Save Batch Automation can save the BatchList in a multitude of ways, but it is most commonly used for file format conversions. You can combine this process with a user-defined script while saving the files.

- **Save with SuperPalette:** You can both save into a different file format *and* apply a SuperPalette. You can also combine this Batch Automation with a script while saving the files.

- **Print:** You can print a series of files in a BatchList. This process is great for client approval, or if you need to have hard copy for handing off artwork to a programmer.

The beauty of these Batch Automations is that you can run them unattended. Combining the Batch Automation with a script is like having a whole team of people working for you. For those who are nervous about leaving a computer to work on its own, you can always review the BatchList Log to make sure all went as planned.

BatchLists

All these Batch Automations are similar in that they require a Source. The Source is the files that are going to be run through the Batch Automation. One of the Source options is a BatchList; a BatchList is simply a DeBabelizer Pro document that contains a list of files. The files in the BatchList are those to which the scripts or Batch Automations are applied.

You can create a new BatchList by selecting New: BatchList from the **File** menu. The files in the BatchList can be in different file formats. You can have a collection of AVIs, 24-bit images, and so on in a BatchList. You can also drag and drop files from one open BatchList into another. Figure 6.1 is an example of a BatchList.

After you have created your BatchList and saved it, you can edit it at anytime. By default, the files in the BatchList are arranged alphabetically unless you purposely add them out of alphabetical order by adding them in a specific order. You can Shift-click and highlight the files in the BatchList independently. The highlighted file can be manipulated by itself, and you can delete it. You can open a file directly by double-clicking its name in a BatchList. If you click the BatchList Folder, you automatically highlight all the files in a BatchList.

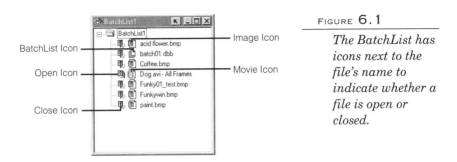

BatchList Icon ——

Open Icon ——

Close Icon ——

—— Image Icon

—— Movie Icon

FIGURE 6.1

The BatchList has icons next to the file's name to indicate whether a file is open or closed.

What Can You Do with BatchLists?

After you have created a BatchList, you can apply any of the Batch Automations DeBabelizer Pro offers to the BatchList. You can also create scripts and apply the script's actions to a BatchList.

You can drag the script's ActionArrow onto an open BatchList and the script's actions are applied to the list's files. By dragging a palette's ActionArrow onto a BatchList, you can quickly palettize all the files in the BatchList. You can also highlight only one file in the BatchList and drag it onto an open script or palette. Dragging one file is a useful way to test a script or palette to make sure it runs the way you want. You can also print BatchLists to document a project or to help in file management.

BatchList Icons

The BatchList contains icons that provide visual information about the files in the list. By looking at the icons, you can ascertain what the file type is and whether the file is open on the desktop or not.

The first column of icons to the left of the file's names in a BatchList in Figure 6.1 are the Open/Close icons. Open/Close icons tell you whether the BatchList file is open or closed on the desktop. The Open icon is an open book with an arrow going to the right. In Figure 6.1, for example, the file Dog.avi is open. The Closed icon is a semi-closed book with an arrow going to the left. In Figure 6.1, all the files other than Dog.avi are closed.

The next column of icons in the BatchList are the File Type icons; the File Type icons tell you what format the BatchList file is in. Figure 6.1 illustrates some of the File Type icons you can include in your BatchList. The File Type icons resemble the toolbar icons DeBabelizer Pro uses. For example, an Image is represented by a headshot icon; a Movie is represented by a filmstrip icon, and a BatchList is represented by series of papers as an icon.

From the BatchList, you can also see a file's extension. The extension can also show you the file formats included in the BatchList.

129

Adding Files to a BatchList

You can add files to a BatchList in a couple of different ways. One way is directly from the **Open** dialog box. Another way is to use the Add Files option found under the **Batch** menu. Finally, you can drag and drop files from one BatchList to another, or from an Explorer window to a BatchList window.

Add Files Option

When you have an open BatchList on your desktop the **Batch** menu becomes available. From the **Batch** menu you can select the Add Files option, which brings up the Add Files to the **BatchList** dialog box shown in Figure 6.2. The dialog box asks you to locate the files you want to add. You can highlight several files at a time to add to the BatchList and you see the files' names go into the File name field. After you have selected all the files you want to add, click the Add to Batch button, and the files are added to the open BatchList.

FIGURE 6.2

130

By clicking the Files of type arrow, you find the file format for which you are searching. In this example, only Image files appear in the window for you to choose.

In the Add Files to **BatchList** dialog box, you can modify your search for particular file types. The Files of type field acts as a filter to search only for the selected file type. The choices to filter by are images or AVIs.

The Open Dialog Box

The second method to add files to a BatchList is via the **Open** dialog box. The **Open** dialog boxes for images and movies give you the option to add files to a BatchList. You can add files to an existing BatchList by clicking the Open button (see Figure 6.3). DeBabelizer Pro prompts you to find a saved BatchList or to create a new BatchList. After you select a BatchList, the Add to BatchList button becomes active.

FIGURE 6.3

*Adding files to a
BatchList directly
from the Open
Image dialog box.*

Selecting New creates a new BatchList on the desktop. If you select an existing
BatchList, the files are added to the BatchList without ever opening the BatchList.
You do not have to open the files you add to the BatchList. If you click the Cancel
button, the file is still added to the BatchList, but unopened.

Drag and Drop

You can also create BatchLists or modify existing BatchLists by dragging and
dropping files from one BatchList to another. You can make a quick duplicate of an
existing BatchList by creating a new BatchList and dropping the ActionArrow of the
existing BatchList onto the new BatchList.

You can also use the Explorer option to drag and drop entire directories into an open
BatchList. The Explorer option is under the Tools menu. If your company has a
folder structure that it follows for saving artwork to, you can create BatchLists that
are also based on this structure. For example, if you have a folder for your finished
flattened artwork, you can drag this folder from the Explorer window onto an open
BatchList. The entire directory of files is now ready for a Batch Automation or script.

TIP

> You can also drag and drop files into a BatchList by using Explorer. This process
> is helpful for dragging a complete Web page with all its GIFs and JPEGs onto a
> BatchList. Open the Explore option from under the Tools menu. Find the Web page
> that contains your GIFs and JPEGs. Drag the Web page onto an open BatchList.
> Depending on your Naming conventions settings the files can be saved out with their
> original path—a nice feature for converting Web graphics.

The Right-Click

DeBabelizer Pro uses the right-click of the mouse for quick access to more options. Figure 6.4 is the menu for the right-click on an open BatchList. The right-click menu is the same menu as the Batch menu with the additional option of Show Log. Remember, the Batch menu is only available when a BatchList or Batch Log is active.

FIGURE **6.4**

The right-click gives quick access to the Batch menu with the added bonus of showing the BatchList Log.

BatchList Log

A BatchList Log records all the actions done to the BatchList including any errors which occur during the Batch Automation. You can take items from the BatchList Log and drag and drop them into a script or onto an open image. BatchList Logs are also useful for double checking that the files were processed.

The column headings for a BatchList Log are Operation, Parameters, Document Name, Date and Time, and Errors. BatchList Logs can be saved as independent files and reviewed at a later date. The following is a description of the BatchList's column headings:

- **Operation:** The actions applied to the BatchList

- **Parameters:** The specific details of the Operations. For example, how much dithering was applied, or is it a 256-color palette.

- **Document Name:** The name of the file being processed.

- **Date and Time:** The date and time that the files were manipulated.

- **Errors:** If there was a problem with the file and it could not be processed, it would be reported in the Errors column.

TIP

You can clear a BatchList Log by right-clicking the Log window. Clearing a BatchList Log is helpful when you are running tests on a BatchList. You want the most immediate information up front, instead of having to scroll down or getting it confused with similar actions.

You can also print the BatchList Log. Printing the BatchList Log is a useful tool for project management. It can provide a paper trail of events. Figure 6.5 is an example of a BatchList Log.

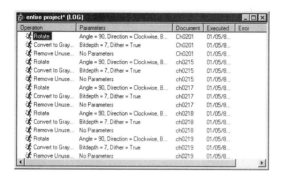

FIGURE 6.5

The BatchList Log keeps track of all the actions done to each of the images in your list.

The Batch Menu

The Batch menu can be confusing. At first glance, it appears that the Batch menu and the Batch Automation menus offer similar options. This is not true; the options the Batch menu offers can *only* be applied to an open BatchList. When a BatchList or a BatchList Log is open on the desktop, the Batch menu is available. Figure 6.6 shows the choices found under the Batch menu.

FIGURE 6.6

From this menu, one of your choices is to do a Batch Save to an open BatchList.

Batch Save

You can only do a Batch Save to an open and active BatchList. You can designate a naming convention for the files and choose the destination to which the files are saved. A Batch Save has all the same features as a Batch Automation Save under the Tools menu, except that it can *only* be applied to an open BatchList.

Create SuperPalette

You can create a SuperPalette based on an open and active BatchList. Creating this type of SuperPalette has all the same features as a Batch Automation SuperPalette under the menu. The only difference is that it can only have an open BatchList as the source.

TIP

Remember that **Batch** menu functions can only be applied to an open BatchList.

Create Movie

You can take an active BatchList and create a movie (.AVI file) from it. Your BatchList can be the single frames of the movie file. By choosing the Create Movie option under the **Batch** menu, a prompt comes up to tell you how many files were added to the movie and warns you if any files didn't make it into the movie.

BatchLists default to an alphabetical listing. If this is not the order you want the frames of your movie to be in, your naming convention needs to reflect this difference. Figure 6.7 shows the dialog box for creating a movie from the **Batch** menu.

Figure **6.7**

Creating a movie from a series of still images. If the images are not alike, then some images can be rejected.

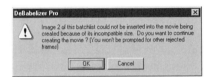

134

The movie takes on the attributes of the first image in the BatchList; the color depth and size of the first file become the attributes for the entire movie. Any subsequent files that do not meet this initial criteria are rejected. DeBabelizer Pro tells you how many images make it into the movie and how many are rejected (see Figure 6.8).

Figure **6.8**

DeBabelizer Pro informs you of how many images made it into the movie. This is a good proofing device for ensuring all the images make it into your AVI file.

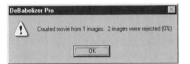

After a movie is created in DeBabelizer Pro, the **Movie** menu becomes available. You have three options under this menu: Create SuperPalette, Create BatchList, and Compression Options.

- **Create SuperPalette:** You can create a SuperPalette for your movie and apply it. You get a prompt asking if you would like to apply it to just selected frames or the entire movie. The movie SuperPalette has the same characteristics as any DeBabelizer Pro SuperPalettes.

- **Create BatchList:** Each frame in the movie becomes a file in the new BatchList, which is useful for saving frames for applying image manipulations you cannot directly apply to a movie file.

- **Compression Options:** From within DeBabelizer Pro, you can apply different forms of compression to the movie. Your choices are built into Windows 95/NT 4.0 operating systems.

You will learn more about creating movies and what you can do with them in Chapter 9, "Working with Digital Video and Animations."

Batch Automations

Batch Automations are one of DeBabelizer Pro's strengths. Being able to apply a process to a large number of files is very efficient and productive. Not only are they easy to use, but you can also create your own "Batches" by creating a script that then can be piggybacked on to a Batch Automation. You learn more about scripts in Chapter 7, "Scripting."

TIP

You can cancel a Batch Automation at any time by hitting the Esc key.

Selecting the Source

All the Batch Automations require you to select a Source on which to apply their process. Selecting the Source identifies the files to which the process is applied. Figure 6.9 shows the choices you have as the source. These are Image, Open Image, All open images, BatchList, Open BatchList, or a Directory.

FIGURE 6.9

You can select an entire directory as your Source, which is convenient if you have a network directory structure in place.

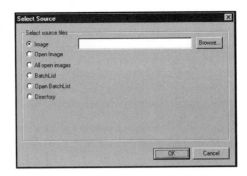

- **Image:** Choosing the Image option as the source enables you to Browse the hard drive to find the image you want. You can search the hard drive or connected servers by using the Browse button.

- **Open Image:** This option enables you to use the open and active image on the desktop as the source. All open images are listed under the Browse button.

- **All open images:** This option enables you to use *all* open images on the desktop as the source. No Browse option is available for this choice.

- **BatchList:** This option enables you to use a BatchList as the source. You can search the hard drive or connected servers for the BatchList by using the Browse button.

- **Open BatchList:** This option enables you to use an open and active BatchList on the desktop as the source. All open BatchLists are listed under the Browse button.

- **Directory:** This option enables you to use a directory as the source, which is convenient if your company has a network file structure it follows. For example, if you save all your final artwork to a folder titled "FINRGB," then you can select this entire folder to create a SuperPalette. You can search the hard drive or connected servers for the desired Directory by using the Browse button.

After you have selected the Source for the Batch Automation, the following screens vary depending on which Batch Automation you are running.

Why Use SuperPalette?

SuperPalette is an incredibly vital part of putting together any multimedia title. The importance of palettes is right up there next to file size. You don't want to see palette flashing during a presentation or title. Palette flashing looks crass and the technology has come along far enough that it doesn't have to be something you have to live with anymore. Optimizing palettes is an important part of every project on which you work. Also, custom palettes reduce the artwork size, enabling you to save on space as well.

After you have a SuperPalette in place, you can bring it into an image editing software as a custom palette and create additional art using the optimized palette colors. It can be used as a swatch of custom colors artists use for text or highlights. Using the SuperPalette colors for text and highlights can be done after a substantial amount of work has been done to create the custom palette. Having certain colors in mind as you create the artwork also ensures that those colors will definitely find their way into the project's custom palette. It works both ways, finding the palette based on the files in the project and creating artwork using consistent colors to then be polled into the palette.

Create SuperPalette

DeBabelizer Pro has two places where Create SuperPalette lives, under the **Batch** menu and under the **Tools: Batch Automation** submenu. Why two places? The two Create SuperPalette options handle creating SuperPalettes differently. The Create SuperPalette under the **Batch** menu *only* works with an open and active BatchList. The Batch Automation Create SuperPalette has more options for its source.

The first screen to come up when running the Create SuperPalette is the **Select Source** dialog box (see Figure 6.9). You can create a SuperPalette from the standard sources: Image, Open Image, All open images, BatchList, Open BatchList, or a Directory.

After you designate the source to use to create your SuperPalette, the **SuperPalette Properties** dialog box comes up (see Figure 6.10). Creating a SuperPalette follows all the information discussed in Chapter 5, "Working with Palettes."

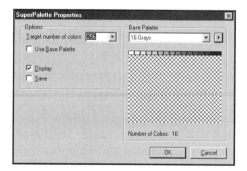

FIGURE 6.10

*The difference in creating a Batch Automation Super-Palette is that in the **SuperPalette Properties** dialog box you can choose to either automatically save or display the SuperPalette, which is not an option for creating a **Batch** menu SuperPalette.*

TIP

You can choose to do both save and display, but at least one of them needs to be chosen when creating the SuperPalette. If you choose to save, DeBabelizer Pro prompts you to name the SuperPalette and to designate where it should be saved to.

In the **SuperPalette Properties** dialog box, you can choose how many colors the SuperPalette has. You can also choose to have a Base Palette used in the creation of the SuperPalette.

You can save your SuperPalette and use it at a later time. All the color information stays with the SuperPalette. If you decide later to increase or decrease a SuperPalette's colors, you can easily do this with the information retained in the SuperPalette Properties dialog box.

After polling the files, the resulting SuperPalette displays the index colors for you and tells you how many images and pixels were reviewed in creating it. This information can serve as a proofing device to make sure you have the latest SuperPalette and it is based on all the files you need it to be.

You can also create a stand-alone palette from the SuperPalette with the **Create Palette** command from the **Palette** menu. The stand-alone palette can then be used in other dialog boxes within DeBabelizer Pro.

Naming Custom Palettes

Saving custom palettes with a job number or a name you recognize as being a part of a particular project is useful—especially if you are working on more than one project at a time. Each project can have its own SuperPalette.

Why Create SuperPalette and Remap?

The Create SuperPalette and Remap Batch Automation combines two powerful functions, creating a SuperPalette and applying it. The SuperPalette and Remap is efficient because you can see the changes made to the files as they are remapped. You can see what images are going to have banding or artifacts with the new SuperPalette. You can also keep track of those images and tweak them further to ensure that they look their best in the final project.

Create SuperPalette and Remap

The Create SuperPalette and Remap Batch Automation works very much like Create SuperPalette, with the added plus of being able to automatically remap the files to the newly created SuperPalette. You can create and apply an optimized palette to the files in one process.

The first step in the Create SuperPalette and Remap Batch Automation is to select a Source for the SuperPalette. After you have selected the source, the **SuperPalette Properties** dialog box appears. From the SuperPalette Properties dialog box, you can designate how many colors the SuperPalette has. You can also designate a Base Palette for the SuperPalette to include. After all the parameters are set for the SuperPalette, the **Set Palette and Remap** dialog box appears (see Figure 6.11). Notice that the **SuperPalette** dialog box automatically defaults to the new SuperPalette being created, which is used in remapping.

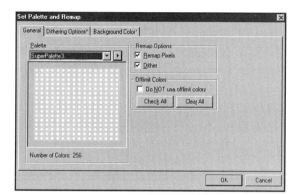

FIGURE 6.11

Applying the created SuperPalette means you need to tell DeBabelizer Pro how you want to remap or dither the files.

139

From the **Set Palette and Remap** dialog box, you can modify the Dithering Options* if you need to. If you know you need a particular amount applied from your dithering tests, you can change it here. After all the options are set to your liking, you can click OK. The files are instantly remapped to the new SuperPalette. As the files are remapped to the new SuperPalette, DeBabelizer Pro opens them on the desktop. You can watch as they are remapped to the new SuperPalette. If you like the way they look, you can use the **Close All** command from the **File** menu. The Close All option prompts you to Save All the files you have open on the desktop. Figure 6.12 shows the dialog box for the Close All option.

FIGURE 6.12

*The **Close All** dialog box tells you how many documents you have open.*

Why Batch Save?

Batch saving is often combined with customized scripts, making it a very useful and productive feature of DeBabelizer Pro. For example, you can use the Save Batch

Automation to crop a series of files as you convert them to another file format. After the crop is applied, you can then pass them off to the next production step.

Being able to save files to other file formats is important for CD-ROM titles. For example, some authoring or programming tools require that files be saved in a specific file format. You can convert your files to the desired format easily with the Save Batch Automation.

Each branch of the New Media industry has its own optimum format. For example, for Web graphics you want to save images as GIFs or JPEGs, DeBabelizer Pro makes this process much more efficient by converting files into compatible file formats for their final destination whether it is print, CD-ROM, or the Web.

Save

Using the Save Batch Automation, you can automatically save the files in the BatchList. The BatchList files can be saved with new names or with different file formats. You can also piggyback a script onto the Save Batch Automation, which allows for a large group of files to be converted and manipulated in the same process. Save Batch Automation is a very efficient process and can be used in more than one way.

The first step in the Save Batch Automation is selecting your Source. You have the standard set of choices (refer to Figure 6.9). The next step is to set up a naming convention for the files. The **Naming Options** dialog box automatically appears after selecting your Source, which you can use to designate a naming convention for your files. Figure 6.13 shows the Naming Options dialog box for the Save Batch Automation.

FIGURE 6.13

*The **Naming Options** dialog box for the Save Batch Automation.*

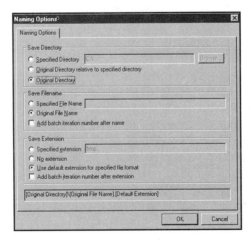

Naming Options

Naming Options specify the naming conventions you apply to your files and the destination of the final files as they are saved. The Naming Options dialog box has three main sections: Save Directory, Save Filename, and Save Extension. At the bottom of the dialog box is an example of the path and how the naming convention will read.

Save Directory

The Save Directory section of the Naming Options dialog box enables you to select the final destination of the saved files. You have three choices within this section: Specified Directory, Original Directory relative to the specified directory, and Original Directory.

- **Specified Directory:** You can choose the specific directory in which you would like to save the files. By using the Browse button, you can search your hard drive or any connected servers to select the exact directory you want.

- **Original Directory relative to specified directory:** You can save the files into a new directory that is relative to the Original folder from which the files came. In order to use this option, you need to recreate the directory hierarchy that the original files followed. DeBabelizer Pro does not recreate the path for you, so in the new destination directory that you specify you need to recreate that path.

- **Original Directory:** Using this option enables you to save into the Original Directory from which the files came. Unless you have a naming convention established you overwrite your original files. For example, if you add an extension or a batch iteration number, your original files are protected from being overwritten.

Save Filename

Save Filename enables you to designate a naming convention for your files after they have been processed. You have two options to choose from: Specified File Name and Original File Name. You can also choose to add a batch numbering to the file name by using the Add batch iteration number after name option.

- **Specified File Name:** You can use this option to designate a naming convention you would like DeBabelizer Pro to use. For example, you could use CH07DE as a beginning. All following files will have this same beginning, and the last two remaining character spaces can be provided by the batch iteration number. DeBabelizer Pro names the files sequentially through the BatchList. Make sure your BatchList reflects the order you desire. Double check that the Specified File Name you have chosen appears in the File name field of the Save As dialog box. If it does not appear there, press the Naming Options button and reenter your specified file name.

- **Original File Name:** You can choose this option to use the same naming convention as the original file. When using this option be careful not to overwrite your original files, unless that is your plan. You can prevent rewriting by adding a new extension or batch iteration number to the files. Changing the destination directory of the processed files can also prevent the original files from being overwritten.

- **Add batch iteration number after name:** This option enables you to sequentially add numbers to the end of your files. For example, if you named your files "AABBCC," DeBabelizer Pro adds 01, 02, and so on to the end of your filename as it goes down the BatchList. This option is useful for programmers who have macros to enter their assets into their programming software according to the file's sequential order.

Save Extension

Save Extension option enables you to save your files with an extension. The file extension can be an instant visual clue to the file's format. You can use DeBabelizer Pro's standard default extension. (Appendix A has a listing of all the extensions DeBabelizer Pro uses.) You can also designate your own extension; it may be a visual clue for you to know where the file is in your own in-house process. For example, if it has a certain extension, you know the file has been indexed. The choices for the Save Extension are Specified extension, No extension, and Use default extension for the specified file format.

- **Specified extension:** You can use this option to create your own extension, which could be an extension that follows a set in-house protocol. The extension provides a label for staff to know exactly where the file is according to the process it goes through from artist to programmer.

- **No extension:** By using this option, no file extension is added to the end of the filename.

- **Use default extension for the specified file format:** You can use DeBabelizer Pro's default file format extensions. For example, a Photoshop file would have an extension of .PSD at the end of it. A complete list of these extension is provided in Appendix A.

- **Add batch iteration number after extension:** You can add a sequential numbering to the end of the file name's extension. This option is similar to the batch iteration file name feature except that the numbers appear *after* the extension.

At the very bottom of the **Naming Options** dialog box is a text box. This text box provides an example of the naming convention you have chosen. It is useful to check here to ensure the name reflects what you need.

At any time, you can access the Naming Options button from the **Save As** dialog box. You can go back to the Naming Options and reset the naming conventions if need be.

Saving the Files

After you designate the naming conventions for the new files, you are ready to save them. After you hit OK on the **Naming Options** dialog box, the **Save As** dialog box comes up. Figure 6.14 shows the Save As dialog box.

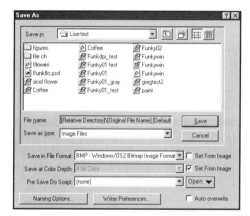

FIGURE 6.14

You have the option to go back into the Naming Options and change your naming convention.

143

From the **Save As** dialog box, you have access to a few more choices, which make the Save Batch Automation truly user-specific. The choices you have left to make for the files are the file format, the bit depth, applying a script, and naming conventions.

File Format

You can pull down the Save in File Format arrow to change the file format of files to be saved. If you check the Set From Image box, the file format remains the same as the original file. To access the **Save in File Format** menu you may have to uncheck this box. Once the box is unchecked you can change the file format to one of the many file formats DeBabelizer Pro offers.

If the file format you have chosen has a Writer Preference, you can also manipulate the file format by clicking the Writer Preferences button. You can make changes to the way the specific file format is written from the Writer Preference option.

Bit Depth

You can also designate a new bit depth for the saved files. The choices for your bit depth depend upon the file format chosen. Some file formats only support certain bit depths; for a complete listing see Appendix A. If you check the Set From Image box, the file's bit depth remains the same as the original file. You can only have access to the Save at Color Depth menu if the Set From Image box is unchecked.

Applying Scripts

You can apply a script directly from the **Save As** dialog box. By clicking the Open button, you can access the **Open Script** dialog box to locate the script you want to apply. The default is to apply none. This option is useful to piggyback a script onto the Save Batch Automation.

Why Batch Save with SuperPalette?

The reason this option is so useful is because you can change the file format. There are many times you create a SuperPalette and apply it to a series of files. Generally you want to palettize a file and then save it to another file format. Save with SuperPalette combines two of the most common uses of DeBabelizer Pro—file conversions and palettizing—into one batch run. You can create an optimum custom palette, apply it, and then convert the files to what is needed for the final project. For example, you could run Save with SuperPalette and pass the files off to a programmer, the last step of a multimedia project.

Save with SuperPalette

Save with SuperPalette enables you to apply a SuperPalette to a BatchList and then save the files to a different file format. Using the Create Palette and Remap doesn't enable you to change the file format of the files.

Using the Save with SuperPalette is a direct process. DeBabelizer Pro prompts you with text screens as you go through the process (see Figure 6.15). DeBabelizer Pro tells you all the steps you need to follow and what will happen next. The steps should look familiar to you because they are the same as both Create SuperPalette and Remap and Save.

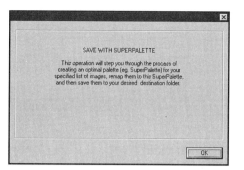

FIGURE 6.15

Nothing is left to chance. The text screen tells you exactly what you are going to do next.

Why Batch Print?

Batch Printing is useful for many different reasons. The most common reason has to do with organizing a project. You can organize a project before you start by having a printout of all the assets you have to create. If you run a Batch Print, the art director and production artist can easily pick the best images to use.

You can also organize on the backend as you are archiving the project. Being able to recreate a CD-ROM title, if you have to, is important for titles that get translated into other languages.

Running a Batch print is crucial for file management. You can Print all the pieces that make up a project and keep track of what has been revised or needs to be revised. You can quickly keep track of images no longer in the show.

Batch print keeps your work organized as the project passes hands, whether it goes onto a programmer or another artist. You can create Batch printouts of finished indexed art files along to a programmer. After all the art has been palletized and saved in the right final format, the printouts help the programmer to keep track of various assets if there should be a problem.

The final reason a Batch Print is helpful is for client approval so that text can be proofread, for example, or to make sure the latest revisions were made.

Print

You can do batch printing from DeBabelizer Pro, which is helpful for organizing your project. The first step in running the Print Batch Automation is selecting a Source. Your Source options are the standard Batch Automation selection as shown in Figure 6.9. You can only print images; you cannot print movie files.

The Printed page can have only one image per page. The default for the image to print is from the upper left corner of the page. If your image is very small, it will take up only the upper left corner of the page. The printing size of the image depends on the DPI of the file. Using the Set DPI Resolution before you run the Batch Automation can change the size of the image (see Figure 6.16).

145

FIGURE 6.16

Changing the file's DPI makes your files print in different sizes.

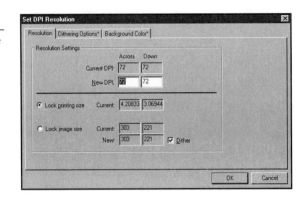

Changing the File's DPI

You can change the print size of your image by going into the Set DPI Resolution dialog box. You can find the current printing size your image has from this dialog box. In Figure 6.16, the image prints at 4.2 inches wide by 3 inches high.

If you would like your image to print larger than this, you need to decrease the DPI. Entering a value of 35 for the New DPI increases the printing size of the image to 8 inches wide by 6.3 inches high. The Lock image size box has to be checked in order for you to affect the printing size. Increasing the DPI to a higher number makes the printing size for the image smaller. You can run a script to change the printing sizes of your images before you do a Batch Print.

Page Setup

As you set the Batch Print to run, the **Print** dialog box automatically comes up (see Figure 6.17). The **Print** dialog box tells you to which printer you are printing. Clicking the Properties button enables you to change the orientation of the page; your choices are portrait and landscape. The Print dialog box comes up for each image in the BatchList. The setting for the orientation of the page is retained, but the Print dialog box still comes up with each file on BatchList.

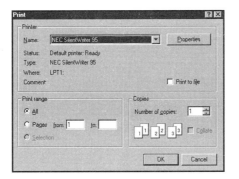

FIGURE 6.17

You can select the number of copies of each image.

Print to File

You can also choose to print a file to disk. Printing a file to disk is a convenient way of sending files for output to a Service Bureau. Most Service Bureaus help you setup your files correctly for their printers.

As you print to file, DeBabelizer Pro prompts you with the **Print to File** dialog box on every file of a BatchList (see Figure 6.18). The Print to File dialog box asks you to name the file and to select where it should be saved. DeBabelizer Pro adds the extension of .prn to files printed to disk.

147

FIGURE 6.18

You can select the destination and the names of the .prn files.

CHAPTER 7

Scripting

Scripting is one of the most powerful functions of DeBabelizer Pro—especially when you combine it with a Batch Automation. A script is a customized list of tasks you set DeBabelizer Pro to do for you. If you are creating artwork on one platform and need to resize it for another, you can create a script to resize your artwork. A script might, for example, take an image, resize it, convert it to grayscale, flip it, then save it out as a JPEG. It is basically a macro.

All of the manipulations you can do to a file via the pull down main menus can be put into a script. You can create scripts to do the work for you by applying a script to a BatchList of files. Scripts often include actions that you do routinely as a part of the production process. For example, you can run a script to remove the unused and duplicate colors in your indexed images before including the images in your Web page. Why would you want to create a script? If you routinely perform the same set of functions over and over again, a script is the perfect way to store those functions and execute them with a single command.

DeBabelizer Pro uses its own proprietary method to create the scripts. You can create scripts with DeBabelizer Pro easily—you don't need to be a programmer to do it. You can create a script by assigning which DeBabelizer Pro functions should be included in it. After you create the script, it is important to test it to be sure it does exactly what you had in mind. In this chapter, you learn how to create a script and what you can accomplish with them.

What Scripts Can Do for You

Scripts enable you to apply a whole list of functions to a BatchList. Applying a script enables you to have some standardization of your manipulations. This ensures that no matter who is sitting behind the computer, there is a consistency with the resulting graphics. Scripts also help you to automate functions so that you can leave your computer unattended while you move onto another aspect of the project. The ease of use and productivity of scripts is an important asset in any production cycle.

You can take an entire series of images and apply a script to it; opening that same list of files one by one to make the same changes would take twice as long. It is a huge time saver, with the added bonus of performing all the manipulations *consistently*.

You don't have to apply scripts to a BatchList, although that is the most effective use. You can also apply scripts to single files. You can drag and drop a script's ActionArrow onto a open file, and the script is executed.

Not only can you apply scripts to individual files and BatchLists, but you can also apply scripts to palettes. Not all of DeBabelizer Pro's functions can be applied to palettes via a script. You can apply the Sorting functions and color manipulations to a palette via scripts. For example, you could write a script that made particular index colors within your palette, transparent, or offlimit. Applying a transparency property to an index color is useful for images with a color designated to be a mask.

The Script Window

A script window lists the commands you want to be applied to a file, BatchList, or palette. To create a new script, chose **File:New:Script**. This calls up an empty script window. Script commands should go in the order of their application. For instance, if you are creating a script that removes unused or duplicate colors in a palette, you may need to have the script repalettize the files first. You wouldn't want to remove the unused and duplicate colors before the file is in the palette you want. Writing scripts requires a linear reasoning. Any manipulation you can apply to an image or movie file can be recorded as a script. The script holds the commands and the specifics or parameters of how each command is to be applied. See Figure 7.1 for an example of a Script window.

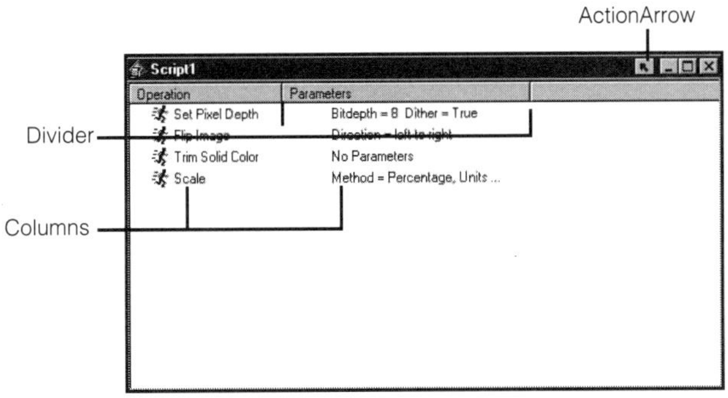

ActionArrow

Divider

Columns

FIGURE 7.1

The Script window lists the commands in sequence.

You can double-click on a Script command to set its parameters. Double-clicking the parameters brings up the function's dialog box where you can enter your own values. For example, if you double-click the Scale Command in the Script window, the Scale dialog box appears. You can set the Scale options to whatever you presently need. Not all commands require parameters. For example, if you add the Trim: Solid Edges Command to your script, no parameters need to be set. The parameters option is only for commands that have a Specify dialog box.

The Script window has two columns: Operation and Parameters. The Operation column lists the commands by their names. For example, a script for scaling an image would have "Scale" written in the Operation column. The Parameters column is for the settings each command uses. Depending on how wide you make this column, you can see all the settings or only a subset. You can make the column wider or shorter by dragging the divider to the left or the right.

You can rearrange the order of the commands in a script by dragging and dropping a command above or below another command. The order your Script commands follows is important, especially when one command must happen before another. You can highlight a Script command and press the Delete key to remove commands from your script.

Items in the Script window can be dragged and dropped into other scripts. You can also take items from logs and drag and drop them into open scripts. You can make a quick copy of a script by dragging its ActionArrow onto a new Script window; all the commands from the original script are copied into the new script. You can also repeat a series of commands by dragging the script's own ActionArrow onto itself. (This is convenient to use when you troubleshoot scripts; more on this later in the chapter.)

A right-click on a Script window gives you access to the **Script** menu as shown in Figure 7.2. It also lists the options under the **Script** menu. Remember, the Script menu is only available when a script is open and active on the desktop.

151

FIGURE 7.2

*Right-clicking a
Script window
gives you quick
access to the Script
Commands.*

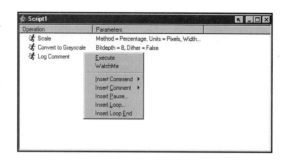

Why Scripts?

Creating scripts is useful for several reasons. Scripts enable certain functions to become automated. The most obvious benefit of the automation is the time saved, but an added benefit of this is that it also ensures your files will be manipulated consistently. For example, if you have images that were used in a color brochure that you intend to use in another product but cannot afford color, you could create a script to convert your color images to grayscale.

The alternative to this is to take each file one by one and convert it to grayscale. This can be long and tedious, but with a program like DeBabelizer Pro, you can create a script to do the work for you. This frees up time for you to go on to another task while DeBabelizer Pro does the work for you. Or, let's say you didn't have the time to do the operation yourself, you could hand the script to an intern and have them do it, with a minimal amount of training.

Another reason writing scripts is beneficial is that scripts, like BatchLists and palettes, can be saved as individual files. The script can be easily edited later or saved to a floppy disk or even e-mailed for people to use remotely—a great convenience when you are working with freelancers or if the art director and programmer are at separate locations. The scripts can once again ensure your files are being processed the way you want them done.

Having scripts on hand is also useful for project management; you can have all the pieces of a project, its BatchLists, palettes, and scripts archived should the project ever need to be recreated. For example, if a CD-ROM title is to be re-released in a foreign language, you have the artwork, palette, and scripts archived. Reinventing the wheel is an arduous task—you don't need to recreate artwork, palettes, and scripts for just changing text, audio, and sound files. The bulk of your production process is already figured out for you.

Creating a Script

To create a script, you need to have a script window open, which can be done by going under **File** and choosing **New:Script**. After you have a script window open, you have three possible ways to create your script:

1. Choose the **Script** menu and select **Insert Commands**.

2. Select the **WatchMe** mode under the **Script** menu.

3. Drag and drop actions from a Log or another script into the open script window.

Each method of creating a script gives you the ability to prioritize commands and to set the Parameters of each command accordingly. The script can then be saved as an independent file by whatever name you choose. DeBabelizer Pro adds the default extension of .dbs to scripts. Saved scripts can be reopened and edited at any time.

Creating a Script by Inserting Commands

After you have a script window open on the desktop, the Script menu becomes available. By using the Script menu, you can insert Commands into the script. DeBabelizer Pro's **Insert Command** submenus are a mirror of the Commands found under the main menus. When you select the Commands, they immediately go into an open script. Figure 7.3 shows the **Script** menu.

FIGURE **7.3**

The Script menu is only available when a script is active on the desktop.

153

You cannot add the commands from the main menus directly to a script. For example, if you want to create a script involving the **Set Palette and Remap** function, you have to go to the **Script** menu to add it. The options in the main menus are grayed out and unavailable.

Let's test writing a script using this method. You will create a simple script that will resize using the Scale Command and rotate your images. First, open a new Script window and right-click with the mouse button. The menus you are going to use to add the commands to the script are listed.

Let's add the Scale command. You want to resize the image first before you rotate it, just as a personal preference. From the right-click menus, you will find the Scale Command listed under the **Image** menu. By selecting **Scale**, the command is automatically added to your new script. Your script now reads "Unspecified Parameters" under the Parameters column. By double-clicking on "Unspecified Parameters," the Scale dialog box appears.

From within the Scale dialog box, you can set the new size of your images. For our purposes here, we are going to resize everything to 640 × 400 pixels. Our originals were 640 × 480. Choose Common under the Method choices and pull down on the size menu and you will find 640 × 400 listed as one of the choices. You can choose to dither the image as it shrinks. You can also keep the proportions of the image constrained. Press OK and you are ready for the next step.

Next we are ready to add the **Rotate** command to the new script. Right-click the window to get quick access to the **Insert Commands** menu. Add **Rotate** to the script by choosing the **Image** menu. You can select a preset DeBabelizer Pro degree of rotation. For example, you can choose 90°, 180°, 270° (all clockwise) or add your own degree of rotation by choosing **Specify**. For purposes here, we are going to choose the preset 90° clockwise. The 90° rotation is automatically added to your script.

You have just created a script that is ready to use. You can save it and use it whenever you are ready. Make sure that the list of commands in your scripts reads in the order you want. For this example, the script should read "Scale" first followed by "Rotate." If it doesn't, just click and drag the command to the order you want.

You should always test your script on one image to be sure to get the results you are looking for. You can go back into the script and modify the parameters of each command at any time. Once you have tested it and achieved the results you wanted, you are ready to apply it to the rest of your graphics.

Creating a Script in the WatchMe Mode

Using the **WatchMe** mode enables you to record movements as you pull down the main menus. You must have a script window and an image open to use the **WatchMe** mode. DeBabelizer Pro records your movements directly into the script window as you make the changes to the open image. To stop writing the script in **WatchMe** mode, select **Stop Recording** from the **Script** menu. You need to click back on the open script to get the Script menu back in order to have access to Stop Recording. Unlike the Insert Commands method of creating a script, you use the main menus in the **WatchMe** mode as you make changes to the image.

WatchMe mode is convenient for instances when you want to record exact movements. For example, if you need to move a pasted selection into an exact location, DeBabelizer Pro records the precise X,Y coordinates. The selection's move is documented in the script and you can apply it to all the files in your BatchList.

Here is an example of creating a script using the **WatchMe** mode. Open your image and open a new script. Because the script window is active and the **Script** menu is available, select **WatchMe** from under the **Script** menu.

Now make a selection in an open image, by copying the selection and pasting it into another open image. As you make these manipulations to your files, the script is recording your actions. Click back on the Script window to select **Stop Recording** from the **Script** menu. The script in Figure 7.4 is an example of the actions recorded into a script during the **WatchMe** mode.

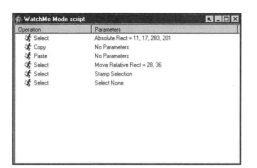

FIGURE 7.4

An example of creating a script using the WatchMe mode.

If you look at your Script window, it will have a list of all the actions you did. When using the **WatchMe** mode, however, some subtleties of a script may not get included. For example, if you open a document to copy a selection and then close the document, the opening and closing of the document won't appear in the script.

If closing the document needs to be in your script then you need to refine your script. When using the **WatchMe** mode you need to pay extra attention to the script's details. As always, it is best to test a script on one or two files to make sure it works before you apply it to entire BatchList.

In Figure 7.4, notice that the size of the selection is listed in the script under the first line "Absolute Rect = 11, 17, 283, 201." DeBabelizer Pro retains this information by watching the selection to the open image. This is a quick and convenient way of setting the selection size instead of entering the numbers into the **Selection** dialog box.

Further down in the script you will see the selection was moved, where it says "Move Relative Rect = 28, 36." This is another convenient way to get the results you want without having to do the math yourself. You can graphically move the selection by eye using the **WatchMe** mode to have the numbers recorded for you.

Having DeBabelizer Pro do the math for you is a nice shortcut. You can use this example to composite images into one another. If you have several foreground images that must be pasted into a common background image, you can use the method described to help achieve that end. Using the **WatchMe** mode when working with selections is useful because it can be done visually, by physically moving the selection to where it needs to go.

Creating Scripts by Drag and Drop

You can drag and drop commands recorded in one script into another script. You can also drag and drop items from an Image or BatchList Log. Using commands from a log is useful when you are testing manipulations to an image. As you perfect the manipulations, you can then drag the commands into a script.

Using the log approach to creating scripts is also helpful when working with selections. As you manipulate the image, the log records the exact size of the selection for you. You can take this data and drop it into a script. The selection size is automatically added to your script.

Another example of using the log approach to script writing is to keep the settings you used for one image and apply them to a series. For example, let's say you have a series of images that were scanned. The images are consistently washed out and need to be adjusted using the Adjust HSV Command. You can open one image in the series and make changes to it. Because the scanned images are consistently light, the changes you make to one should be applicable to all. You can take a tweaked image's setting from the image's log and drop it into a script.

Troubleshooting Scripts

There is an art to creating scripts. It's not that it is difficult; it just requires a certain mode of reasoning. A very linear approach is helpful, but, like anything in life, the more practice you have creating scripts, the more easily it comes to you.

After you create a script, it is a good idea to test it on one or two images to be certain it is doing what you want it to do. Some of the pitfalls to not getting the results you want is forgetting to add a step in the process you are automating.

Most of the pitfalls to scripts are in the small details of the process you are scripting. For example, if you are processing a series of files you will want to add a command that saves and closes your files. Always go back to the parameters you set and re-analyze them. Thinking in very concrete linear terms helps you to create successful scripts.

Other ways of troubleshooting your scripts is to think in steps. If you have a long complex script, break it down. Get each piece to work; after you have the smaller pieces working you can then try combining them into one script.

If you have a script that you cannot get to work the way you'd like, you can try to let DeBabelizer figure it out for you. Try creating the script using the **WatchMe** mode. After you have your original script and the **WatchMe** mode script, compare them. See where the differences are—the answer may be there as well.

Applying Scripts

You can apply a script in several different ways. The quickest way is to drag and drop the script's ActionArrow onto an open file or a BatchList. The script is instantly executed.

Another way to apply a script is to go to the **Script** menu and select **Execute**. You have access to **Execute** from the right-click of a mouse.

Going to the **Tools** menu and selecting **Apply Script** is another way to apply a script. Any open scripts on the desktop are available from the **Apply Script** menu. The last way to apply a script is directly from the **Save As** dialog box. You can apply a script as you save the new files. Figure 7.5 is an example of applying a script from the **Save As** dialog box. You can apply an existing script by clicking on the Open button next to the Pre Save Do Script menu. When you click the Open button, the **Open Script** dialog box comes up, prompting you to find the script you want to apply. The Script pull-down menu lists any script open on the desktop.

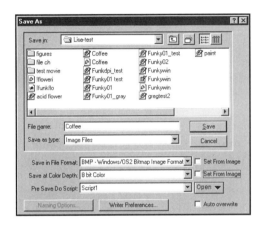

FIGURE 7.5

For an immediate result, you can apply a script as you save the file in a new format.

157

Dragging and Dropping Commands

You can also drag and drop *one* highlighted command from a script onto an open image or onto a BatchList. Only the highlighted command dragged and dropped is executed, not the entire script.

The Commands for Creating Scripts

Under the **Script** menu, you see a list of functions you can use for the creation of scripts. The functions you can add are commands, comments, and special Script functions such as pause and loop.

These functions help you to create a script. They also give you more control over how the commands are applied to your files. For example, instead of having to repeat the commands six times in a script you can insert a Loop telling DeBabelizer Pro to repeat the commands six times.

Insert Command

Basically, the command list mirrors the functions that are available in the main menus. For instance, you could go to the **Palette** menu in the **Insert Commands** to select **Set Pixel Depth**. After the command goes into the script, you can double-click it to give the specifics of **Set Pixel Depth**. If you have a script window active and you try to go directly to the main **Palette** menu, the options are grayed out. **Insert Command** is the most common way to create a script.

The best way to familiarize yourself with the particulars of writing scripts is to practice creating them. Play with the Commands—it is a matter of getting used to the order or sequence of events. After you get the timing down, scripting falls into place. It is also a matter of thinking concretely—if a documents opens it must also close. If I copy a selection it must also paste it into something. If you think with an "if, then" approach, you will be able to master scripts.

Adding Close/Save

When you are creating scripts, remember to add a Close or Save command. If you do not, when you run the script, DeBabelizer Pro reminds you and asks you to save the files or keep them open on the desktop.

Remember to double-check your program Preferences. If you are applying a dithering in a script, you need to make sure that you reset it according to what you need this time around, because Preferences settings are retained from the last execution. If you ran a script that had 50 percent dithering in it, the next time you go into the **Dithering Option*** preferences, it is set at 50 percent. This also applies to the **Writer Preferences** for certain file formats. Remember what your settings are, because you may run a script and get unexpected results. If something weird is happening, check your **Preferences** settings.

Another thing to keep in mind when creating scripts is that you don't need to overlap their functions with the custom Batch Automations. For example, if you are going to dither a group of images, set the script to do the dithering only. The **Save As** Batch Automation handles the opening and saving of the files. You need to think in steps like this and allow DeBabelizer Pro to do most of the work for you.

Insert Comment

A *comment* is a piece of information that DeBabelizer Pro can give you while a script is running. Comments are entered into an Image or BatchList log. You have the choice of four different comments you can insert into a script. The comments are Date and Time, Available Memory, Free Space on Drive, and a user-specified comment. Figure 7.6 is the example of the comment in the Script window, and Figure 7.7 is the final result.

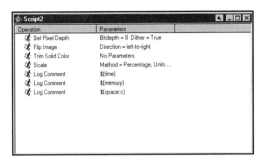

FIGURE 7.6

You could insert the time each file was processed for keeping track of your processed files.

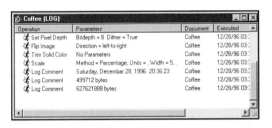

FIGURE 7.7

The log entry is a good proofing device for what actually gets done to a file. In order, the log comments are Date and Time, Available Memory, and Free Space on Drive.

159

Inserting comments is a good way to know what your computer is doing as it runs a script. For example, if you want to know how much a space is being taken up while running a script, you can have a comment keep track of the free space on your disk for you. You can monitor your computer to check the comment as the script is being executed, ensuring that your computer is being filled up by newly processed images.

Date and Time Comment

The date and time comment records the date and time a command took place on a file. Using the date and time comment is helpful for file management. You can use it to keep track of your files and their versions. If you apply a script with the date and time comment to a BatchList, the BatchList Log lists the date and time for each file. Figure 7.8 is an example of a BatchList Log with the date and time comment listed.

FIGURE 7.8

Keeping track of processed files is an important part of file management.

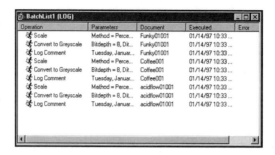

You can keep track of the versions of your files. File management is an important part of any multimedia project.

Available Memory Comment

If you have complex scripts to be applied to large BatchLists, you may use up your computer's resources. The available memory comment keeps track of what resources your computer has available as you apply the script.

Free Space on Drive Comment

You may want to calculate the drive space remaining as you process large BatchLists, especially if new files are being created that are not overwriting the original files in the BatchList.

User-Specified Comment

You can create your own comment to be entered into the Log. To create your own Comment, select **Specified** from the **Insert Comment** submenu. The dialog box in Figure 7.9 comes up; it resembles the dialog box for the text overlay function.

FIGURE 7.9

You can enter specific keywords and manipulate the way they look on the Log window by adding a new line character between keyword information.

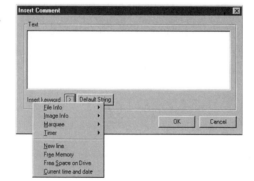

You can enter your own comment by typing into the window. The comment you type appears in your image or BatchList Log. Figure 7.9 also displays the menu for DeBabelizer Pro's list of keywords you can add. You can access the **Keyword** menu by clicking on the arrow button next to **Insert keyword**.

At first glance, it may appear that some of these options are redundant, but they aren't because you can group several keywords together. You are creating your own specific comment for the information you want to be listed in the Log.

You may select more than one comment from each submenu to make a list of information you want displayed in the Log. For example, you can choose to have the file path comment *and* the bits per pixel comment listed on one line in the Log. All the user-specified comments can be grouped together and listed in different orders. You can mix and match them to your own liking.

You should add your own user-specified comment to keep track of your files. Each one offers a different way to manage your processed files. For example, you may want to make a comment contain information about the name of the files. You can then print your log as a proofing device to keep track of the files that underwent the script.

161

File Info

You can choose to have a file's information listed as a comment in a log. The options you have are Filename, File Path, File Size, and File Date. Keeping track of this information in a log is a good proofing device to ensure your files have been processed.

- **Filename:** You can specify to have the Filename listed in the log. This can serve as a running list of the files processed.

- **File Path:** You can have a file's path added as a comment. Adding the path can be very helpful for file management. You can be certain the images you wanted to be processed where indeed processed. For example, if your company has a naming convention it follows and it is the same naming convention for all in-house projects, adding the file path to your log ensures the correct project files were processed. Keeping track of the file path can also be useful for retaining the integrity of your path for Web design.

- **File Size:** You can list the file size of a document. This size is the size of the original document prior to applying the script. For example, if your script applies a convert to grayscale command, the size of the file decreases as the color information is removed. The file size comment lists the original file's size not the file's new size. This can be a useful way to make sure your project will fit onto a CD-ROM. You can also use this to keep track of the sizes of images you are using on your Web page.

- **File Date:** Using this option, you can choose to have your file's last modified date listed. It does not list today's date, even if you have applied manipulations to the file. This is another way to manage your files, to ensure you have the latest version.

Image Info

You can choose to have an image's information listed as a comment into a log. Adding image info to a log is an excellent proofing device. The following list indicates the choices you have from the Image Info to be entered into a log.

- **Horizontal size:** This comment option lists the horizontal dimension of the file. DeBabelizer Pro lists the value in pixels. You can make sure your images are the correct size—this is especially applicable to situations where you are repurposing artwork, for instance, reformatting a project run on the PC to run on the Mac.

- **Vertical size:** This comment option lists the vertical dimension of the file. DeBabelizer Pro lists the value in pixels. This is a good method to ensure your images are the correct size.

- **Bits per Pixel:** This comment option tells you the bit depth of a file. You can use the Log comment as a way to ensure all your images are indeed palettized and not in 24-bit.

- **Colors per Pixel:** This comment option tells you how many colors are in a file; normally, it would list a file as having 256 colors. This option is tied to the bit depth of a file. For example, when a Netscape palette is applied to an image the image has 216 colors. Even though there are only 216 colors, the comment listing for a Netscape image reads 256 colors in the Log. Despite the fact that the Netscape palette has only 216 colors in it the image is still thought of by DeBabelizer Pro as 8-bit.

- **Cell number in animation file:** This comment options lists the cell number for an animation file. You may want to keep track of the cells in your animations.

- **Horizontal offset from upper left of corner page:** This comment option lists the X coordinate for your file. Some file formats have X coordinate that do not begin at 0.

- **Vertical offset from upper left of corner page:** This comment option lists the Y coordinate for your file. Some file formats have Y coordinate that do not begin at 0.

- **Horizontal DPI:** This comment option lists the DPI for the image horizontally.

- **Vertical DPI:** This comment option lists the DPI for the image vertically.

Marquee

Inserting a log comment is a useful feature for the X,Y coordinates of a marquee selection. You can use it to verify your selection or the placement of a stamped selection.

- **Upper left H coordinate:** This log comment lists the upper left horizontal coordinate of an active selection. It is the X axis of the upper left corner of an active selection.

- **Upper left V coordinate:** This log comment lists the upper left vertical coordinate of an active selection. It is the Y axis of the upper left corner of an active selection.

- **Lower right H coordinate:** This log comment lists the lower right horizontal coordinate of an active selection. It is the X axis of the lower right corner of an active selection.

- **Lower right V coordinate:** This log comment lists the lower right vertical coordinate of an active selection. It is the Y axis of the lower right corner of an active selection.

163

Timer

You can calculate the time it takes to apply a script to a BatchList by using the Timer Log comment. You may want to use this to time the process being applied to the files. From the Log you can ascertain how long a process may take.

- **Zero timer:** This comment option sets the timer to zero. You would want to use this feature before beginning your timer.

- **Display timer:** This comment option displays the timer in the Log. You can set this option sporadically through your script to time the script commands.

- **Pause timer:** This option pauses the Timer. You see a Log Comment listed in the Log but with no parameters.

- **Run timer:** This option usually follows a Pauses Timer Comment. This option resumes the Timer. You see a Log Comment listed in the Log but with no parameters.

Additional Comment Entries

You can add the following options as part of a series of comments you have created. They are options you could enter as a single comment but are offered here so you can group them with other comments: Free Memory, Free space on drive, Current Time and Date, and New Line.

- **Free Memory:** This log comment calculates your computer's resources. The available memory comment keeps track of what resources your computer has available as you apply the script. This a good comment to use when you have a long and complicated script to apply.

- **Free Space on Drive:** This log comment calculates the drive space remaining as you process large BatchLists, especially if new files are being created that are not overwriting the original files in the BatchList.

- **Date and Time:** This log comment records the date and time a command took place on a file. Using the date and time comment is helpful for file management. You can use it to keep track of your files and their versions.

- **New Line:** This comment option separates comments from one another in a log.

Special Script Functions

You can add other special functions to a script such as a Pause or a Loop. A Script Loop cycles a script through a series of commands. A Pause enables you to temporarily delay a series of commands. Pausing a script enables you to see what is happening onscreen. Special script functions help to fine-tune a script to get the best results.

Pause

You add a Pause to a script if you want to view the changes as the commands are happening onscreen. The Pause enables you to see the script executed. There are three different ways to execute a Pause in a script: a user-specified amount of seconds, stop and wait, and delay off.

- **Delay for X seconds:** You can delay the script for user-specified amount of time. You can use this to pause the screen as you watch the file being manipulated by the script. For example, if you have a script that scales images, you can watch the files onscreen as the scaling takes place occurs.

- **Stop and Wait:** The Stop and Wait Pause requires the OK to Continue button be hit in order for DeBabelizer Pro to keep running. When implementing this Pause, the user should be watching over the execution of the script or else the process is halted. Figure 7.10 is an example of a script with a stop and wait Pause.

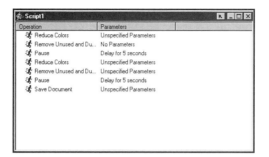

FIGURE 7.10

You can use a Pause to make sure you get the results you want. When reducing colors in an image, it is a good idea to watch as you go, to see where the image may break up.

- **Delay Off:** Another pause option is to use the delay off option. If you are testing a script or if you have a script you want to use but it already has the Pause inserted, you can toggle it off with the display off option. You can override the Pause temporarily by turning off the delay. To turn off the delay permanently, you can delete the Pause from the script.

- **Display Message:** Another option is to have a message displayed. You can make up your own message to display as the Pause takes place. Figure 7.11 is the dialog box for the Pause settings.

165

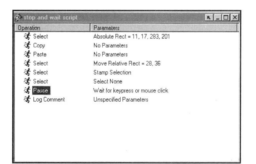

FIGURE 7.11

You can insert a Pause command into a script to interrupt the execution of the script.

You can create a message for yourself or coworkers to view while the script is being executed. You can press the Enter button in the message box to make the message box disappear. The message box will also disappear if the time runs out. The message window will display for a user-specified amount of time; if the Enter button is not hit in that amount of time the scripting process will proceed. The amount of time the Message box is onscreen depends on the value entered in the user-specified box. Figure 7.12 shows a sample of a message box.

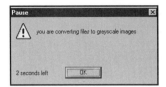

FIGURE 7.12

You can display a pertinent message as the script is running.

Looping

If you create a script where you want a few commands repeated, you can add a Loop. Looping enables the repetition of commands to continue until you add a Loop End into the script or the specifications for the Loop no longer exist. Figure 7.13 shows the dialog box for Loop settings.

FIGURE 7.13

You can loop a script while it has an active selection—a handy tool for manipulating files.

The trickiest part about setting up Loops is knowing where to enter the Loop in the list of commands in a script. It should go before the Command you need applied as a Loop. In the case of the Reduce Colors script, you list the Loop before the Reduce Colors Command. Also, a Loop should have a Loop End so that the script's commands stop, unless you plan on hitting the Esc key.

The following is a list of different types of Loops you can have:

- **Loop Forever:** You can have a Script loop forever until you press the Esc key. If you try to close out the image or script, it crashes. For example, you may want to Loop forever in a Script if you are trying to Reduce an image to the fewest colors it can handle.

- **User-specified Loop:** You can designate how many times you would like a Loop to last. You can Loop a script's Commands as many times as you need. After the number of Loops has been executed, the script proceeds with any Commands coming after the Loop.

- **Loop with a Selection:** You can set DeBabelizer Pro to Loop the script while there is a selection. DeBabelizer Pro continues to Loop until there is no longer an active selection.

TIP

While testing your script, if you get stuck in an endless loop unintentionally, you can press the Esc key to cancel the process.

ProScripts—A Hybrid Script

A ProScript is a hybrid between a script and an automated process. ProScripts are DeBabelizer Pro's way of creating commonly used scripts for you. You can download these from Equilibrium's home page at http:\\www.equilibrium.com. ProScripts are to scripting what Batch Automations are to DeBabelizer Pro.

ProScripts started as a way for Equilibrium to support the Web, and DeBabelizer Pro stays current by creating custom scripts. Equilibrium intends to keep adding to the list. There are four ProScripts presently available: Internet Remap to Custom Palette, Internet Remap to Netscape Palette, Remap to Windows Compatible Palette, and Trim and Scale. The ProScripts can be applied directly to files similar to the way a Batch Automation can be applied.

Although they read like a script, they are also similar to a Batch Automation. Like other Batch Automations, they require you to select a Source to which the ProScript is applied. Figure 7.14 shows the options you can select as source.

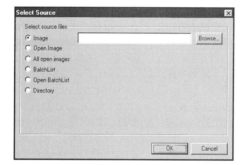

FIGURE 7.14

You must select a source for ProScripts.

167

You can open the ProScripts as a script to see the way they are written. They can be found in the Scripts folder in the DeBabelizer Pro directory. You can open ProScripts like you would any other script, by using the Open Script dialog box; they look like any other script.

Internet Remap to Custom Palette

To continue their support of the Web, Equilibrium has developed a ProScript to create a 128-color SuperPalette for your Web graphics. This ProScript also saves the files in your BatchList in three formats. The BatchList files are saved as an interlaced GIF, a non-interlaced thumbnail GIF, and a standard JPEG.

Equilibrium walks you through the step-by-step process of creating a SuperPalette via text screens. The first screen to come up is the SuperPalette dialog box (see Figure 7.15). You can specify a Base Palette to be included and you can save the SuperPalette immediately or display it.

FIGURE **7.15**

The SuperPalette-Properties dialog box automatically defaults to 128 colors.

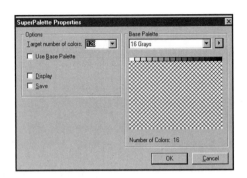

After you have created your SuperPalette of 128 colors, the Set Palette and Remap dialog box comes up, prompting you to set the dithering amount. The new GIF files are remapped, but the JPEG file is not. In running the ProScript, DeBabelizer Pro prompts you to save them to their original directory so you do not have to recreate paths. They are saved with the default extensions of .7bt for thumbnail GIF and .7bp for non-interlaced GIF.

Internet Remap to Netscape Palette

This ProScript is similar to the Internet—Remap to Custom Palette ProScript, except that instead of creating a 128-color SuperPalette, you can apply the 216-color Netscape Palette to your files.

You must also select a Source to use in this ProScript. The ProScript remaps the files and then saves the BatchList files. The BatchList files are saved in three formats: an interlaced GIF, a non-interlaced thumbnail GIF, and a standard JPEG. The files are saved to their original directory with the default extensions of .ntt for a thumbnail GIF and .net for non-interlaced GIF.

Remap to Windows Compatible Palette

The Remapping with Windows Palette ProScript automatically saves files by applying a SuperPalette with the Windows default 20 set as the Base Palette. This is a quick way to create a SuperPalette, with the Windows palette included in it. After you create the SuperPalette, you can remap your files to it.

The program prompts you to select a source on which the ProScript will run and leads you through the SuperPalette Properties dialog box and the Set Palette and Remap dialog box. Unlike the previous ProScripts, you can select the final destination of the files as they are saved; the standard Naming Options dialog box prompts you to name the files. After you have given your files a naming convention, the Save As dialog box comes up prompting you to select the destination directory for the saved files.

Trim and Scale

The Trim and Scale ProScript trims your files to the their solid edges and scales them while maintaining their original proportions. You must select a source to which you will apply the ProScript. You are also given the options of naming your files and saving them to a designated directory. This ProScript scales your files to 400 × 400 pixels.

Sample Scripts

In the next section, we have created some sample scripts for you to use and practice with. You can add your own variations to these scripts; they are not exclusive. They are just to give you an idea of what you can do with scripts. The best way to write great scripts is to practice and explore what DeBabelizer Pro can do for you. The idea is to get DeBabelizer Pro to do the most that it can for you and writing scripts is the best way to achieve this.

Multiple Copy and Paste

In DeBabelizer Toolbox, you can run a batch process called Place and Save. Essentially, this process takes an image or a selection of an image and pastes it into another document. You can use this option in situations where you are merging two images, such as pasting an image into a background image.

In DeBabelizer Pro, this Batch Automation isn't available, but you can create a script to do exactly the same thing. Figure 7.16 shows an example of the script order; you are opening one document and pasting that selection into all the files in a BatchList.

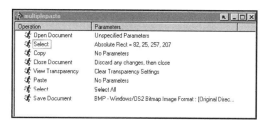

FIGURE 7.16

The basic script for pasting one selection continuously.

There are several variations to this basic script. Other options for this script include applying it to the frames of a movie, applying a different transparency setting to the paste, and moving the selection around. The key to making this script work is to insert the Close document command after you copy the selection.

This particular script saves the images as BMPs, but you can alter the script to save in any format that you need by double-clicking on the Save Document command at the end of the script. This example does not have a document specified to open, so when the script is run, it prompts you to Open an image. You can also add a Move Selection command to this script if you want the paste to be placed in a particular position.

Optimize Palette

If you need to optimize your Image palettes for taking out colors that are not used or are duplicates, you can create a script to do it. Figure 7.17 shows an example of the script and Figures 7.18 and 7.19 demonstrate how an image palette changes before and after the script is run. This will optimize your graphics for the Web.

FIGURE **7.17**

The basic script for optimizing images for the Web.

FIGURE **7.18**

The image palette before the script is run.

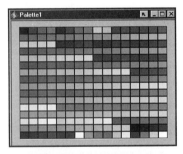

170

FIGURE **7.19**

The image palette after the script is run.

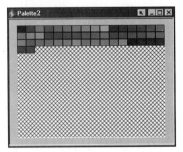

You can also use this script to create a Macintized palette. If you add a Sort palette Command to the script, you could have the palette sorted by RGB in descending order. You can add or change any of the settings of this basic script to create your own Palette optimizer script. The Macintosh needs to have Black (255) and White (0) placed in specific index numbers.

CHAPTER 8

Working with Web Graphics

Since the release of the NCSA Mosaic browser in 1993 when users were first able to browse graphic images on the Web, DeBabelizer has garnered a special place as the premier tool for preparing and optimizing Web graphics. DeBabelizer's capability to automate tasks, open nearly any file type, create custom palettes, and produce the smallest files with the highest level of quality have made it an indispensable tool for any serious Web developer. Many professional Web houses and independent artists use DeBabelizer for graphics production, and for good reason. This chapter explains why DeBabelizer is such a powerful Web tool and provides you with the information you need to know to make the most of your Web graphics.

The Challenges of the Web

As with all forms of new media, the Web presents designers with unique challenges—and limitations—for which they must devise solutions or find compromises. The three biggest challenges of the Web for graphics creators today are:

- The inherent quality limitations of the two major graphics file formats used on the Web today: GIF and JPEG.

- The complexity of palette optimization for limited resolution monitors and cross-platform viewing conformity.

- The necessity of creating the smallest graphics possible in light of the limited bandwidth available on the Internet.

Fortunately, DeBabelizer provides us with the best tools to meet these challenges.

Web Graphics Formats

The first problem faced in creating graphics for the Web is that browsers only support a small number of file formats. Initially, when the Web first came into use in 1989, it was used only for transferring text files in the form of HTML (Hyper Text Markup Language). Around 1993, the National Center for Supercomputing Applications (NCSA) developed a browser called Mosaic, which for the first time enabled the transfer and viewing of graphics files in the GIF format over the Web. With the advent of Netscape's Navigator a short time later, native support was added for the JPEG format and today the two file formats, GIF and JPEG, comprise the most popular graphic formats utilized on the Web. DeBabelizer can read and write both these formats and provides us with many extra options for fully optimizing them for the Web. Understanding the limitations and strengths of these file formats is the first step towards producing the best Web graphics. Let's now take a look at these file formats more closely.

Web Graphics Formats Supported by DeBabelizer Pro

Format	Compression Ratio	Description	Best Use	Drawbacks
GIF	4:1-10:1	8-bit color or less. Lossless LZW compression. Allows for transparent colors and interlacing.	Flat color images, images with text, images with small, sharp details, line art.	Limited to 8-bit color. Can result in color shifting and dithering in images with many colors. Less compression than JPEG format.
JPEG (JFIF)	10:1-100:1	24 bit color and 8-bit greyscale. Lossy compression.	High quality photographic and continuous tone images.	Small details often get lost or look muddy. Image quality suffers with very high compression ratios. No support for transparent colors.
PNG	10-30% better compression than GIF	Lossless compression. Up to 48-bit color and many improvements over GIF format.	Same as GIF.	Not yet widely supported by Web browsers.

Format	Compression Ratio	Description	Best Use	Drawbacks
Progres-sive JPEG	10:1-100:1	Same as JPEG but provides for incremental image display.	Same as JPEG.	Can slow display down with a slow CPU. No benefit on very fast Internet connections.

The GIF Format

GIF stands for Graphics Interchange Format. It was originally developed for use on the CompuServe network in the mid-1980s and was tuned toward the limited resolution 256-color displays of that time. It allows for data streaming and lossless LZW compression. (Lossless means that the compression algorithm doesn't delete any image data to compress the file.) It's generally the best file format for saving images with flat colors, text, line art, or images with great detail. It also performs better compression on images with horizontally oriented bands of color than verti-cally oriented ones so some images compress better than others. GIFs only support 8-bit color depth or less, so if you've got an image at a higher bit depth, you will need to convert it to an indexed color image before saving it as a GIF.

Let's take a look at the process of preparing and saving a GIF image for Web use. With GIFs, you always need to choose an 8-bit or lower color depth because they don't support any higher depths. It's generally a good idea to choose one of the dithered options because this provides better gradations between colors and better overall image quality. The depth you choose depends on what you consider accept-able image quality versus how small you want your file size to be. Almost always, the lower the bit depth and the fewer the number of colors in the palette, the smaller the file size.

The following steps cover the process of creating a GIF file for the Web. For now, we won't worry about specific browser palettes. The example we'll use starts as a 24-bit color Tiff. You can use any of the formats supported by DeBabelizer Pro, but in this case we will start with a Tiff image. Figure 8.1 shows the original 24-bit color Tiff image.

First, convert the image to indexed color by reducing it to an 8-bit or lower color depth. The easiest way of doing this is by accessing the **Palette** menu and selecting one of two menu items: **Set Pixel Depth** or **Reduce colors**.

The Set Pixel Depth Command

Choosing **Set Pixel Depth** provides predefined depth values from 1 to 32 bits. Try the different pixel depths to get an idea how your image looks at each setting. The trick here is to find the best compromise between file size and image quality. Differ-ent images, based on the types and numbers of colors they use, compress better or worse than others; experimenting with your images is the only way to find out. The best thing to do is to try each option to find the lowest bit depth you can use without losing too much quality. We usually try the lowest bit depth that will look good, undo it, and then try the next lowest until a good compromise is found between quality and file size. We always weigh smaller file size as more important than image quality with Web graphics, but the real trick is in finding the best balance between the two. Figures 8.2, 8.3, and 8.4 show the results of several bit depths applied to the same image (please refer to the CD to view the figures in this chapter in color). The best result is Figure 8.3, with the best balance of image quality versus file size.

FIGURE **8.1**

The original 24-bit color image opened in Tiff format. File size is 64K.

174

FIGURE **8.2**

Compare the original image in Figure 8.1, this one, 8.3, and 8.4; this image has been reduced to 8 bits/256 colors, and it has a final file size of 16K while maintaining very good image quality.

FIGURE 8.3

This image has been reduced to 5 bits/32 colors— notice the banding in the shadows. Final file size is 11K.

FIGURE 8.4

This image has been reduced to 4 bits/16 colors, producing heavy dithering in the shadows. Final file size is 9K.

TIP

Other programs that save GIF and JPEG files, such as Adobe Photoshop, LView, and CorelDraw, tend to compress files less efficiently than DeBabelizer. Also, they usually include more information in the final saved file, such as preview icons and other info that add to the file size. This extra information is unnecessary for graphics residing on a Web server. DeBabelizer Pro by default doesn't include this extra information and compresses images more efficiently, almost always producing smaller file sizes than the other programs when saving the same images.

The Reduce Colors Command

Choosing **Reduce Colors** from the **Palette** menu instead of **Set Pixel Depth** brings up the Reduce Colors dialog box, allowing you much greater control over the final number of colors in your image (see Figure 8.5). With this dialog box, you can specify the exact number of colors in your indexed image to bring the file size down even more using much smaller increments. Rather than having a choice between

5 bits/32 colors and 4 bits/16 colors, you could choose something like 24 colors, which would make for a smaller file size than 5 bits but still provide better image quality than the 4-bit option. Again, you need to experiment with different color depths to find the ideal one; it can be a tedious task, but a savings of a few K per image adds up to a lot on a multi-image Web site. Figure 8.6 shows the results of the image saved with only 24 colors.

FIGURE 8.5

The Reduce Colors dialog box enables you to enter the exact target number of image colors.

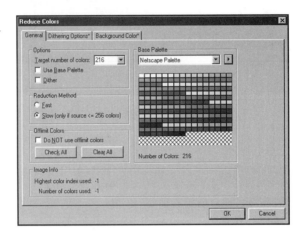

FIGURE 8.6

After trial and error, a minimum color depth of 24 colors is decided on; final file size is just under 10K, halfway between the 5-bit and 4-bit file sizes.

The rest of the options in the Reduce Colors dialog box provide for additional tweaks. For the moment, you don't have to worry about the Base Palette; this is covered later in the chapter. The Reduction Methods refer to DeBabelizer Pro's algorithms for analyzing and reducing color use. The Fast method uses an algorithm based on Median Cut whereas the Slow method algorithm is based on color clusters. It is usually best to stick with the Fast method, but you can experiment to see which method works best for you. The Marked Colors option enables you to designate off-limit colors in the palette. More about this later.

Once you finally select the proper color depth for your GIF file, it's time to save it. Save a GIF file by choosing **Save As** from the **File** menu and designating the GIF format in the Save in File Format pull-down menu. The Save at Color Depth pull-down menu enables you to choose predefined color depths that will override the current image depth once you press OK and exit the box. Be sure that the color depth listed here matches your desired color depth, or if it is not listed, check the Set from Image option to use your current image's color depth values. More options are available by clicking the Writer Preferences button. These are covered in the next section.

GIF Format Options

The GIF format provides several options and extensions for Web graphics that can be utilized by DeBabelizer Pro. Besides the standard GIF format, DeBabelizer Pro also supports interlacing and transparent colors as well as dithering when reducing colors. Though DeBabelizer Pro is capable of generating multi-image GIFs, they only provide slide-show capabilities and currently cannot be saved directly in a GIF animation format (GIF89a). To create GIF animations, you need to export individual frames into a third party utility, such as GIFBuilder by Yves Piguet for the Macintosh or Alchemy Mindworks' GIF Construction Set for Windows.

Dithering

Dithering is the process of simulating a greater range of colors by mixing patterns to make the eye perceive additional colors. It is introduced into an image as its color depth is reduced to lessen the effect of a smaller color palette.

Though a dithered image usually looks better then a non-dithered one, under some circumstances it's desirable to avoid dithering. The reason for this is that browsers perform their own dithering when using a limited palette that can create unexpected results with your images. Another reason is that dithering makes for poorer image compression by the GIF algorithm, which works best with large areas of uniform color. In general, if you can get away without dithering your Web graphics, they'll be smaller in size and less likely to dither poorly in the Web browser. As a rule of thumb, we analyze the image first to decide if it should be dithered. Images with lots of subtle shading and gradual transitions between lots of colors are best with dithering. Flat color images, especially ones with a small range of colors, usually do well without dithering. Ultimately though, experimenting with your images is often the best way to tell which method works best. In time, you'll gain a good sense as to how an image will respond to dithering just by looking at it.

DeBabelizer Pro easily lets you turn on or off dithering when reducing an image's color depth. The Set Pixel Depth, Set Palette and Remap, Reduce Colors, and Convert to Greyscale dialog boxes all turn on or off dithering through a check box in each of their dialog windows. You can also access the dithering options from these windows by clicking the dithering options tab where you can change the dithering amount by specifying a percentage. The ability to change the dithering amount is useful for Web graphics and worth experimenting with because it has an effect on image quality and final image size. To lower the amount of dithering, choose a smaller number using the slider or by typing a number manually. You can also designate a background color not to dither even when dithering the rest of the image. This is useful if you need to make a background color in the image transparent, because dithering can introduce other colors into the background and ruin your transparent effect.

Interlacing

Interlaced GIFs display incrementally as they load into the browser, gradually coming into focus, rather than waiting for the entire image to download. This enables the viewer to see an early low-res approximation of what the image looks like before it is completely downloaded. This is accomplished by displaying regularly spaced horizontal lines of the image and gradually filling in the missing lines until all of them have been displayed. Interlacing adds a few K to an image size, but it's generally a desirable option for GIFs destined for the Web, especially for people with slow connections. The interlacing option is available via the GIF Output Options window accessible by clicking the Writer Preferences button in the Save As dialog box. To make your GIFs interlaced, check the Interlaced box in the File Options area as shown in Figure 8.7.

178

FIGURE 8.7

The option for interlacing images is available in the File Options area of the GIF Output Options window.

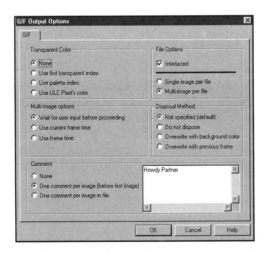

Transparency

The GIF format also supports the capability to designate one or more colors in the image as transparent. Designating a transparent color enables you to create images that knock out of the Web page's underlying background (see Figure 8.8) rather than having images with opaque rectangles of color (see Figure 8.9) surrounding the main image. Though the GIF format can support multiple transparent colors, DeBabelizer Pro currently only supports one transparent color in its writer preferences. The option is available via the GIF Output Options dialog box accessible by clicking Writer Preferences in the Save As dialog box and selecting one of the transparent color options (refer to Figure 8.7).

FIGURE **8.8**

A GIF with transparency applied to the background color, allowing it to knock-out of the page.

FIGURE **8.9**

A GIF without any transparency applied appears as an image in a rectangular box with an opaque background.

179

The following is a list and description of the four different transparency options available:

- **None.** This turns off the transparency option.

- **Use first transparent index.** Because DeBabelizer can only create one transparent color, this option takes the first index color that has been designated as transparent in the Palette Properties for that color (see Figure 8.10).

- **Use palette index.** This option enables you to specify the index number of any color in the current palette to designate as the transparent color. This requires you to look at the image's palette in order to determine the index number of the desired color.

- **Use ULC Pixel's color.** This option takes the first color in the upper-left corner of the palette (at index value 0) and uses this to define the transparent color.

FIGURE 8.10

Double-clicking any color in a palette brings up the Palette Properties window where you can designate that color as transparent.

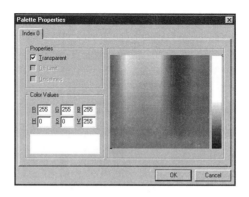

TIP

You can hold the Eyedropper over any portion of an image to determine which color is being used in the palette (the color in the palette window will highlight when the Eyedropper hovers over the corresponding color in the image). Double-click the color in the palette to bring up the Palette Properties where you can designate the color as transparent.

After you've defined the transparent color, click OK and save your image in the GIF format. You won't be able to see the transparent effect until you place the GIF over a background or another image on your Web page and preview it with your browser.

The JPEG Format

JPEG stands for Joint Photographic Experts Group, the name of the committee that wrote the standard. The JPEG or JFIF (JPEG File Interchange Format) standard is the second major file format for Web graphics and started to come into use on the Web around 1994. It is tuned for 24-bit color images and uses a more efficient DCT-based algorithm for image compression, which can achieve compression ratios as high as 100:1. The format is dependent upon the CPU speed of the client computer because JPEG is decoded on the fly, but this is usually not an issue with today's faster computer processors.

One of the main distinctions between the JPEG and GIF formats is that JPEG provides lossy compression. This means that the JPEG format achieves its compression by throwing out image data. Once the file is saved in the JPEG format, this image data is permanently lost, unlike with the GIF format, which retains all its image data. This isn't necessarily a problem provided you keep copies of your original images before saving them as JPEGs. Another major distinction is that the JPEG format allows images to be saved at 24-bit color, allowing for much greater image quality and color variation than with the GIF format. Note that unlike GIFs, JPEGs support only two bit depths, 24-bit color and 8-bit grayscale, and nothing inbetween.

When attempting to save a color image that has been palletized or reduced from 24-bit as a JPEG, DeBabelizer will either resample it to 24 bits or convert it to 8-bit grayscale. You need not reduce color images when saving them as JPEGs. Because of this, DeBabelizer Pro offers only two color depth options in the Save As dialog box when you select the JPG format, 8-bit grayscale or 24-bit color. Make sure you select the proper bit depth for your image before saving it.

TIP

The JPEG format only supports two bit-depths: 8-bit grayscale and 24-bit color. Palettizing or reducing a 24-bit color image in DeBabelizer Toolbox will cause it to convert to grayscale when you try to save it as a JPEG. DeBabelizer Pro will only enable you to save in 24-bit color or 8-bit grayscale when you attempt to save it. Make sure your images are either 24-bit color or 8-bit grayscale before saving them in the JPEG format. Attempting to reduce the palette beyond 24 or 8 bits will not result in any savings in file size and will compromise the quality of your images.

Knowing which format to use, GIF or JPEG, is one of the most important skills for a good Web graphics creator. Although the GIF format works best for flat color and sharp-edged art, the JPEG format works much better for full color, grayscale, photographically real, or continuous tone images. It does a much poorer job with text and smaller images having tighter detail. Figure 8.11 shows a comparison of the same photographic image saved as both a JPEG and a GIF. In this example, not only does the GIF image dither, but it compresses poorly due to the lack of any large areas of uniform color.

FIGURE 8.11

The image on the left has been saved in JPEG format, on the right in GIF format. Notice the difference in image quality. File size for JPEG is 12K, for GIF 26K.

In Figure 8.12, an image with text has been saved in both GIF and JPEG formats to illustrate the differences between the two. Here the GIF format works much better, producing better image quality and even achieving better compression due to the large area of solid white in the image, which works well with the GIF compression algorithm.

181

FIGURE 8.12

This image is better suited for the GIF format. The image on the left has been saved in JPEG format, on the right in GIF format. File size for JPEG is 7K, for GIF only 3K.

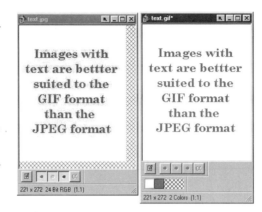

Let's take a look now at the process of preparing and saving a JPEG image for Web use. Because it's a 24-bit format, you don't have to worry about palettes.

To save your image as a JPEG, perform the following steps.

1. Once you've decided that your image is best suited for the JPEG format, choose **Save As** and Designate JPG in the Save in File Format entry box by selecting it from the pull-down menu (see Figure 8.13).

FIGURE 8.13

The Save As dialog box enables you to select the JPG format. Notice only two color depths are supported in the color depth pull-down menu.

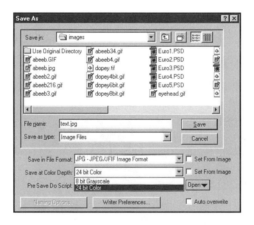

2. Take a look at the Save at Color Depth entry box. Make sure you select the correct bit depth depending on whether your image is grayscale or color.

3. Select the appropriate compression setting with the JPEG Output Options by clicking on the Writer Preferences button. The JPEG Output Options dialog box (see Figure 8.14) enables you to select a compression setting between one and 100; the lower the number, the smaller the file size will be. You can use the slider or simply type a value. You'll have to experiment with different values to get the optimal balance between image quality and compression, but we find the best setting usually falls somewhere between 65 and 75 percent.

The Force baseline compatibility option forces a setting between 25 and 100 percent even if you choose a setting of, say, 15 percent. The reason for this is that baseline compatibility is a required standard of all applications supporting the JPEG standard. Some JPEG applications won't recognize a JPEG saved lower than a 25 percent setting, so forcing a cut-off of 25 percent ensures compatibility with all applications that can read JPEGs.

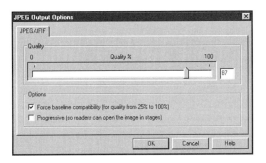

FIGURE 8.14

You can select a compression / quality level from 1 to 100 for a JPEG file.

5. The Progressive option enables you to save the image as a Progressive JPEG. A Progressive JPEG acts like an interlaced GIF that displays incrementally in the browser as it downloads. Progressive JPEGs are a newer subset of the JPEG format and are not supported by all browsers, although both Netscape Navigator (2.0 and later) and Microsoft Internet Explorer (3.0 and later) do have built-in support.

183

The PNG Format

PNG (pronounced "ping") stands for Portable Network Graphic. It evolved as a grass-roots effort among graphics developers on the Internet to replace the GIF format in response to the attempt by CompuServe and Unisys to demand royalties from applications that implemented GIF. Although royalties were never collected, the PNG format stands as a substantial improvement over the GIF format. For the Web, it has some excellent advantages over GIF:

● 48-bit color and 16-bit alpha channels

● Built-in gamma correction, which allows for cross-platform control of image brightness

● Two-dimensional interlacing

● An average of 10–30 percent better compression

As for drawbacks, PNG does not support multiple images such as GIF animation files and it still has not received wide support on the Web as a graphics standard, although it is now being officially recommended by the W3C committee and other companies such as Apple Computer. If your targeted audience only includes the major browsers such as Netscape and Explorer, PNG is a great way to go. More browsers are adding support all the time and the latest info can be found on the PNG home page at: http://www.wco.com/~png/.

The method for saving a PNG file in DeBabelizer Pro simply involves selecting the PNG format in the Save As dialog box and indicating the desired bit depth (1- to 32-bit depths are supported). DeBabelizer Pro can also open PNG files created in other graphics programs. You'll achieve better compression on images that don't use dithering when using PNG.

Color Palettes and Web Graphics

One of the big challenges of working with Web graphics is dealing with limited resolution computer monitors and the problems they pose when trying to display more than 256 colors in the browser window. Naturally, monitor resolution is dependent on the capabilities of the monitor and the video card driving it. Although higher resolution video cards are becoming standard these days, many Web users are still only capable of viewing sites with a maximum of just 256 colors. Some estimations say that 70 to 80 percent of the users on the Net have only 256 color displays.

With the capability to display only 256 colors, a browser window with multiple GIFs, JPEGs, and screen resources (windows, scroll bars, menus, and so on), will require more than 256 colors to display all of its information. In this case, colors falling beyond the 256 color limit will shift in color or become dithered so that only 256 colors are displayed at any one time. This phenomenon is known as *palette flashing* and can adversely effect the quality of your displayed Web graphics. In addition to the 256 color limit, different computer platforms use different color palettes so that the range of colors viewable on one platform will be different from another. This presents a major problem for Web designers. Fortunately, DeBabelizer facilitates making graphics that fall within the limited color ranges displayable on lower resolution monitors and are optimized for cross-platform palette differences. In Chapters 4 and 5, you learned about using DeBabelizer to create custom palettes for your images. Now you'll learn about DeBabelizer's capability to create and save a cross-platform, 256-color-optimized palette.

NOTE

Remember you need not worry about color palettes and color reduction with JPEG files. JPEG images dither to the same browser palette as GIFs on lower resolution displays, but the image quality is usually more acceptable. Color palette optimization applies only to GIF images.

A lot of talk and confusion surrounds color palettes on the Web. Anybody who has designed a Web site on a high resolution monitor and then looked at the results on a

256-color display was probably in for a surprise. This is especially true if they used one computer platform to create the site and then another platform to view it.

One of the principal problems with Web graphics is that Windows, Macintosh, and Unix all utilize different system palettes to display screen colors. That means that at 256 colors, not all of the colors are the same across the three platforms. Netscape on the Macintosh and XWindows (Unix) platform use a 256-color palette. Other Unix versions of Netscape vary the palette according to the number of available colors, while Netscape for Windows uses a 223-color palette.

To deal with this problem, Netscape devised a common palette, or color cube, based on the 216 colors common to both the Mac and Windows platforms because they comprise the vast majority of Web users. Remapping all or some of your GIFs to the Netscape palette helps to ensure cross-platform color fidelity and minimal dithering and works equally well with Microsoft's Internet Explorer. Another advantage of the Netscape palette is that it tends to lend itself well to GIF compression. Often, a 216-color image mapped to the Netscape palette will compress better than images with fewer colors mapped to a different palette.

TIP

DeBabelizer Pro ships with the Netscape palette built into the palette menu, making it easily accessible when you index your color images. DeBabelizer Toolbox requires you to load the Netscape palette separately. For Toolbox users, the palette is included on the CD-ROM.

So what about JPEGs? Remapping is not necessary or even possible with JPEGs because they can't be made into palletized images. The browser applies its own dithering to JPEGs using the same browser palette as for GIFs. With JPEG images, however, the worst results tend to look better onscreen than the worst results for GIF images. Another benefit of JPEGs is that they look great on higher resolution displays whereas GIFs do not improve with higher resolution.

Using the 216-Color Netscape Palette

To conform a graphic to the Netscape palette, select **Set Palette and Remap** from the **Palette** menu while your target image is open. This brings up the Set Palette and Remap window, enabling you to choose the Netscape palette from a pull-down menu (see Figure 8.18). Notice that once you select the palette, the 216 colors are displayed in the palette window. Make sure that the Remap Pixels option is checked and click OK. The image will then remap the pixels to the Netscape palette, which uses only 216 colors.

TIP

The Netscape palette not only reduces the chances of palette flashing on 8-bit color monitors, but images utilizing the Netscape palette tend to compress better than images saved to other palettes, even ones with fewer colors!

FIGURE 8.15

Designating the Netscape palette in the Set Palette and Remap window.

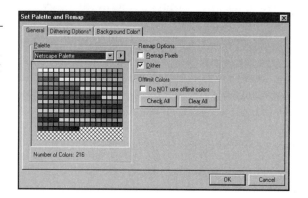

186

The visual results of setting your image to this palette vary greatly from one image to another. You'll generally find you get the most visually pleasing results using the dither option, though it's preferable to turn this off if you can. The reason for this is that the browser performs its own dithering even if you pre-dither an image. It's ultimately best to let the browser do your dithering for you if possible. If all of your images on the page conform to the Netscape palette already, then it's less of an issue. Ideally, the best results are obtained by creating your graphics in the first place using only Netscape palette colors. This eliminates the need to dither the image in the browser and it makes for smaller files since the GIF format performs better compression when using Netscape palette colors. You can load the Netscape palette into a program like Adobe Photoshop and use the palette colors to draw your image. Because GIFs work best for flat color art, you can usually get away with using a minimum of colors in your art, which is the ideal scenario and produces the best results for Web graphics. We recommend doing this for all your buttons, logos, and other artwork saved in the GIF format.

Create Your Images Using the Netscape Palette

One of the most important things you can do to improve the look and size of your GIF files is to create them using the Netscape palette from the start. This palette can be loaded into many image editing programs and used to draw your logos, buttons, and graphics. Doing this consistently prior to DeBabelizing your images will make a big difference in image quality and file size and avoid all of the problems with palette flashing.

Figures 8.16 and 8.17 illustrate the results of using the Netscape palette versus not using it. The first example in each figure shows the original image before reducing to the Netscape palette. Figure 8.16 was created without using the Netscape palette and then shows the results of the 216-color palletized image. Figure 8.17 was created using Netscape colors from the start and was then saved to the same palette. Notice the difference in quality between the two different images.

FIGURE 8.16

The image on the left was created without using any particular palette colors. The image on the right shows the results when reduced to the 216-color Netscape palette.

187

FIGURE 8.17

The image on the left was created from the start using only the Netscape palette colors. The image on the right shows the results when reduced to the 216-color Netscape palette.

Using the Netscape Palette ProScripts Wizard

ProScipt Wizards are built-in scripts made available by Equilibrium, using Wizard technology to walk you through the steps of carrying out operations in DeBabelizer Pro. They are available for DeBabelizer Toolbox as plug-ins and can be downloaded from Equilibrium's Web site. In DeBabelizer Pro, they are accessible under the **Tools** menu by selecting **Tools:Batch Automation:ProScripts Wizard**. Choosing the Remap to Netscape Palette ProScript steps you through the process of remapping a specified list of images to the Netscape 216-color palette. The script allows you to save each as an interlaced GIF, a thumbnail GIF (non-interlaced), and a JPEG, all to the directory you specify.

The 7-Bit, 128-Color Palette

One of the problems with the 216-color Netscape palette is that the available colors can result in poor image quality with certain images. One of the reasons for this is that the Netscape palette is based on the limited Windows palette and most of its colors are ones that don't occur in nature. Consequently, certain images containing a lot of fleshtones, earthy colors, and other subdued colors tend not to look good when remapped to the Netscape palette. In cases like these, using an adaptive 7-bit 128-color adaptive palette will yield better results. An adaptive palette is a custom palette, created by analyzing an image's colors and then figuring out the best colors to represent the image when its color depth is reduced. The Netscape palette is not an adaptive palette because it forces the same 216 colors on an image regardless of the original colors in that image. Anytime you reduce an image's colors in DeBabelizer *without* selecting a pre-existing palette, you create an adaptive palette, unique to that image.

The reason for using a 128-color adaptive palette rather than a larger one is that 128 colors are less likely to dither than 216 or 256 colors. They usually provide for good image quality versus file size. Also, images saved to a 128-color adaptive palette usually look better than 216-color Netscape palette images on higher resolution displays, unless the images were created using Netscape colors from the start.

There are some trade-offs, however. Netscape palette images tend to compress better as GIFs, even more so than 128-color adaptive palette images. Also, with a lot of images set to 128 colors in a browser window, the images are more likely to dither than if they all used the same Netscape palette. Again, it's an issue of trial and error to find the best solution for each particular image. If you've got only a few images on the page and quality is of utmost importance, or your images are also intended for downloading, go with the 128-color adaptive palette. If you're using lots of images intended only for viewing on the Web and the Netscape palette yields acceptable results, you'll get smaller file sizes and less chance of dithering if all your images conform to the same Netscape palette.

To convert an image to a 128-color adaptive palette, select **Set Pixel Depth** from the **Palette** menu and choose one of the two 7-bit 128-color options. Whether you choose dithering or not depends on which one provides the best results. No dithering is preferable, but turning dithering on will usually make for better looking images. Remember also that you can always alter the amount of dithering in the Dithering Options preferences available in most of the Palette dialog boxes. You can also convert to 128 colors by selecting **Reduce Colors** from the **Palette** menu to call up the Reduce Colors dialog box. Here you type in the target number of colors (128), make sure Use Base Palette is unchecked, and check or uncheck the dithering option based on your results with the particular image.

Using the Custom Palette ProScripts Wizard

DeBabelizer Pro also offers a built-in ProScripts Wizard for creating a custom 7-bit SuperPalette. The ProScripts Wizard simplifies this process and allows it to be completely automated after walking you through a few initial steps. The ProScripts Wizard not only creates a SuperPalette based on all of the images you specify, but it remaps them, and saves multiple versions, an interlaced GIF, a thumbnail GIF (non-interlaced), and a JPEG file, all ready to be displayed on the Web.

To access the ProScripts Wizard for the 128-color palette, select **Tools:Batch Automation:ProScripts Wizard:Internet-Remap to Custom Palette**. The ProScript does most of what the above operation does, except that it walks you through the process step-by-step and prompts you for the pertinent info before applying it.

Creating a Custom SuperPalette for Your Web Site

If you're designing graphics for a single Web site, one of the best ways to control dithering and maintain image quality is to create a custom SuperPalette based on all of the images in the site. Some of the top Web sites on the Net such as *HotWired* use this strategy. By creating a custom SuperPalette, you take into account all of the images you intend to display and can optimize the Palette based on the most commonly occurring colors in your images. The size of your SuperPalette can vary, but in essence it is like a Netscape palette but uses the *best* colors to represent your images, not the ones Netscape has chosen. Unwanted dithering and palette flashing are controlled because the browser will always be displaying the same colors no matter which images are being viewed.

189

Before deciding to create a SuperPalette, you should assess whether a SuperPalette is the best option for your particular site. The problem with SuperPalettes is that the more images they have to represent, the wider the color variation and the lower the quality of each individual image will be once it's remapped, especially at lower bit depths. Web sites with a very large number of images with widely divergent colors may not be well suited to a SuperPalette. On the other hand, a SuperPaletted site, especially one with fewer colors will not cause any problems with palette flashing, even with many images on the same page. A Web site well-suited to Super-Palettization is one where most of the images use similar colors that don't conform well to a Netscape/Windows palette. For instance, a Web site composed mostly of screenshots from a Macintosh computer would do well with a SuperPalette, as would a site composed mostly of artwork from an artist that always uses the same earthy colors. The overall image quality of the graphics using a SuperPalette, provided the number of images isn't too large and their colors not too divergent, will be better than those using a Netscape palette.

You can create and implement a SuperPalette for your Web site the same way you would any SuperPalette. You can also use DeBabelizer Pro's SuperPalette creation wizard, which steps you through the process. The following steps cover the creation and implementation of a SuperPalette as it pertains to Web graphics. Consult Chapter 6, "Batch Automations," for more information on creating and implementing SuperPalettes through Batch Automation.

Creating a SuperPalette Using a BatchList

Since a SuperPalette uses a bunch of graphics to arrive at a common palette based on color popularity, a BatchList is a perfect way to organize your images in order to apply the SuperPalette. The following steps describe how to apply a SuperPalette to a group of images using a BatchList.

1. Create a new BatchList and add all of the images you want factored into the SuperPalette. You can also use the HTML parsing function described in the next section to do this. For the best results, use original unindexed images rather than reduced palette images.

2. Once all of the desired images are listed in the BatchList window, right-click the window and select Create SuperPalette. This brings up the New SuperPalette dialog box displayed in Figure 8.18.

FIGURE 8.18

The New SuperPalette dialog box enables you to specify the number of colors for the SuperPalette.

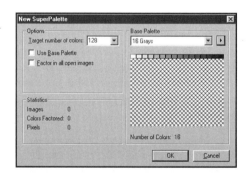

3. Pick the target number of colors to use for the SuperPalette. A 128-color palette provides a good starting point. Because your graphics are going to conform to the same palette, you could get away with more colors, but you'll need to do some experimentation. To play it safe, start with a 128-color palette or something close to it, then go down from there.

   Clicking OK brings up the SuperPalette in a new window. Notice the SuperPalette lists the number of images, colors, and pixels factored in at the bottom of the window (see Figure 8.19). You can use this to check that all of your images listed in the BatchList window are indeed factored into the SuperPalette.

4. To apply the SuperPalette to the images in the BatchList, drag the ActionArrow™ from the SuperPalette window to the BatchList window. DeBabelizer Pro then opens and remaps all the listed images to the new SuperPalette. Because all the images now open in their own windows, you can check their quality before finally saving them.

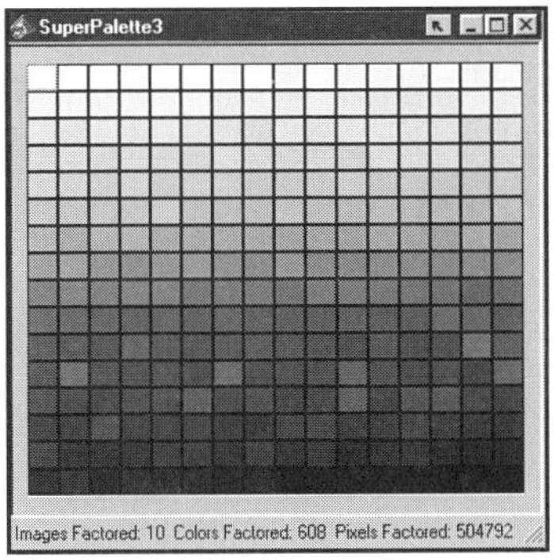

FIGURE 8.19

A SuperPalette is a custom palette derived by polling all the images in the BatchList to determine the most popular ones based on the target number of colors.

TIP

Once you have a SuperPalette window on the screen, you can factor in new images by dragging them directly from a system window or from the Explorer onto the SuperPalette window.

Creating a SuperPalette Using the Built-In Wizard

DeBabelizer Pro offers some built-in Batch Automation wizards for walking you through the process of creating a SuperPalette. **Create SuperPalette** and **Create SuperPalette and Remap** are two options available in the **Batch Automation** submenu of the **Tools** menu. Both of these options enable you to create SuperPalettes using a Wizard to take you through each step.

Saving and Exporting Palettes

DeBabelizer Pro can save palette files using the .pal extension and SuperPalettes using the .dbp extension. To save either of these files while a palette or SuperPalette is open and active, select **Save As** from the **File** menu. This enables you to save either file type with the proper extension.

Because other programs—including DeBabelizer Toolbox—do not currently read or write DeBabelizer Pro's palette file types, the best way to import a foreign palette or export a DeBabelizer palette is to save an indexed image using the exact palette you want as a regular GIF file. If you've got a standalone palette you want to export from DeBabelizer Pro, with no associated image or images, you can create a "dummy" image and remap it to that palette. Then you can open the image in the other program, which will make the image's palette available to that program. The same is true for importing palettes from other programs into DeBabelizer Pro.

Tweaking Graphics Even Further

The ability to create elegant graphics at the smallest file size is one of the standards that a good Web designer is judged by. The fewer the number of colors in your image, the smaller the file size and the less chance of problems with unwanted dithering and palette flashing. Even the ability to extract a few kilobytes of information from a file can pay off on a large multi-image Web site and is worth the extra time spent. DeBabelizer offers more ways of tweaking your Web graphics files than any other program available.

Removing Unused and Duplicate Colors

Assuming you've already converted your image to a reduced palette, it's still possible to reduce the color depth even further for greater savings in file size. Because images converted to the Netscape palette don't necessarily use all the colors in the palette, your final palette probably will contain some unused color information. Adaptive palettes like the 128-color palette that are optimized to the original image usually use all the colors in those palettes, but sometimes they contain duplicate colors. Removing the unused and duplicate colors reduces your file sizes even more.

The image in Figure 8.17 was reduced to a 216-color palette but actually only uses a total of 33 colors from that palette. Saving the image with 216 colors results in a file size of 12K. Since 182 of those colors are actually unused in the image, it makes for a lot of needless additional colors. DeBabelizer Pro provides a convenient way of removing these unused colors and finds the lowest possible bit depth to save at while retaining the exact same image quality. This is done by selecting from the **Main** menu, **Palette:Remove Colors:Unused and Duplicates**. After performing this function, the resulting palette is stripped of any unused or duplicate colors and the new palette is displayed beneath the image in Figure 8.20.

Figure 8.20

By removing unused colors, the 216-color image (4.8K) is reduced to only 33 colors (3.9K) without affecting image quality.

TIP

When saving the file to the GIF format, be sure to check the Set from Image option in the Save at Color Depth field in the Save As dialog box. This ensures that the image retains the color depth you set when the image is saved.

Removing Less Popular Colors by Replacing with Closest Color

Now we're really getting into some palette hacking. If you've performed the Remove Unused and Duplicates command and gotten your palette down to a comfortable size, it's still possible to reduce it further by removing more colors. Although removing random colors can bring the file size down, it can have an adverse and unpredictable effect on image quality. One way to deal with this is to selectively remove the least used colors in the image and replace them with similar, more commonly occurring colors. Remember, even if only one pixel in the image uses a particular color, it will be represented in the palette. Replacing less common colors with more popular colors that are similar in color value usually has an imperceptible effect on image quality. We'll perform this function now for the 33-color image in Figure 8.20.

First you need to figure out which colors are the most/least used in your image. DeBabelizer enables you to view the number of occurrences of each color in the image by sorting the palette based on popularity. This is accomplished from the palette menu by choosing **Palette:Sort:Popularity**. Sorting the palette by popularity rearranges the palette so that the least popular color is positioned in the upper-left corner of the palette (index value 0) and the most popular one in the lower-right corner as shown. You can see this in Figure 8.21 in which white, the most common color in the image, is listed at the highest index number. If you perform a sort by popularity and your image colors suddenly shift radically, you'll need to undo the operation and check the settings in the palette pop-up menu by right-clicking the palette (see Figure 8.22). Make sure that Rearrange Palette is checked and that Replace with Closest is unchecked before performing the sort to avoid the color shift in your image.

FIGURE 8.21

Palette sorting by ascending popularity. The most common color, white, now appears in the last index position.

Now that you know which colors occur the least in your image you can replace them with a closely matching color. This creates a duplicate color in the palette, which you can remove by using the remove duplicates command. The reason for replacing the color with the closest matching color is that it has the least effect on image quality and performing this operation on a color-by-color basis lets you see the immediate effect on image quality.

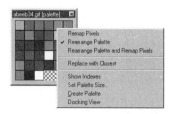

Figure 8.22

The Image Palette pop-up menu is accessible by right-clicking the mouse on the palette window.

DeBabelizer Pro enables you to replace a color in the palette window with its closest equivalent color with just one mouse click. After you are done sorting the palette, right-click the palette window and make sure that Replace with Closest is checked, as is Rearrange Palette. Now left-click the first color (it will turn into an eyedropper) in the palette in the upper-left corner representing the least commonly used color in the image. Its color automatically changes to the next closest color in the palette—that is, the next color in the palette that most closely approximates it. This replaces the color you just clicked and creates two instances of the same color in the palette. Remember, you need only have one instance of a color in the palette; any extra instances are redundant. Take a look at your image to see what effect this has on final quality. If it's acceptable, keep going and clicking on more colors until you reach the threshold of acceptable image quality. When done, you can remove the duplicate colors using the Remove Duplicates command, **Palette:Remove Colors:Duplicates Only**. The great thing about doing this manually is that you can see the effects of changing each individual palette color directly in the image window. As long as Replace with Closest is checked (right-click the palette to check or uncheck it) you can continue clicking palette colors from left to right until you reach the threshold of acceptable image quality. Once you've determined the most amount of colors you can acceptably change to the next nearest color, remove the duplicates to minimize the palette. This gives you a custom image with the absolute lowest possible number of colors based on your standards of acceptable image quality—a superbly crafted Web graphic! For our sample image, this operation resulted in bringing down the final number of colors to only 13 (see Figure 8.23) with almost no perceptible decrease in image quality.

Figure 8.23

After converting the least popular colors to their closest equivalents and removing the duplicates, the image uses only 13 colors, suffers little image degradation, and is a mere 3.2K in size.

Translating Colors

If you've used DeBabelizer Toolbox before, you might be familiar with the translate color function. Translating a color enables you to take any color in the palette and use it to replace another color. This is almost like replacing it with the closest color except that translating it allows you to manually decide which color will replace the target color. To replace any color in the palette, click on the color you want to replace it with in the palette bar. Hold down the Control key and drag that color over the one you want to replace. This changes the first color to the new color, creating another instance of that color in the palette. Again, use the remove duplicates function to remove the duplicate color.

Parsing HTML Files

DeBabelizer Pro provides the unique capability of parsing (interpreting) HTML files to extract graphics and add them to a BatchList for further processing. This only requires that the HTML file and embedded graphics reside locally on the hard drive. With a powerful feature like this, it makes it easy to access existing Web sites and apply any function to the existing graphics without having to search throughout the directory structure. The parsing feature supports JPEG, GIF, and PNG file formats. The following steps describe how to parse an HTML file and add the graphics to a BatchList:

1. Open the desired BatchList or create a new one.

2. Drag the HTML file from the Windows Explorer or system directory directly into the BatchList window.

3. Provided the graphics are valid files and reside in the same directories indicated in the HTML file, they will appear in the BatchList window.

Once the graphics are displayed in the BatchList window, you can perform any function on them or save the BatchList as a standalone file (see Figure 8.24).

FIGURE 8.24

Parsing an HTML file displays all the valid linked graphics in the BatchList window.

GIF Animations

The GIF89a specification lets you create a single GIF file with multiple frames, enabling you to create an animation to play in a Web browser, commonly referred to as GIF animation. Neither DeBabelizer Toolbox nor DeBabelizer Pro, however, currently enable you to create GIF animations or read all the frames in a GIF animation by themselves (though Equilibrium is working on adding this functionality via a plug-in in the near future). For DeBabelizer Toolbox, the plug-in is available as a Custom Code Module and is included on the CD-ROM. In the meantime, DeBabelizer helps you make better GIF animations when used in conjunction with a third party GIF animation utility such as Alchemy Mindworks' GIF Construction Set for Windows or Yves Piguet's GIFBuilder for Macintosh. Both utilities allow for importing GIF images that have been pre-processed in DeBabelizer.

TIP

DeBabelizer doesn't allow you to make GIF animation files by itself, but it is an excellent tool for making better ones when used with third party GIF animation software. You can use DeBabelizer to create a custom SuperPalette for all the frames of your animation to ensure the best image quality, least amount of dithering, and smallest possible file size before importing the GIFs into your animation utility.

Because GIF animations are composed of multiple GIF images, they can be quite large, especially when there are a lot of frames in the animation. Running your GIFs through DeBabelizer is a must to get them as small as possible for the tightest animation file sizes. Fortunately, because GIF animations are composed of multiple views or frames of the same image or object, the frames use a similar palette of colors. This creates an ideal scenario for a custom SuperPalette. Remapping your GIFs to a custom SuperPalette reduces the files to the absolute minimum number of colors to avoid any palette flashing and makes for the smallest possible animation.

Optimizing a Series of Graphics for a GIF Animation

To optimize your images before importing them to a GIF animation utility, it's best to create a SuperPalette using all of the images destined for the animation. We'll use a series of 30 PICT images in this example, outputted as a series of individual frames from a MacroMedia Director animation.

1. First, you need to get the images into a BatchList by adding them individually or drag and dropping them from the Windows Explorer to a BatchList window (see Figure 8.25). You'll get the best image quality by starting out with non-indexed color images rather than with palletized images.

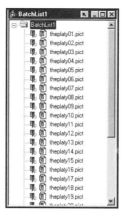

FIGURE 8.25

Creating a BatchList for all of the animation files.

2. Because most of the frames probably contain similar colors, you should be able to get a very useable SuperPalette that doesn't use a lot of colors. For best image quality, try using the 7-bit 128-color palette or less. With GIF animations, file size is critical so go with the least number of colors you can. The easiest way to make a SuperPalette for all the images in your BatchList is to right-click the palette and select Create SuperPalette. This brings up the window in Figure 8.26. Click OK to create the SuperPalette.

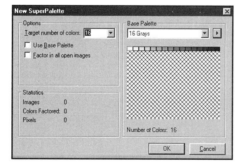

FIGURE 8.26

The New SuperPalette window can be called up by right-clicking on a palette window.

3. Apply the SuperPalette to the images by dragging the palette's ActionArrow™ to the BatchList, which opens all of the image files (if they are not already open) in the application after remapping them to the SuperPalette.

4. At this point, remove all the unused and duplicate colors for each image. After that, you can reduce the file size even more by manually reducing the colors of each image file using the Reduce Colors command (making sure that the Use Base Palette option is *not* checked). You can also replace the least used colors with their closest value in the palette. Manually reducing the colors enables you

to tailor the reduction for each image while still conforming to the same SuperPalette. The goal is to use as few colors as possible in the image, so you'll need to experiment to see what the lowest setting can be for each one. When you are done, save the image (making sure you keep copies of the originals) to a different directory and import them into your GIF animation utility. You can also remap the images in your animations to the Netscape palette if that provides decent image quality. For most animation files though, unless created using the Netscape colors to begin with, a 128-color palette or less yields the best results.

CHAPTER

9

Working with Digital Video and Animations

Up until now, you've seen how to use DeBabelizer Pro with still images. DeBabelizer Pro can also manipulate digital video (Audio and Video Interlaced or AVI) files as well as multiple image files (MIFs).

DeBabelizer Pro handles AVIs and MIFs in very different ways. In this chapter, you will learn the how DeBabelizer Pro handles each format.

Differences Between AVIs and MIFs

Both file types support multiple frames within one file. What makes them different from one another is that the frames are made of contain different images. DeBabelizer Pro handles them differently as well.

Digital video—or AVI—is a file that has both a video and audio stream. For example, a talking head video on a CD-ROM is digital video. Although DeBabelizer Pro can manipulate the video stream of an AVI file, it has no audio capability. DeBabelizer

Pro refers to AVI files as movies. A MIF is generally an animation of computer-generated images. An animated GIF, for example, is a MIF file.

DeBabelizer Pro handles these two formats in very different ways. You have greater flexibility in manipulating a MIF file than an AVI file; DeBabelizer Pro can only apply limited functionality directly to AVI files. To compensate for this limited capability, you can create a BatchList from an AVI. Each frame in the AVI is saved as an independent file. You then can apply any image manipulation to the series of AVI frmaes in the BatchList.

You are not as limited in the functionality you can apply to MIF files. On MIF files, you can use all of DeBabelizer's image manipulation techniques. You can also create a BatchList for a MIF, which is useful when you want to convert the MIF file to a AVI file. After you create the MIF BatchList, you can then apply the **Create Movie** command from the **Batch** menu.

The Movie Window

When opening an AVI file, the DeBabelizer Pro Movie window appears as shown in Figure 9.1. The Movie window has playback controls; you can play the file all the way through or you can step through the movie file a frame at a time with the Frame Counter arrows or Frame Selector arrows.

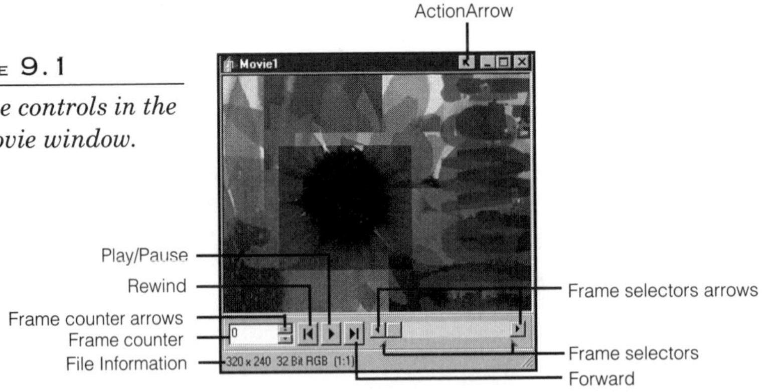

FIGURE 9.1

The controls in the Movie window.

If you enter a number in the Frame Counter, DeBabelizer Pro automatically displays the corresponding frame. Movie files begin at Frame "0." The arrows next to the Frame Counter, called the Frame Counter arrows, move the file forward or backward one frame at a time.

You can select a portion of your movie by dragging the Frame Selectors. Using the red (left) and green (right) Frame Selectors, you can drag them to select a series of frames. If an image manipulation or palette is applied, only the selected portion of the movie file is affected. Notice, however, that no palette is displayed in the Movie window, even if an AVI is indexed.

The Movie window sports an ActionArrow which works like the standard DeBabelizer Pro ActionArrow. You can drag the ActionArrow for a script or palette onto a Movie file to execute the changes. Dragging the movie's ActionArrow onto a SuperPalette automatically adds the movie's colors into the SuperPalette. While you are in the Movie window, the right mouse button has no function.

The MIF Window

When opening a MIF file, DeBabelizer Pro uses a hybrid of the Movie and Image windows as shown in Figure 9.2. Like the Movie window, it has playback controls. You can either play the file all the way through continuously or step through one frame at a time with the Frame Counter arrows or Frame Selector arrows. You can also drag the Frame Selectors to select a series of frames.

Unlike a Movie window—but similar to an Image window—the MIF window has a palette displayed (only for indexed MIFs). Also, similar to an Image window, you can access the RGB and alpha channels for the MIF frame. You can also access the Log directly from the MIF windows via the Log icon, and you can right-click on a MIF window to have quick access to the **Image** menu.

201

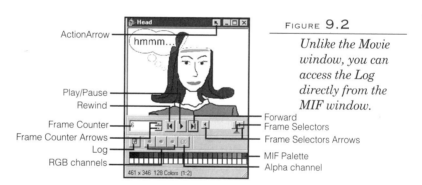

FIGURE 9.2

Unlike the Movie window, you can access the Log directly from the MIF window.

Movie and MIF Logs

Both AVIs and MIFs support a Log; the Log lists all the actions applied to a file. You can *only* access a Movie's Log by going to the **View** menu and selecting Log. You can access a MIF log directly from the icon on the MIF window or by going to the **View** menu and selecting Log.

The Movie and MIF Logs list the individual actions for each frame of the file. For example, if you have an AVI or MIF with six frames and apply the **Convert to Grayscale** Command, both the Movie and MIF Log would have Convert to Grayscale listed six times as shown in Figure 9.3.

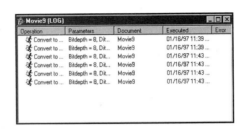

FIGURE 9.3

A Movie Log records actions done to each frame in the movie.

You can take items from a Movie or MIF Log and drag and drop them into a script or onto another open image or movie file. Logs are a useful tool for keeping track of the changes applied to a file.

The Movie and MIF Logs have the standard Log column headings of: Operation, Parameters, Document Name, Date and Time, and Errors. Logs can be saved out as independent files. DeBabelizer Pro adds the default extension of .dbl. to logs, which can be a helpful proofing device.

Manipulating AVI Files

DeBabelizer Pro handles AVIs and MIFs differently. In this section, you will learn the capabilities specific to working with AVI files. In the next section, you will learn about what functions you can apply to MIF files.

Movie Menu

You manipulate movie files via the **Movie** menu; the **Movie** menu is only available when an AVI file is open and active on the desktop. A MIF file does *not* activate it. The Movie menu contains the functions you can perform to a Movie file only: Create a SuperPalette, Create BatchList, View Properties, and Compression Options. Figure 9.4 shows the **Movie** menu.

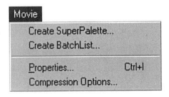

FIGURE 9.4

*From the **Movie** menu, you can do several tasks including creating a SuperPalette for your movie.*

TIP

While the functions under the **Movie** menu cannot be applied to MIF files directly, you can access the comparable functions for MIFs via other menus.

Before you can apply an action to a Movie file, the Apply Movie Operation dialog box appears as shown in Figure 9.5. This dialog box appears any time you manipulate the frames in a Movie *or* a MIF file. You select the source for the manipulation being applied to the Movie file. You have a choice of applying it to Current frame only, Selected frames only, or Entire movie.

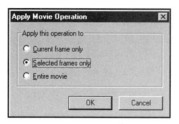

FIGURE 9.5

The Apply Movie Operation dialog box appears with every function you apply to a movie or MIF file.

You may want only to apply a function to just selected frames. Later you will earn about applying filters to movies or MIFs. You can select just a few of the frames to be affected if you so please. Applying filters to just a few frames can have some interesting affects on your files.

203

Creating a SuperPalette

You can create a SuperPalette specific to your Movie file. The SuperPalette would be based solely on the frames of the movie. This can be useful for comparisons to other movie files if there is trouble getting the movies to index to the project's SuperPalette well. You can create each movie's own SuperPalette and then do a comparison of the colors to see where the differences in colors are. Differences in the AVIs is not uncommon and can be attributed to the AVIs being shot with different backgrounds and significantly different lighting. Being able to work with each AVIs SuperPalette is useful for trying to create an optimum project palette.

Creating a SuperPalette from the **Movie** menu is similar to creating a SuperPalette from the **Batch Automation** submenu. The exception is that the Movie menu SuperPalette is only for a movie file. DeBabelizer Pro scans each frame in the movie file polling all the colors to create the SuperPalette. If you have a long movie with a lot of frames, this can take a while.

Before you can create the SuperPalette, the Apply Movie Operation dialog box shown in Figure 9.5 appears. It requires that you select the source for the SuperPalette. After you have selected the portion of the movie to be affected, the standard SuperPalette dialog box appears. The Movie SuperPalette has the same characteristics as any SuperPalette does in DeBabelizer Pro. You can designate a target number of colors and a Base Palette to be used.

TIP

It is a good idea to use the entire movie to establish a SuperPalette. If you do so, the colors in the SuperPalette are representative of the entire movie.

The Movie SuperPalette can be saved independently for use on other movie files. DeBabelizer Pro adds the default extension of .dbp to SuperPalettes. You can also go back into the SuperPalette at any time to factor in other files or movies.

Including AVIs Within a SuperPalette

If you are having significant problems with getting the AVIs to conform to the entire project's SuperPalette, you can create its own SuperPalette. Drag the AVI SuperPalette's ActionArrow onto the entire Project's SuperPalette. It will automatically add the colors again and it may help the movies. Just be careful it doesn't compromise the rest of the graphics in the project.

Creating a BatchList

You can create a BatchList from a movie, and each frame becomes an individual file in the BatchList. You would want to use this option to apply image manipulations to movie files that cannot be applied directly to the AVI file but can be applied to stand-alone images. Figure 9.6 illustrates a BatchList created from a movie file.

FIGURE 9.6

A BatchList created from a Movie file makes more choices available for file manipulation than an AVI file.

For example, suppose you wanted to apply a the NTSC/PAL Hot Fixer function to your AVIs. This function ensures the colors in your AVIs are NTSC/PAL color-safe for going to TV or video. You cannot apply this directly to the AVI file. By creating a movie BatchList you can create a script with the NTSC/PAL Hot Fixer function set to your desired level and apply it to the individual BatchList movie frames.

Before you save the movie frames as individual BatchList files, the Save As dialog box appears. In the Save As dialog box, you can choose the file format in which the frames are saved. The Files are automatically given a name consisting of the title of the Movie file with the word "Frame" added and a sequential frame number starting with "00000."

The Naming Options is grayed out in the Save As dialog box. You cannot change the naming convention of the files when creating a BatchList. The files must remain in sequential order for DeBabelizer Pro to recognize them, to convert them back into an AVI file later. The Create Movie command is also available with a right-click on the open Movie BatchList.

View Properties

Movies, like images, have their own Properties. The Properties dialog box brings up information about the movie file. You can view the Movie Properties from two locations: from the **View** menu and choose Properties, or you can choose Properties from the **Movie** menu. As mentioned earlier, the **Movie** menu becomes available when an AVI file is open on the desktop.

Selecting Properties brings up the Movie Info dialog box. The Movie Info dialog box has two tab indices, one for the Image Info, the other for the Movie Info. If a Movie has a palette associated with it, then a third tab, Palette Info is available.

The Image Info section tells you the name of the file, its path, and the horizontal and vertical dimensions of a file. It lists the file's horizontal and vertical dpi, its bit depth, how many colors per pixel, and if a marquee is selected.

The Movie Info section, shown in Figure 9.7, gives you the following information: the Frame Rate, Number of Streams, Length of Movie by frames, Length by time, Current Frame, Color Depth, Palette Changes, and Compression Settings:

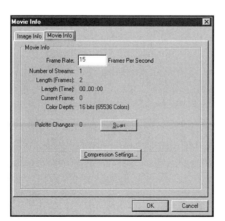

FIGURE 9.7

Movie Properties hold information regarding the file's dpi and color depth.

- **Frame Rate:** The Frame Rate is how many frames are displayed per second. The default is 15 Frames per Second (fps), but you can change it.

- **Number of Streams:** A Movie can have several streams, usually one is for audio and another for video, although a Movie can have more than one video stream, or track. DeBabelizer Pro displays and affects only the primary video stream.

AVI Multimedia Restrictions

AVIs used in multimedia have only one video track/stream because they are limited by the playback speed of CD-ROM players. Digital video files going out to tape may have more than one video stream.

- **Length (Frames):** This option tells you how many frames are in the movie file. You can divide this number by the Frame Rate to get the length of the movie file in chronological time.

- **Length (Time):** This options tells you how long the file is in hours, minutes, and seconds. You won't want to change the length of Movie if it has audio; it becomes unsynched.

- **Current Frame:** This option tells what frame you currently have displayed in the movie window.

- **Color Depth:** This option displays the bit depth of the movie.

- **Palette Changes:** Some movie files have more than one palette, although it is better to have as few palette changes as possible. Having several palettes results in a slower playback. You can press the Scan button to scan the movie file to see if there is more than one palette.

- **Compression Settings:** You can apply a compression algorithm to the movie file to reduce its size. This is important for movies used in CD-ROM titles, since you are limited to the playback speed of the CD-ROM player. You are given a choice of several different, commonly used compression methods.

The Palette Info section holds the information regarding the colors used in the movie's palette. It lists all the colors used in the movie's palette by their index numbers. You can also find out the RGB or HSV values for each specific index color.

Compression Options

Movie files can take up a lot of space; one way to be efficient with space is to apply a Compression method to them. For example, it is also important to apply compression to movie files so that the CD-ROM players can read them. A double-speed CD-ROM player can sustain transfer rates of 150kbs. If you have a 10 frame AVI each frame must be at the most 15 kb. Applying compression brings the size of each frame down. You have access to the compression option from the Movie Info screen in the Movie Properties dialog box.

Applying different compression methods gives you different file sizes. DeBabelizer Pro gives you several choices: CinePak, No recompression, Intel Indeo® Video R32, Microsoft Video 1, Microsoft RLE, Intel Indeo® Video Interactive, Intel Video® Video Raw R1.1, and Full Frame (Uncompressed). Figure 9.8 shows the dialog box for Compression Options.

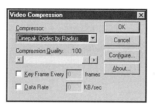

FIGURE 9.8

Compression methods for a movie file.

Compression enables you to cut a file's size and increase playback time or download time. Compression methods also affect the quality of the file you are saving. In general, the higher the quality of the image retained, the less compression applied.

You can also set the Keyframes and data rate of your movie files. To save space, your movie is shown by displaying only the differences between each frame, rather than showing the entire next frame. Frames that are shown in their entirety are Keyframes. The Keyframe becomes the reference point for the frames in between whose changes are only saved. The playback application uses Keyframes to reference for reading the other frames. Having many Keyframes adds to the size of your file.

By using different Compression methods you can change the data rate of your movie, which is usually listed in kilobytes or megabytes per second. The data rate is important for playback of your movie, especially if your final destination is a CD-ROM or the Web. The higher the data rate, the more information that is trying to be read by your CD-ROM player or squeeze through your modem lines. High data rates can cause bottlenecks when trying to display the movie.

The various compression options are:

- **CinePak:** This compression option offers high quality but takes longer to compress the file. It does a great job at compressing file sizes. It supports 5-bit to 24-bit movie files. You can compress in color or black and white by selecting the Configure button. You can change the compression quality, applying less or more compression, as well as set keyframes and the data rate. This method is one of the most popular, offering high-quality compression at small file sizes. The only drawback is it takes a longer time to compress. CinePak offers a Lossy compression method. This compression method works best on animation and graphics. It has been a long time standard for CD-ROM titles.

- **Intel Indeo® Video 3.2:** This option is the precursor to Intel Indeo® Video Interactive. This method enables you to change compression quality, set keyframes, and set data rate. It supports 5-bit to 24-bit movie files.

- **Intel Indeo® Video Interactive (IVI):** This option offers many new options (such as quick compress, scalability, Bidirectional prediction, Transparency, Quality control, Access Key, and Minimum viewpoint) to your movie file. As well as setting its own proprietary settings, you can also change compression quality, set keyframes, and set data rate. It supports 5-bit to 24-bit movie files. This method is considered the best method to use because it offers the most flexibility. This method is better for photographic-based images as opposed to CinePak, which is better suited for graphics.

- **Intel Indeo® Video Raw 1.1:** This is raw, as in no compression at all. It does *not* allow you to set keyframes or a data rate. It does, however, support 24-bit to 5-bit movie files.

- **Microsoft Video 1:** Originally created by MediaVision, this option is best used for straight digital video. This method enables you to change compression quality, set keyframes and set data rate. It supports 5-bit to 24-bit movie files.

- **Microsoft RLE:** Microsoft's compression method uses Run Length Encoding to compress the file. This option is useful for computer-generated images such as 3d renderings. It is not well-suited for drastic color changes from frame to frame. This method allows you to change compression quality, set keyframes, and set data rate. It supports 5-bit to 24-bit files. This option is comparable to Apple's Animation compression. It is best used for computer-generated images or animations.

- **Full Frame (Uncompressed):** No compression is applied to the file. This method does *not* allow you to change compression quality, set keyframes, and set data rate. This is not generally the way you want to go.

Functions You Can Apply Directly to Movies

DeBabelizer Pro has limited functionality in manipulating AVI files directly. For the most part, you need to create a BatchList to apply *all* the image manipulation to each frame of the movie. You can, however, perform a few operations directly to movie files: Set Pixel Depth, Set Palette and Remap, Reduce Colors, Convert to Grayscale, and Convert to Black and White.

> **TIP**
>
> All these operations can also be applied directly to MIF files.

Before you can apply these functions to a movie, you have to decide if you want to affect the entire file or only part of it. You can select a frame range by dragging the green and red arrows on your movie window. The Apply Movie Operation dialog box appears for any function that you apply to a movie file. From the dialog box, you have the choice of applying the action to the current frame, selected frames, or the entire movie.

Set Pixel Depth

The quickest way to change a movie's bit depth is to use Set Pixel Depth under the **Palette** menu. The **Set Pixel Depth** submenu gives you a choice of several pre-set values for changing the bit depth of the movie. You have a choice of the standard bit depths, or you can use Specify from under the Set Pixel Depth submenu for more choices. Using Set Pixel Depth on an image creates an instant custom palette based on the colors already in the movie, and each frame of the movie is changed to the desired bit depth.

AVI Option Restrictions

You cannot use the Revert to Original or Undo options on AVIs. If you need to revert, you can only close the file (without saving the changes, of course) and reopen it. The reason you can't undo AVIs is the memory required to keep revisions for each would max out most systems.

Conforming each frame of the movie file to the new selected bit depth can get tricky because the colors in each frame may vary due to scenery changes or the introduction of new characters from frame to frame of your AVI. In a sense, a new palette is created for each frame since each frame can be quite different. Due to this, a warning message, shown in Figure 9.9, appears. If you have a 15 frame movie or MIF file, you could essentially have 15 different palettes, one for each frame. DeBabelizer Pro prevents this dilemma by automatically using the palette from the first frame to undergo the bit depth change.

FIGURE 9.9

Warning message to prevent you from creating multiple palettes in a movie file.

Because each frame conforms to the first frame in your movie or selection's palette, you run the risk of having a movie with undesirable remapping. Using Set Pixel Depth is only useful for movies with minor changes in color and action from frame to frame. The optimum way to come up with a standard palette for your AVIs is to use the Create SuperPalette command from under the **Movie** menu.

Set Palette and Remap

You can change the movie's bit depth by using the Set Palette and Remap option from the **Palette** menu. Not only does this change your movie's bit depth, it enables you to apply a specific palette. You can also choose to apply one of the default palettes DeBabelizer Proofers. See Figure 9.10 for the Set Palette and Remap dialog box.

FIGURE 9.10

You can quickly apply your movie SuperPalette if it is open on the desktop by pulling down the arrow next to the Palette menu.

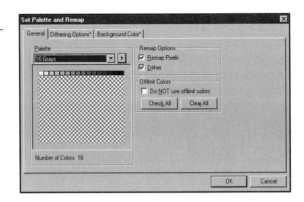

Using this option conforms your movie to 8 bits or less consistently from frame to frame. Reducing to 8 bits is significant because movies can take up a lot of space. By using palettes and compression methods, you can reduce the size of a movie file and increase playback time for the user. The goal is to have frames with small sizes so that the CD-ROM player or modem do not bottleneck.

You can choose to remap the pixels to the palette's closest color as the palette is applied. Remapping replaces the original colors with the closest color equivalent in the new palette. When this option is checked, the image gets the best color changes to the new palette. You also have access to the Dithering Options* and Background Color* from this dialog box.

You can set Offlimit Colors in the palette from the Set Palette and Remap dialog box. The Offlimit Color is useful if your movie has a blue screen or chroma key process in it. The Offlimit index color is protected from modification and also prevents a palettized movie from remapping to the safe color. If your movie has a blue screen, no other color will be remapped to the blue screen color.

Reduce Colors

You can reduce the number of colors in your movie file by using the Reduce Colors option on the **Palette** menu. If 256 colors are too many, you can reduce the number of colors by using the Reduce Colors option to save space and increase playback time for the user; the constraints are CD-ROM players and modems. You can test your movie to see how it handles the color reduction.

You can use Reduce Colors to create a custom palette as well. You can apply Reduce Colors to an open 24-bit movie and by designating 256 colors as your Target palette. It will create a palette based on whatever choices you make in the **Base Palette** pull-down menu. For example, you could open a movie file and select 256 for the Target palette and select the Windows Default 20 as the Base Palette. The result would be a custom palette with the Windows default 20 included, but it would not have all the information a SuperPalette would.

Convert to Grayscale

You can convert your movie or MIF file to grayscale. Palettes do not only have to be palettes of color; you can also create palettes out of black and white or shades of gray. DeBabelizer Pro can create a grayscale palette based on your movie and apply it to your entire movie or MIF file.

The Convert to Grayscale option on the **Palette** menu contains choices similar to Set Pixel Depth. You can change a movie from color into grayscale by applying this option and creating a grayscale palette.

Each frame is converted to grayscale according to the first selected frame to undergo the process. With the Set Pixel Depth function, sometimes the first selected frame's palette is not optimal for all the frames. The grayscale palette can camouflage this problem better than a color palette can.

You can also make a 24-bit movie grayscale, but by using a different method. You have to create a Movie BatchList for the frames of the movie. After they are independent frames, you can apply the Adjust the Hue, Saturation, and Brightness values via Image-Adjust HSV Values. This function automatically and temporarily remaps the movie to 15-bit to base the color adjustments on. You can bring the Saturation level down to –255 to remove all color from the image, and the movie frames are converted to grayscale. You can then re-create a movie from the BatchList.

Convert to Black and White

You have two options to convert your movie or MIF file into black and white and create a monochromatic or black-and-white palette. The two options are Black and White Dither and Threshold; each applies a different method to convert the movies to black and white.

Black and White Dither

Using the Black and White Dither option creates a black and white movie by dithering each image to black and white. The Black and White Dither dialog box appears and immediately applies the dithering setting last used. If you want to change the dithering setting, you should do it before running this function. There is no time to access the dithering amount before DeBabelizer Pro applies it. You can set the Dithering Options* from Set Preferences under the **File** menu and can also change the dithering method to either Albie or Diffusion.

Threshold

You can also create black and white movie and MIF files by using the Threshold option. From the Threshold dialog box, you have two ways to change the movie or MIF file to black and white. You can change the image by black percentage values or by threshold values. You can enter in values for each method or use the slider to affect the image.

The Black Percentage option uses the value you enter as the percentage for the amount of the file to be converted to black. For example, entering in 25 percent means 25 percent of the image is converted to black. The Threshold option uses the value you enter in the threshold value box as a cutoff point, anything below this value is changed to black. For example, if you enter in 216, any color level below 216 is changed to black. In the example of 216 as the cut off number, the result would be a frame that is mostly black.

DeBabelizer Pro applies both options according to values in the dialog boxes as they come up. There is no time to change the settings. The dialog boxes are not dynamic as they are when applying to an image. If you manipulate the levels, you do not see the changes occurring in the movie file as they happen.

Manipulating MIF Files

MIF files have greater flexibility than AVI files. MIFs are like the favored child; you can apply *all* the image manipulations directly to them. The following section explains basic functions you can apply to MIF files, such as creating a SuperPalette. Unlike movie files, there is no separate menu to manipulate MIFs.

Creating a SuperPalette

The optimum way to create a palette for an MIF is to open a new SuperPalette. Then, open your MIF file and drag the MIF's ActionArrow onto the new SuperPalette. Voilà! You have a SuperPalette based on your MIF file.

You can use the **Batch Automation: Create SuperPalette** from under the **Tools** menu to also create a SuperPalette. It requires additional steps than the previous method. You must, however, first save the MIF file as a BatchList. If you apply Create SuperPalette directly to the MIF file, only the first frame is used as source for the SuperPalette. Using the first frame is fine for some animation files because they are conformed to a palette as they are saved. For example, an animated GIF created by GifBuilder already has a palette associated with it. For most animations, however, using the first frame is not an ideal situation.

Creating a MIF BatchList

You can create a BatchList from a MIF file. Each frame of the MIF file becomes an individual file in the BatchList. You may want to create a BatchList so that you can convert the MIF to an AVI file by using the **Create Movie** command. The Create Movie command is available from a right-click on an open BatchList window.

As with the Movie BatchList, before you save the frames as individual files, the Save As dialog box appears. In the Save As dialog box, you can choose the file format in which the frames are saved. The Files are automatically given a name consisting of the title of the Movie file with the word "Frame" added and a sequential frame number starting with "00000." Note that MIF BatchList images begin with "00001" in the BatchList window, unlike AVI BatchLists that begin with "00000." See Figures 9.11 and 9.6 for a comparison.

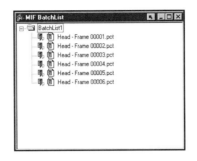

FIGURE 9.11

A MIF BatchList with the frames starting with "00001."

The Naming Options is grayed in the Save As dialog box. You cannot change the naming convention when creating a BatchList. The files must remain in sequential order for DeBabelizer Pro to recognize them, in order to convert the files into a Movie file.

You should also be aware of the file format in which you are saving the frames. You may get a warning that the new file format does not support the color depth of the frames. The color depth option is grayed out to you from the Save As dialog box. You can look up which file formats can save to your desired color depth in Appendix A.

213

Viewing MIF Properties

MIFs also have their own Properties. You can view the MIF file's Properties by going to the **View** menu and selecting Properties.

Selecting Properties brings up the Image Info dialog box as shown in Figure 9.12. The Image Info dialog box has two tab indices, one for the Image Info and the other for Palette Info.

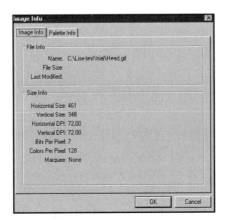

FIGURE 9.12

MIF Properties do not have a Movie Info tab as AVI files do.

The Image Info tab gives you all the pertinent Image information for the file. It tells you the name of the file, its path, and the horizontal and vertical dimensions of a file. It also lists the file's horizontal and vertical dpi, its bit depth, how many colors per pixel, and if a marquee is selected.

The Palette Info sections hold the information regarding the colors included in the MIF file's palette. It can list all the colors *used* in the MIF. You can also find out the RGB or HSV values for each specific index color.

TIP

You cannot apply compression to a MIF file. The animation format you choose generally has a compression method associated with it.

Directly Manipulating MIFs

MIF files have greater flexibility in what can be done to them. Any of the image manipulation actions under the **Image** menu can be applied directly to the MIF file. You can apply the Palette functions as well. Before you apply any operation, DeBabelizer Pro prompts you with the Apply Movie Operation dialog box, as shown in Figure 9.5. You can select what frames to change in the MIF file.

Manipulating Movie BatchLists and MIFs

You can generate a BatchList from a movie file, which is extremely useful because you are limited in the functions you can apply to a movie file directly. You can also save a MIF file as a BatchList. After you export the MIF frames into a BatchList, you can create an AVI from them.

Using a Movie BatchList, you can manipulate the frames using all the image manipulation power of DeBabelizer Pro. You can create scripts to manipulate the BatchList, or you can use other tools geared toward AVI BatchLists and MIF files. The following is a list of tools you can apply to AVI BatchLists or MIFs:

- **Filters:** You can apply third party Photoshop filters from within DeBabelizer Pro. You can set the Preference for DeBabelizer Pro to find the Plug-ins folder.

- **Filter Interpolate:** You can apply a third party Photoshop filter over a segment of BatchList images or MIF frames with varying levels.

- **Blue Screen Removal:** You can remove the blue screen or chroma key applied to an image or MIF.

- **Field Interpolate:** An image has two fields also called scan lines. You can manipulate these fields from within DeBabelizer Pro.

- **NTSC/PAL Hot Pixel Fixer:** For images, Movie BatchList files, and MIFs going to TV, you can ensure that the pixels are NTSC/PAL-safe colors.

- **Gamma:** Important for images, Movie BatchList files, and MIFs going out to TV, Gamma can be set for NTSC and PAL standards.

TIP

Note that these processes can also be applied to images.

You need to be careful of the manipulations you perform to the Movie or MIF BatchList files. When you convert either BatchList to an AVI, frames may be rejected if their color depth and size vary from one another. The color depth and size of the first file become the attributes for the entire movie. Any subsequent files that do not meet this initial criteria are rejected.

Applying Filters

You can apply third party Photoshop filters to images and MIFs. The number of filters you have depends on how many filters you have loaded in your Photoshop Plug-ins directory. You can set DeBabelizer Pro to find your Plug-ins folder from the Directories Screen of the Set Preferences option on the **File** menu. The DeBabelizer Pro software CD-ROM comes with several demo versions of Plug-ins for you to try out. You can access the Filters options from the **Tools** menu.

Be wary of filters that add colors to your files. If you have an indexed file, DeBabelizer Pro shuts down on you. For example, the Aged Film filter from DigiEffects does not enable you to select index colors for the filter effects, and you would be trying to add colors that do not exist in the file's palette. You run into this with MIFs that have a specific palette as well, you don't have to worry about this problem with files in 24-bit. One way around it is to increase the bit depth of the indexed files to 24 bit, and no new color information will be added—it will just be recognized as a 24-bit file. After you run the filter, you can reduce the bit depth back to 8-bit or create a SuperPalette based on a file with the new effects.

When applying a filter to a MIF file, you are prompted at each frame if the filter has a setting dialog box. If a filter has a dialog box for its settings, you can apply the same or different settings to each frame of a MIF file. A more efficient way would be to use the Filter Interpolate function.

You can also add filters to scripts. After you create a filter script, you can apply it to any BatchList, including a Movie BatchList. Remember that you cannot apply a filter directly to a Movie file, but you can affect the frames in the Movie BatchList.

Using Filter Interpolate

You can apply filters over a range of frames by using the **Filter Interpolate** command. The filter can be applied to the frames in increments. Any third party filter can be applied directly to a MIF file or to a BatchList. You can apply it to a Movie

BatchList and recreate a movie from the manipulated frames. Figure 9.13 shows the dialog box for Filter Interpolate.

FIGURE 9.13

Under the Directories tab, you can designate where the Photoshop plug-ins reside.

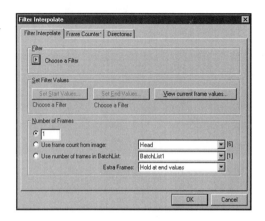

From this dialog box, you must first choose a filter to apply. Then, you must Set Start and End Values for your first and last frame or image. These vary for each filter you apply. Some filters have a dialog box to make the settings to and others do not.

You have three ways to specify the number of frames to which the filter is applied. The first choice of a value field with the number "1" in it is the number of the current frame. You can choose this option to apply the filter to the current frame.

TIP

DeBabelizer Pro prompts before you apply the Filter Interpolate with the Apply Movie Operation dialog box. You can select the portion of the MIF you want to affect.

Second, you can use the frame count from the file. For example, if you have a six frame MIF, checking this option applies the filter to all six frames. The pull-down menu next to it lists all the open image and MIF files on the desktop. Note the number in brackets next to it. This number tells you how many frames are in the file designated in the pull-down menu. You can use this to proof the values you are entering.

The third way to set the frames in this dialog box is to pick the Use Number of Frames from BatchList. The pull-down menu next to it lists all the open BatchLists on the desktop. The number next to it designates the number of files in the BatchList.

You can tell DeBabelizer Pro how to apply the filter to the extra frames that are not included in the filter selection. For example, if you have a 10 frame MIF and are going to apply the filter to only five of the 10 frames, DeBabelizer Pro offers ways to handle the left over frames. The choices are: Hold at End Values, Wrap Around, Backwards and Forwards, and No Filtering.

- **Hold at End Values:** This option holds the End Value you set as the setting for any remaining frames, which is useful when the unselected frames are at the end of the file. The filtering amount remains constant to the end.

- **Wrap Around:** This option repeats the filter amount to the unselected frames. DeBabelizer Pro applies the same filter amount to the first unselected frame as if it were the first frame in the selected range. For example, if you have a MIF with 10 frames and you selected the first five frames to be filtered, frame 6 is treated like frame 1. The filtering amount repeats itself.

- **Backwards and Forwards:** This option applies the filter amount to the unselected frames in reverse. For example, if you have a MIF with 15 frames and the first five are the selected frames to which you apply your filter, frame 6 is given the same filtering value as frame five, is would be treated like frame 4, and so on. After you hit frame 10, the process goes forward again.

- **No Filtering:** This option applies no filtering to the additional frames.

After you have designated your values and the number of frames you want to manipulate, you can apply the filter.

Two additional tabs off of this dialog box are Frame Counter* and Directories. Both are important to how the **Filter Interpolation** command works. The Directories preference designates where the third party Photoshop filters reside on your hard drive, or else DeBabelizer Pro won't know to load the filters. The Frame Counter* Preference designates the way DeBabelizer counts frames. DeBabelizer needs to count the frames as it applies the filters.

Frame Counter Settings

You can change the way DeBabelizer Pro counts your frames by changing the Frame Counter Preference setting. You can access this option in a few different ways. You can get to it from the Filter Interpolation dialog box. You can also find the Frame Counter Preference under **File: Set Preferences**. Lastly, you can choose the Set Filter Interpolate Frame Counter from under the **Tools** menu. Figure 9.14 shows the Frame Counter tab of the Filter Interpolate dialog box.

FIGURE 9.14

Counting your frames can be important when applying a filter to your files.

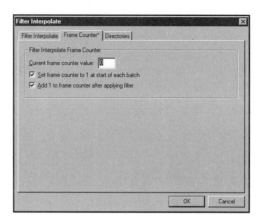

The Current frame counter value tells you what frame you are at currently. If you ran a Filter Interpolation process and then selected the Set Filter Interpolate Frame Counter from under the **Tools** menu, the Current frame counter value would read the next frame value from where you left off. For example, if you processed 6 frames via Filter Interpolation, the value would read 7. Only the **Tools** menu **Set Filter Interpolation** tells you what your current frame is. The Preferences dialog box defaults to 1.

You can have DeBabelizer Pro automatically reset the Frame Counter to 1 for each BatchList, which is handy when you are manipulating several BatchLists at a time with scripts written with filters to occur at certain frames. You need to check the Set Filter Interpolate Frame Counter to 1 at the start of each BatchList for this to happen. You can also access this by going to the **Tools** menu and choosing **Set Filter Interpolate Frame Counter**.

The last option to help DeBabelizer Pro keep frame count is to automatically add 1 to the frame counter after applying a filter. The Automatically add 1 to the frame counter option adds 1 to each frame as the file is filtered. You want this option to be checked so the filter processes all the frames you have selected.

Blue Screen Removal

Sometimes movies or images are digitized against a set background. This process is called blue screening or chroma keying. The idea is to have a solid background so you can composite the image onto another background. The file's original background is shot against a solid blue color so that you can mask it out. (The color does not have to be blue—this term is borrowed from the film industry.) On the computer, you can make any color this safe background color just as long as it is not used in any other portion of your image. If the color is used, you will have holes in the image wherever that color appears.

During the digitizing process the background color can have artifacts added to it. If this happens, it is no longer one color but a range of colors. DeBabelizer Pro enables you to select a color or a range of colors that make up this masked background color. You can replace the range of colors with one single color. You can also replace the range or replace any background color with the **Blue Screen Removal** Command under the **Tools** menu. Figure 9.15 is an example of the Blue Screen Removal dialog box. Blue Screen Removal can be applied to MIFs and BatchList images.

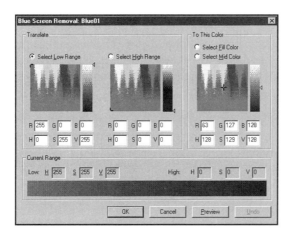

FIGURE 9.15

You can use this process to create a mask for your files that can be used later during programming.

This is a dynamic dialog box; you can click your image while the dialog box is open. You can use your Eyedropper tool to click the image to select the color(s) you want to be replaced. You can also enter in the RGB or HSV values if you know them. Entering the values is useful for the color to which you are converting the background.

The left side of the dialog box is for designating the range of colors presently in the file. You can select a range for the colors already present, a low range, and a high range. The column to the right is the color to which it will be remapped to. The To This Color section has two options: you can remap the present background to a new color, or use a mid color based on the Low and High ranges you selected.

You can preview the color choices to make sure that all the pixels convert to the new color, which is especially handy for when you are choosing a new color altogether. If from the preview you see that you have stray pixels, you can go in and set new high and low ranges by clicking with the Eyedropper tool in the areas with the stray pixels seen in the preview. You can also Undo any color selections you have made from within the dialog box.

Image Fields

Images are made up of two fields, even and odd horizontal lines. The fields are horizontal lines or rows of pixels, one pixel in height. Fields are also referred to as scan lines. The Even field starts at the top of an image with 0, followed by an Odd field at 1. Fields are alternated or interlaced from top to bottom of an image between even and odd. The interlacing prevents flickering when the image is displayed on TV. If a file is going to be output to video or to TV, it needs to have fields. DeBabelizer Pro can manipulate fields of images and MIFs by using Field Interpolate.

Field Interpolate

During digitization, fields or scan lines can become fuzzy or damaged. To correct this problem, DeBabelizer Pro enables you to isolate even or odd fields. You can replace the fuzzy fields with crisper ones. Also different output devices read the field differently, this referred to as field order. The field that is read first is the dominant field. Field order varies from broadcast and video equipment. Debabelizer Pro can change the field order so that your image or movie can be displayed on video accurately. You have several choices for isolating lines and manipulating them.

The **Field Interpolate** menu is broken into three categories: interpolate fields, or repair fuzzy lines; manipulate lines; and rearrange lines. The following is a list of the options you have for your image lines:

- **Interpolate Even Lines:** To clear up fuzzy images you can repair only the even lines in the image. You can make a selection of the image to pinpoint the trouble area. The repaired lines are based on an average of the odd lines above and below the fuzzy even lines. If during digitizing the even lines are distorted you can try to fix them based on the image information in the odd lines. It may not always work, but you can play with the image to fix it as best as you can.

- **Interpolate Odd Lines:** To clear up fuzzy images, you can repair only the odd lines in the image, which are isolated. You can also use this option in conjunction with a selection. The repaired lines are based on an average of the even lines above and below the fuzzy odd lines. If during digitizing the odd lines are distorted, you can try to fix them based on the image information in the even lines.

- **Interpolate Top Lines:** With this selection, the top line is repaired based on the averages of the lines around it. You can try isolating different selection of the image on which to base the image information averages.

You can combine the following two manipulation options together.

- **Delete Even/Odd Lines:** You can delete the Even or Odd lines in an image to make the image half the size it was originally. The image will look stunted. This should be used as a last resort to try to fix very damaged lines.

- **Insert Even/Odd Lines:** You can insert Even or Odd lines into an image. The lines take the color of your selected background color. The image becomes taller and appears skewed because you have inserted more lines.

You can use the next five options to rearrange the lines in an image.

- **Top Half> Odd Lines, Bottom Half> Even Lines:** If your digitizer captures video or your software program renders your fields and separates them into the top and bottom halves of an image, using this option reorganizes the lines so that they will have the appearance of one continuous image. Using this option makes the Odd lines dominant.

- **Odd Lines> Top Half, Even Lines> Bottom Half:** This option separates the fields in the image into halves. The fields may need to be broken up as such in order to be read accurately. This option moves the Odd lines to the top half of the image and the Even lines to the bottom half of the image. It essentially creates a duplicate of the image in the top and bottom halves. Because the Even and Odd lines create a whole image together, they create two smaller versions of the image when separated.

- **Top Half> Even Lines, Bottom Half> Odd Lines:** If your digitizer captures video or software program renders your fields and separates them into the top and bottom halves of an image, using this option reorganize the lines so that they have the appearance of one continuous image and makes the Even lines dominant.

- **Even Lines> Top Half, Odd Lines> Bottom Half:** This option separates the fields in the image into halves. The fields may need to be broken up as such in order to be read accurately. This option moves all Even lines into the top half and all Odd lines into the bottom half of the image. This option essentially creates a duplicate of the image, but on a smaller scale.

- **Swap Even and Odd lines:** This option replaces the Even lines with the Odd lines and the Odd lines with the Even lines. When fields are rendered either the even or odd fields can be designated as dominant. Video equipment requires certain fields be dominant to accurately read the frame. Using this option can change which field is set to be the dominant field.

You can apply Field Interpolate to images and MIF files. You can also use them in scripts to apply to BatchLists.

NTSC/PAL Hot Pixel Fixer

NTSC/PAL Hot Pixel Fixer prepares files for video or television to ensure each pixel is given a NTSC-safe or PAL-safe color. With this option, you have a choice of applying a NTSC or PAL standard. NTSC stands for the National Television Standards Committee (or more affectionately as Never the Same Color Twice). It is the standard used in North and Central America and Japan. PAL stands for Phase Alteration Line and is the European standard. You can access the NTSC/PAL Hot Pixel Fixer option under the **Tools** menu.

The NTSC/PAL Hot Pixel Fixer option can make your images or MIFs color-safe for TV or video. The files use RGB colorspace, so when playing images on a NTSC or

PAL device using NTSC or PAL color space, some of the RGB image's colors will peak. The colors that are most problematic are very saturated or very bright colors. To ensure that your colors can be displayed on the NTSC/PAL device you can apply the NTSC/PAL Hot Pixel Fixer. Figure 9.18 shows the dialog box for NTSC/PAL Hot Pixel Fixer.

FIGURE 9.16

Applying NTSC / PAL Hot Pixel Fixer converts your RGB file to YIQ, the color model for color TV.

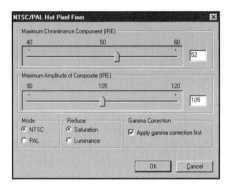

You can choose to apply a NTSC or a PAL standard, depending on where your file is going to go geographically. You can also choose to Reduce the colors by their Saturation or their Luminance (brightness). The colors are adjusted according to the method you choose.

You can also choose to apply the Gamma correction before changing the colors. Gamma is the amount of contrast found in the midtones of your image. NTSC uses a Gamma of 2.2 and PAL uses a Gamma of 2.8.

In the NTSC/PAL Hot Pixel Fixer dialog box, you can also set the Maximum Chrominance Component and the Maximum Amplitude of Composite. Both are measured in IREs (Institute of Radio Engineers). IRE is a unit of amplitude measurement used for TV signals. The Maximum Chrominance Component value serves as the limit for the color or chrominance component of an IRE signal. The value you enter is the highest value the chrominance component can have. The DeBabelizer Pro default is 52.

The Maximum Amplitude of Composite value limits the amplitude of the composite signal. A composite signal carries chrominance (color) and luminance (brightness) information. The DeBabelizer Pro default is 112.

After you have made all the adjustments your file should be color-safe to go to TV or video. You can apply this function to images, MIFs, BatchLists, and stand-alone palettes. Applying it to a palette is useful because you can then remap all your files to the color-safe palette. The NTSC/PAL Hot Pixel Fixer can also be a good feature to use for the new technology of WebTV. You can create the graphics for your Web page and run them through this option to see if check they display correctly on the TV monitor.

Gamma

Gamma is the amount of contrast found in the midtones of your image and affects the midtones without affecting the highlights or shadows. It gives the appearance of brightening an image. Often when creating a movie on the Macintosh and porting it over to the PC, the movies look really dark. You can adjust with Gamma to help the movies look better.

You can set DeBabelizer Pro to display according to a designated Gamma, and you are also given several options. In this chapter, only two Gamma settings are important: Gamma NTSC 2.2 and Gamma PAL 2.8. (See Chapter 3 for complete details on Gamma Control.) You can access Gamma Control from under the **Image** menu. You can apply Gamma Control to images, MIFs, and BatchLists.

In DeBabelizer Toolbox, Gamma is equivalent to Gun Controls.

- **Gamma NTSC 2.2:** This option sets the Gamma to the standard NTSC curve, which is 2.2.

- **Gamma PAL 2.8:** This option sets the Gamma to the standard PAL curve, which is 2.8.

CD-ROM and Multimedia

In this chapter, you'll apply the functions you learned for multimedia projects. This chapter covers the ways you can use DeBabelizer Pro in creating artwork for a multimedia title and the trouble spots you may encounter along the way. It also covers how to create optimized custom palettes, the issues that arise in creating a custom palette, especially when a custom palette doesn't index all your images as beautifully as you'd like.

DeBabelizer Pro is an indispensable tool in a multimedia project, whether you are creating a CD-ROM title, a business presentation, or a game title. It can create palettes, remap your images, and save them into a format a programmer can use all in one process. Although this sounds like a straightforward process, a lot of work goes into each step. Working out the kinks in the custom palette and the artwork, if there are any, takes finesse. Each of these steps is an important part of any project and DeBabelizer Pro's ability to combine these steps into one batch run is very effective. DeBabelizer Pro is also indispensable because it can do this not only to images but to AVIs and animations as well.

DeBabelizer Pro's indispensability, however, does not end there. Often, issues can come up in creating a title that you may not be prepared for, such as resaving your artwork to run on another platform. DeBabelizer Pro can resize your artwork to the new platform's resolution and dimensions. If a problem comes up in working on a title, generally DeBabelizer Pro's functionality offers a solution. The battle between getting the technology to work the way you want can leave designers empty-handed. DeBabelizer Pro can step in and help to get the project done.

Using DeBabelizer Pro is usually the last step in the process of getting your files to the programmer. Whether the files are still images, movies, or animations, they are run through DeBabelizer Pro before being handed off. Palettizing your images and converting them to another file format that the programmer can use is the last thing done to files before they are programmed. By this time, you have worked out the kinks in your graphics and your palette.

Every business I have worked has had some new way to use DeBabelizer. This chapter is in no way exhaustive of all the uses of DeBabelizer. Play with the software and push its envelope—I am sure you will discover your own unique way to use it. Usually what happens is that a problem arises as a deadline looms and you need to come up with a quick way to solve the problem. Nine out of 10 times DeBabelizer will be able to help you.

File Conversions

Using the Batch Save for converting your files from one file format to another is one of the most common uses of DeBabelizer Pro. Being able to convert an entire BatchList to another file format is an efficient process. Couple a Batch Save with a user-defined script and you have the makings of a beautiful project.

Most often your artwork is created on the Macintosh, but the project is programmed on a PC. You must then take your Photoshop files and save them as PICTS, BMPS, or TARGAS, depending on your authoring tool, which may only read specific file formats.

For example, Director 5.0 only reads images in the PICT file format. If you are going to be using Director to program your project, you need to convert all its files to PICTs. Using DeBabelizer Pro, you can take the flattened Photoshop files and apply a custom palette while saving them as PICTs.

Even though DeBabelizer Pro reads layered Photoshop 3.0 or 4.0 files, you are more likely going to create flattened files yourself. The master Photoshop file can have several layers included in it, especially if there are highlighted or depressed states involved with the objects in the screen—such as interface buttons with more than one state. Having to remember which layers stay and which remain off is a tedious task. Saving copies of the files is much quicker.

Reading Photoshop Files

DeBabelizer Toolbox and DeBabelizer Pro can read layered Photoshop 3.0 and 4.0 files if the 2.5 File Compatibility option is checked in Photoshop's preferences (see Figure 10.1). DeBabelizer automatically flattens the file when it opens it. The hitch is making sure all the layers you want included are turned on in Photoshop. (Please refer to the CD to view the figures in this chapter in color.)

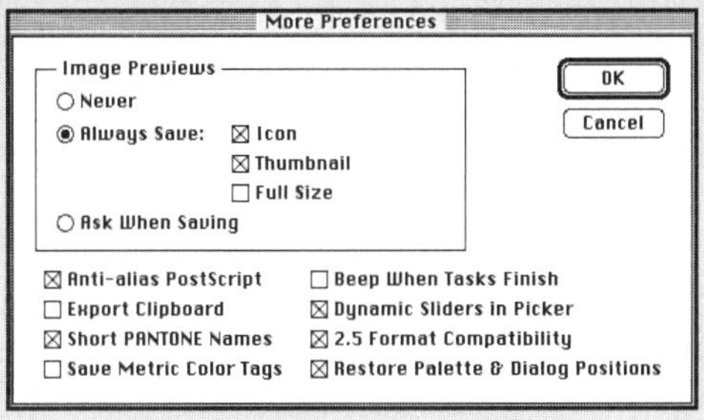

FIGURE 10.1

Photoshop's preference for enabling DeBabelizer Toolbox and DeBabelizer Pro to read 3.0 and 4.0 file formats.

Creating a Project's SuperPalette

227

While converting your files to another file format, you can apply a SuperPalette to them. DeBabelizer Pro offers many efficient ways to create a SuperPalette. You can create a project SuperPalette from all the project's files, including still images, animations, and movies. The SuperPalette becomes representative of all the project's files. To create a SuperPalette for your project:

1. Create a BatchList for all the files in your project. Click the toolbar icon to create a new BatchList and name it by your project title.

2. Right-click the BatchList to access the Add Files command. Add all your movies and images to the project BatchList.

TIP

If you have all the files isolated in directories, you can use the Start Explorer command on the Tools menu and add an entire directory to your BatchList. When the Explorer window is open, drag and drop the desired directory onto the open BatchList. All the files and directories in the selected directory will be included in the BatchList.

3. If your project has animations, you need to do a work-around to include them into the BatchList. Animation files cannot be added directly to BatchLists. If you use the Add file method from the BatchList dialog box, only the first frame of the animation is included. To get around this, open your animation file and drag its

ActionArrow onto your open BatchList. The file will be added to your BatchList as shown in Figure 10.2. The added animation should read "Filename—Frames 1 to 6." This is an excellent way to double-check that all frames of your animation are included.

FIGURE 10.2

You can add animation files by dragging its ActionArrow onto an open BatchList.

TIP

The steps for creating a SuperPalette are similar with the exception that creating a BatchList for all different file formats is straightforward. You can add any file type to the BatchList directly and then run the BatchProcess: Create SuperPalette.

4. Now you can create your SuperPalette by using **Create SuperPalette** from the **Batch** menu. The reason for using this method to create your SuperPalette is it opens AVI files in the BatchList (see Figure 10.3). The Batch Automation Create SuperPalette has an odd quirk; it does not open AVIs.

Separate BatchLists

Another way to add an animation is to generate a separate BatchList for the animation file. To create a separate BatchList for your animation, use the Create BatchList function at the bottom of the Tools menu. The animation's frames are individually saved in the animation BatchList. Drag and drop the Animation BatchList's ActionArrow onto the "Entire Project" BatchList. Now all the frames of the animation file are added to the project BatchList. Unfortunately, DeBabelizer Pro does not support BatchLists within BatchLists. You will have to do this process for every animation you have.

If you use the Batch Automation Create SuperPalette, your SuperPalette does not reflect all the files in the BatchList. I stumbled upon this quirk by comparing the number of images used at the bottom of the SuperPalette windows.

SuperPalette is created by using the Batch menu Create SuperPalette, the Batch Auto SP is the SuperPalette created from the Batch Automation Create SuperPalette. Notice the number of images polled in each SuperPalette.

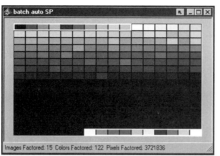

FIGURES 10.3
AND 10.3A

Including AVIs in your SuperPalette is an important part of coming up with a comprehensive project SuperPalette.

229

NOTE

Both Create SuperPalette and Remap and Save with SuperPalette Batch Automations can open AVI files in BatchLists. You get the prompt, shown in Figure 10.4, as the process runs. However, the SuperPalettes are still not as complete as when using the Batch menu Create SuperPalette. Always use the Batch menu method; it gives you better results.

FIGURE 10.4

Each movie in the BatchList brings up this prompt for you to determine whether the entire movie or only specific frames are processed.

5. The New SuperPalette window appears and you need to make some decisions about the attributes of your SuperPalette. In Figure 10.5, The SuperPalette has 256 colors. It uses the Windows Default 20 as the base palette. The SuperPalette's project is a hybrid CD-ROM that will be viewed on the Macintosh and the PC.

FIGURE 10.5

Setting up the specifics of the SuperPalette is an important part of creating an optimum SuperPalette.

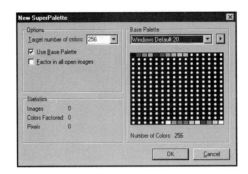

6. The next step is to name the SuperPalette, as shown in Figure 10.6. If you have a company directory structure that you use, you can save the SuperPalette into your company's "Palettes" folder.

FIGURE 10.6

The final SuperPalette for your project.

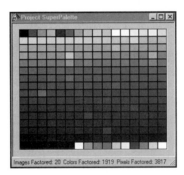

7. After you have saved your SuperPalette, you can use it to automatically remap your project BatchList. You need to create a script with the Set Palette and Remap command in it, as shown in Figure 10.7.

FIGURE 10.7

Creating a script to add to the Batch Save kills two birds with one stone.

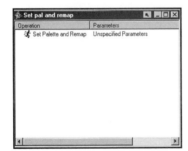

8. Double-click the Set Palette and Remap command and the dialog box in Figure 10.9 appears. If you click the arrow next to the Palette menu, you find the SuperPalette you created on the desktop. After you have chosen the

SuperPalette, you need to set the dithering options. You can close the dialog box and save your script.

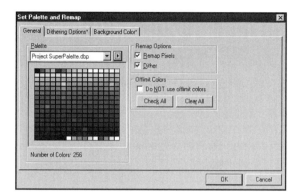

FIGURE 10.8

You can apply the dithering options from this window as well.

9. From the **Tools** menu, select **Batch Automation: Save**. You need to select the project BatchList as your Source, as shown in Figure 10.9. As an alternative, you can have a project BatchList without the animation frames. You can go back in and remap the animation files independently. If you decide to remap the frames within the project BatchList, you have to convert the animation frames back into a movie by using DeBabelizer Pro's Create Movie option from the Batch menu.

231

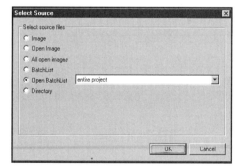

FIGURE 10.9

The source for your Batch Save is the project BatchList unless you create another BatchList without the animation frames.

10. The next step is to decide how to name your new files and where they are to be saved. In Figure 10.10, the saved files are going to be given another extension to reflect their new file format and saved into another folder, not the original. The reason for creating a new folder is in case the SuperPalette needs to be reworked because it does not work well on all the graphics in the project; you can throw away the new folder and start from scratch with the original flattened art. Figure 10.10 shows the Naming options dialog box.

FIGURE 10.10

You can change the naming of your files.

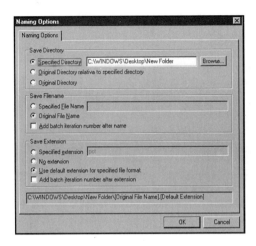

TIP

Naming files by sequential order can help your programmer, if the programmer has macros to insert cast members into the authoring tool based on the filenames.

11. After you have named the files, the Save As dialog box appears. You need to designate a destination folder, if you haven't already done so, and tell DeBabelizer Pro what file format you want to save your new files to. At this point, you can also select a script to be applied as you save the files. Pulldown the script menu, and the "Set pal and remap" script should be listed, as shown in Figure 10.11.

FIGURE 10.11

Applying the script as the files are saved is very efficient.

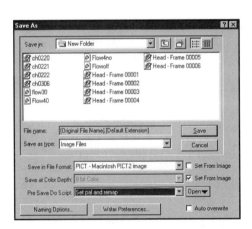

You have created a SuperPalette for images and saved them to a new format. If the SuperPalette worked well on all the images, you are ready to hand the files off to the programmer.

The alternative to using DeBabelizer is painstakingly long. If you had to figure out the palette through a long tedious process in Photoshop by opening each image and creating its own custom CLUT, you would have to reduce your images to 8-bits and then compare the colors in each of their CLUTs.

Most likely what would result is a standard palette like the Windows default Palette, for instance. Not much room for color creativity there. Not to mention that the AVIs and animation files would have to be done in another program altogether. So the time savings on polling all the different files' color information is enormous—not to mention the fact that it gives you complete freedom in developing a palette with colors you choose as opposed to being constrained to a standard palette.

Once you went through the painful process of developing a palette, you would then have to apply it to your images one file at a time. The only bonus would be at this point you could save the file into a new format, one at a time. You also need to figure out how to apply the palette within another program so you could palettize your animations and AVIs.

Designating a Mask Color

Artwork is constrained to be in a rectangular shape despite the shape of an image. If you have a character that you want to use and composite onto a background, the character is constrained to a square form.

When you bring this character into a Authoring tool, you can designate the character's background color as a mask to give the illusion of the character being a free-form shape. This masking process has two parts to it.

The first is to create the artwork with the masking color background. You can do this in your favorite image editing program, such as Photoshop. Secondly, you need to palettize the images but protect and include the mask color in the project's custom palette.

TIP

This mask color technique can also be used for a blue screen removal process.

Creating the artwork in Photoshop is easy; you isolate the character on its own layer and create another layer beneath it to be the mask color. See Figure 10.12 for an example.

After you bring the masking color into DeBabelizer Pro, you need to do two things. First, if it is part of a project, you need to determine how you are going to get the masking color into the SuperPalette. Second, after you add it to the SuperPalette, you need to protect the images with the mask color and prevent other images from using the mask color during remapping. To do so, complete the following steps:

1. Create your project BatchList. It should include all the artwork for the show. The files with the mask should be in the BatchList too.

2. Open one of the files with the mask color. With the Eyedropper tool, capture the color and find out its RGB formula. In this example, it is R=45, G=101, B=242.

3. Using the Open Palette icon on the toolbar, go to your Palettes Folder within the DeBabelizer Directory. Open the Windows Default 20 palette. You are going to use the Windows Default 20 as the base palette for the project SuperPalette. You can also add the mask color to this base palette. Add the RGB formula for the mask color into one of the undefined index positions by double-clicking it. Also, give the color an Off Limit attribute.

FIGURE 10.12

Creating artwork in layers with the masking color in Photoshop.

FIGURE 10.13

Double-click one of the undefined index positions and the Palette Properties dialog box appears; enter in the RGB values for the index color.

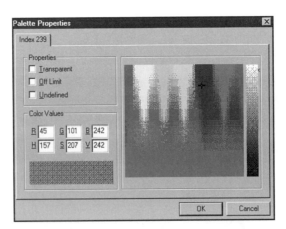

TIP

Creating your own Base Palette is a quick way to get the colors you want incorporated into your SuperPalette. You can use this work-around for other colors as well, such as a client's logo if you are creating an interactive business presentation.

Giving the color an OffLimit attribute prevents other images from being remapped to that color. It also prevents the images with mask color from being given the OffLimit color as well. There is, however, another way to fix this; save the new base palette with another name, as shown in Figure 10.14.

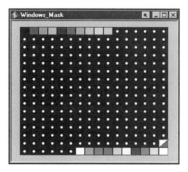

FIGURE 10.14

The Windows_ Mask palette is the final result of adding the mask color to the Windows Default 20 palette.

4. Using a right-click, select the Create SuperPalette option. Choose the new "Windows_Mask" palette as your base palette. A SuperPalette is created based on all the files in your project. Save the new SuperPalette.

235

5. Apply the Set and Remap function from the **Palette** menu to your BatchList. In the Set and Remap dialog box, set your Palette to the new SuperPalette by pulling down the arrow. Make sure you mark the Do Not Use OffLimit colors checkbox, as shown in Figure 10.15.

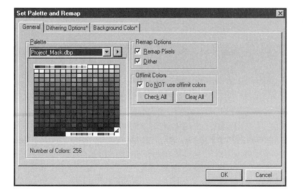

FIGURE 10.15

You need to set the dithering and background color from this dialog box too.

TIP

You can create a script to apply the Set Palette and Remap function, or you can use the Batch Automation Save and Remap option. The choice depends on whether the files need to be saved into another file format.

6. From the Set and Remap dialog box, click the Dithering Options* tab, and set your dithering amount. Make sure the Don't Dither background color box is

checked to protect the files with the mask background from having artifacts added to them during palettizing. You don't want artifacts added to the mask color for later. Also, from the Set and Remap dialog box, click the Background Color* tab. Set your background color to the mask's RGB formula.

7. Open the files with the mask color. In the example used here, the files with the mask color were consistently remapped to a RGB formula of 41, 99, 247. Create a new script with the Blue Screen Removal command in it. Figure 10.16 shows the Blue Screen Removal dialog box. Set the high and low ranges with the 41, 99, 247 RGB formula for the remapped mask color. Set the fill color to the original mask color of 45, 101, 242.

FIGURE 10.16

You can enter the formulas or use the Eyedropper tool.

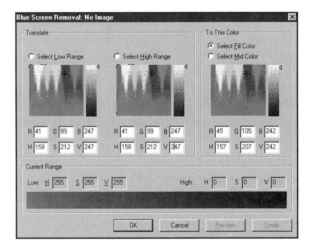

The original mask color is a protected color because in the "Windows_Mask" palette you designated the mask color as offlimits; no images used the original mask color when they were remapped to the SuperPalette. The mask color now is only in the masked files. Apply the Blue Screen Removal script to all the masked images.

Before you pass the art off to the programmer, you can save the files in another format by using one of the Batch Processes. The programmer has to set up the mask color in the Authoring tool. Keep the RGB formula handy in case the programmer needs it.

Tricks for Optimizing Palettes

Sometimes when you apply a SuperPalette to your files *en masse,* some images don't handle the remapping well. This tends to happen mostly in gradients as shown in Figure 10.17. The gradient colors develop a banding effect when remapped.

You have two ways to solve this problem. First, you can reconstruct a new SuperPalette with the trouble colors given more weight in the polling process. Or, second, you can go back to the original artwork in your image editing software and play with the troublesome colors in your images. This way when the images are brought back into DeBabelizer Pro, they may be assigned a different color in the palette, which are more conducive to remapping.

FIGURE 10.17

A stepping effect occurs in your gradient after the image is indexed. Complicated washes or gradients don't always remap well.

The SuperPalette Approaches

One solution is to stack the deck while DeBabelizer Pro polls the color information. When you go back to reconstruct the new SuperPalette, you can add the troublesome files more than once, giving the colors in the file more weight. Adding the files to the BatchList used in creating the SuperPalette will make DeBabelizer Pro pay more attention to the colors used in the files.

Another solution is to cut up the files to include just the gradients. This option is easier if the gradient occurs as a button or easily isolated object. If the background image is giving you trouble, simply add the file to the BatchList several times. Cutting up the buttons helps DeBabelizer Pro give more weight to the colors. Remember that DeBabelizer Pro factors in how much of the image itself uses the colors as it adds the colors to a palette. Crop the gradient buttons and save them as individual files. After they are saved, add them to your BatchList.

In this example, a SuperPalette was created using both methods, stacking the deck and cutting up the files. Figure 10.18 shows a comparison between the palettes created from each method.

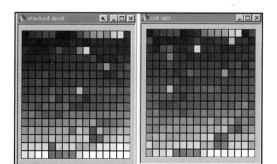

FIGURE 10.18

The Cut up palette offers more of the gradient colors.

After applying the Cut up palette, however, there is still banding in the gradient. (see Figure 10.19.) The bands have been reduced from seven to five. If neither of the previous methods works, then you need to try an alternative method. Use your Eyedropper tool in Photoshop to find the RGB formulas for each end of the gradient. You may not be able to recreate these exact colors in DeBabelizer Pro, but the result will be better than the stepping effect.

FIGURE 10.19

You have five visible bands when the Cut up palette is applied to the image.

The following steps are a way to have smooth gradients in your images, even after images are palettized.

1. Use the Cut up SuperPalette we used in the example above and apply it to the troublesome image. Use the Eyedropper tool to find the RGB values for each of the steps in the gradient. In Figure 10.17, there are five bands, so there are five distinct colors. The banding colors' index numbers and RGB values are listed in the bottom right corner of your desktop. Get the RGB values all five band colors.

2. The colors DeBabelizer Pro has selected for each band may not be anywhere near the colors you originally created in Photoshop. In this example, the first step in the banding is close, but the last is way off. By looking at your Cut up palette, you can see that the colors you want in the gradient are actually in the palette.

3. Before manipulating the SuperPalette, create a stand-alone palette from the SuperPalette by selecting Create Palette from the **Palette** menu. Then, sort the stand-alone palette by its RGB values from the Sort function also from the **Palette** menu. Select Properties from the **View** menu to see the colors listed in your palette. You can get the index positions from the RGB formulas. Using the RGB sort groups similar palette colors together. From your Palette Properties, you should be able to find an index color similar in RGB value to your original gradient color.

4. Find the index color with the closest RGB formula to your original gradient color. As you look at the palette, make sure there are enough colors on either side of it to support the five step gradient you need to create. Select the colors in the palette and hold the Shift key down as you double-click them. The gradient dialog box appears, as shown in Figure 10.20. You are using five colors for the gradient because of the five bands, but you can test to see if you can get away with four.

5. Using the formulas for the original gradient colors, fill the RGB values for each of the end gradient color. Be sure to select the Use gradient checkbox.

6. After the palette has been modified, reapply it by dragging its ActionArrow onto the troublesome images. Figure 10.21 is the end result with a lovely gradient.

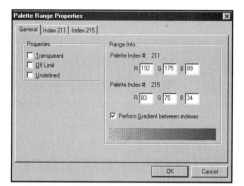

FIGURE 10.20

Creating your own gradient within the palette.

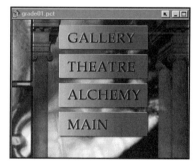

FIGURE 10.21

The end result of your new gradient.

239

The only catch to this solution is to make sure the new gradient does not interfere with the rest of your images. The colors that were in those positions prior to manipulating them should be close enough. If they are not, your images may suffer. For example, pixels associated with the colors before the gradient was created may start to break up with the new colors. Look for the new gradients' colors causing problems in other areas. If this happens, then you have to go back to the drawing board.

The other alternative is to create a Base Palette similar to the Masking operation mentioned earlier. Take the Base Palette and create the gradient from the original Photoshop values. The SuperPalette has to include these colors, so be sure to give the gradient images special attention when applying them to the palette.

Reworking the Images

Which came first, the chicken or the egg? Sometimes when working with palettes you aren't so certain. If you play with a palette long enough, you can usually get it to work even on troublesome images, but if you cannot get the palette to cooperate, you are forced to return to the scene of the crime, Photoshop.

You can add noise to an image and set it up to be dithered by DeBabelizer Pro. You create artifacts in the gradient by adding noise, which forces DeBabelizer to dither it differently. Instead of dithering the bands as pools of colors, DeBabelizer Pro breaks up the pools. This option is useful for banding in background images.

To add noise to image, go into Photoshop and apply the Noise filter to the banding images. A small amount (2 or 3) does the job nicely. In essence, you are forcing DeBabelizer Pro to dither the gradient. Instead of having the gradient form bands, the Noise should be just enough variation for DeBabelizer to not group the colors together. Figure 10.22 illustrates Photoshop's Noise filter.

FIGURE 10.22

Forcing DeBabelizer Pro to see the pixels as independent rather than as a group.

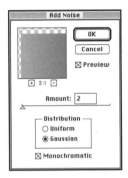

This technique works nicely with background images by reducing the visibility of artifacts, which can be more noticeable on washes or gradients under text. Play with the settings to get the best results for your images.

Creating Aliased Icons or Buttons

When creating artwork for CD-ROM titles, some Authoring tools require buttons or icons to be aliased. This is probably the opposite of everything you have learned about designing for new media.

You alias buttons or icons in a situation where you want to use one button or icon regardless of its background, such as a title that has numerous backgrounds images. An arrow icon is used repeatedly to scroll through each of the background screens. Instead of anti-aliasing the icon to each background screen and having possibly 65 different arrow icons, you can have one aliased icon that is placed on top of all the backgrounds.

You can create the aliased arrow icon in Photoshop. DeBabelizer Pro comes into the picture when the icon needs to be palettized. After you have taken great pains in creating the arrow in its aliased form, you do not want DeBabelizer Pro to anti-alias it when it is palettized.

1. Create a separate BatchList for your aliased icons. See Figure 10.23 for an example of the arrow icon.

FIGURE 10.23

The aliased edges of an icon before it has been palettized.

2. Create a new script with the Set Palette and Remap command. You want to check the Don't Dither Background Color checkbox under the Dithering Option*. You also want to set the background color to white, which is the background color of the icon in Figure 10.23. You can set the Palette in the Set Palette and Remap dialog box to the project palette.

3. The result is an image whose background has been modified (see Figure 10.24). Even with the Don't Dither Background Color checkbox marked, DeBabelizer Pro has changed some pixels. It is okay if pixels are remapped within the body of the arrow, but along the outside of the arrow you don't want any artifacts.

241

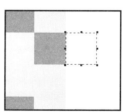

FIGURE 10.24

Reducing the colors in the palette helps you see what you have to work with. If you have a hard time finding stray pixels, double-click the index color and change it to a color that will stand out.

ToolBox Advantage

DeBabelizer Toolbox does a much better job at keeping an image aliased than DeBabelizer Pro. Only two pixels were converted to another color using DeBabelizer Toolbox. Most importantly, the pixels were within the body of the arrow and not along its outside edge. This would hardly be visible to the end-user of the title.

4. To see if artifacts have been added to the outside edge, use the Remove Unused and Duplicate Colors command from the **Palette** menu. The palette shows all the colors used in the image. When you zoom in, you can see artifacts on the outside of the arrow edge. If you are using DeBabelizer Pro, you need to go in and delete the stray pixels.

5. If you are using DeBabelizer Pro, you can use the Pencil tool to make the artifacts white. Keep applying the Remove Unused and Duplicate Colors command from the **Palette** menu, as you remove the artifacts, to make sure you have gotten them all.

A useful way to find the artifacts is to double-click their index color in the palette. Turn the color to a shocking value. The pixels stand out from your original arrow color, and you can go in and turn them white. You should be concerned with the colors on the outside edges.

Project Management

DeBabelizer Pro plays an important role in organizing your project as well. Often a project has many incarnations and is important that all the pieces of a project be archived so you do not need to reinvent the wheel. Keeping your project in order is no easy feat when there can literally be thousands of assets or images included in a project. Keeping revisions straight is also a demanding task, but DeBabelizer Pro can help you with archiving and keeping the project organized in several ways.

DeBabelizer Pro's new unique capability of saving internal files, such as logs or palettes, lends itself to organizing a project. A digital paper trail, if you will, of information can be saved for later use. Each piece provides information about the process a file goes through before it reaches the programmer.

Reasons to Hold onto Everything

Keeping your project organized is important not only for archival reasons but for keeping the day-to-day production running smoothly. The following list gives you reasons to hold on to everything:

- **Logs:** Keeping logs can be useful for recreating the scripts or for establishing an overall production process. BatchList logs can be useful for serving as a checklist for files that underwent a process and were included in the show. Later, when a translation of text is called for, you need to keep track of the screens that get revisions.

- **Palettes:** Keeping track of all your palettes helps the organization, including the Base Palettes you create. You also need to keep all the different levels of the tweaks you perform to the Palette. After you create the SuperPalette, you may create stand-alone palettes to make the changes to the palette for the trouble images, instead of working on the SuperPalette directly.

- **Scripts:** Keep all your scripts; more than likely you will reuse them on other projects.

- **Catalog Pages:** Catalog pages are available only in Toolbox, but you can print all images in a BatchList from Pro. This stage is the last stage for some projects, and the first for others. Having a paper trail of your finished screens for sign off or approval from a client is always a good, especially if text has undergone several revisions. You can also use this to keep track of the source images you used to create the final art. The catalog pages can also be used to determine which screens need work if the project is translated to another language.

- **Naming Conventions:** This is an important part of a project and should ideally be done before the files are brought into DeBabelizer Pro, but it can help you to convert files whose names aren't standardized.

Naming Conventions

Because multimedia projects have so many branches, a good naming convention can tell you exactly where you are in the show. For example, I worked on a CD-ROM title that was based on a book. The CD-ROM had 18 branches off one main screen, each representing a different tribe of Native Americans. If I saw the file name CHBA01SA.bmp, I knew exactly where I was. I knew it was in the Chumash tribe, and it was a main screen for that branch. The naming convention can tell you if a file has been palettized. For instance, the file name has the extension of "BMP." For this project, that meant the file had been palettized. So, if you find stray files, you know where they belong.

You can use DeBabelizer Pro to feed into a naming convention. If you have a BatchList with very different names but you want to apply a standardized naming convention to them, you can do this from a Batch Save by using the naming options:

1. Create a BatchList of the odd-named files.

2. Select Batch Save from the **Batch** menu. The Naming options screen shown in Figure 10.25 comes up. You can select where the newly named files are to be saved. If you have a company directory structure, you can feed DeBabelizer Pro right into it. Type in the new names for your files. In the example, "AABAPA" was typed in. Decide if the batch iteration numbering comes after the name or after the extension. In this example, it should come after the name.

FIGURE 10.25

Giving a new sequential order to your files.

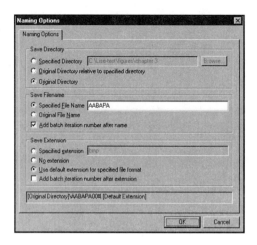

3. After you designate the Naming convention, the Save As dialog box appears. You can tell DeBabelizer Pro where to save the new files. You can also apply a script and change the file format of the files. You are now ready to rename the files.

The end result is files named sequentially, AABAPA01.pct, AABAPA02.pct, AABAPA03.pct, and so on. This is a convenient tool for programmers who have a macro to import cast members in sequentially on the basis of their names. You can save time in two places by having a naming convention in place.

Flattening QuickTimes

The flattening QuickTimes process is for DeBabelizer Toolbox. A Macintosh reads files differently from a PC. On the Macintosh, a file has both a data and resource fork. On the PC, a file only has a data fork. In order for QuickTime movies to be played on the PC, they need to be flattened.

Flattening a Macintosh QuickTime movie means you are taking the resource fork and appending it to the data fork. The result is a QuickTime playable on the PC. You can flatten a QuickTime movie by setting the Writer for QuickTime movies to do so. You can access the QuickTime Writer from the **Misc** menu select **Preferences: Writers**.

TIP

DeBabelizer Pro does not currently support QuickTime for Windows, although it is anticipated in the next release.

When you select the QuickTime Movie Writer, the first dialog box to appear is the compression dialog box. At the bottom of this screen is a More button. Clicking the More button brings up the screen shown in Figure 10.26.

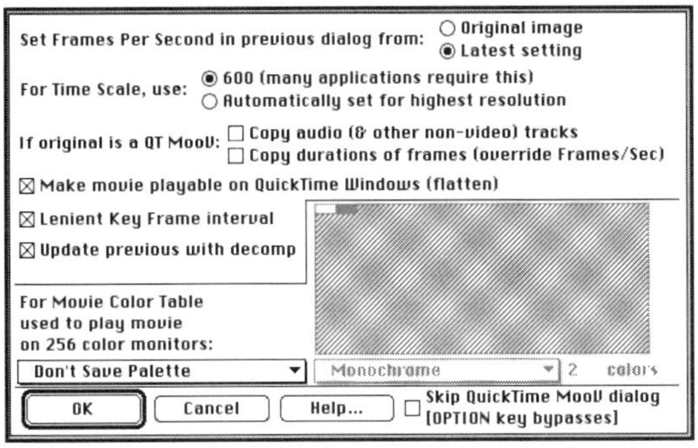

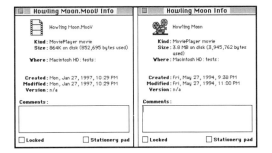

Set Frames Per Second in previous dialog from: ○ Original image
                                          ● Latest setting

For Time Scale, use: ● 600 (many applications require this)
                   ○ Automatically set for highest resolution

If original is a QT MooV: ☐ Copy audio (& other non-video) tracks
                       ☐ Copy durations of frames (override Frames/Sec)

☒ Make movie playable on QuickTime Windows (flatten)

☒ Lenient Key Frame interval

☒ Update previous with decomp

For Movie Color Table
used to play movie
on 256 color monitors:

[Don't Save Palette ▼] [Monochrome ▼] 2 colors

[OK] [Cancel] [Help...] ☐ Skip QuickTime MooV dialog [OPTION key bypasses]

FIGURE 10.26

Flattening your QuickTimes makes them playable on non-Macintosh machines.

Make sure the Make movie playable on QuickTime Windows (flatten) option is marked to flatten your movies as you save them. A good reason for using DeBabelizer over MoviePlayer or ComboWalker is that by using DeBabelizer you can create a custom palette and apply it.

You can include your QuickTime movies as a part of a Batch SuperPalette for all your project files. In Figure 10.27, the QuickTime movie went from 3.8 MB to 864K between flattening and applying a SuperPalette. The savings on space is a big bonus.

Howling Moon.MooV Info

Howling Moon.MooV

Kind: MoviePlayer movie
Size: 864K on disk (852,695 bytes used)

Where: Macintosh HD: tests:

Created: Mon, Jan 27, 1997, 10:29 PM
Modified: Mon, Jan 27, 1997, 10:29 PM
Version: n/a

Comments:

☐ Locked   ☐ Stationery pad

Howling Moon Info

Howling Moon

Kind: MoviePlayer movie
Size: 3.8 MB on disk (3,945,762 bytes used)

Where: Macintosh HD: tests:

Created: Fri, May 27, 1994, 9:38 PM
Modified: Fri, May 27, 1994, 11:00 PM
Version: n/a

Comments:

☐ Locked   ☐ Stationery pad

FIGURE 10.27

Keeping an eye on file size is an important aspect of project management.

DeBabelizer Toolbox

DeBabelizer Toolbox

The second part of this book is devoted to DeBabelizer Toolbox. It provides an overview of the functionality DeBabelizer Toolbox offers.

DeBabelizer Toolbox offers a wide range of functionality and has a unique user interface that can be challenging at times. DeBabelizer Toolbox also has wider capabilities than DeBabelizer Pro. One area in which DeBabelizer Toolbox offers more functionality is in its batch automations. DeBabelizer Toolbox can do several batch processes that DeBabelizer Pro cannot, such as Batch Compare and Batch Catalog.

Although DeBabelizer Toolbox's interface is different from DeBabelizer Pro, the basic functionality of both versions is similar. For example, the past section offered methods for the way palettes are used and created, and these same basic concepts can also be used in DeBabelizer Toolbox. You can refer to the Windows chapters to help you with the concepts also used in DeBabelizer Toolbox. For instance, to understand the concepts behind palettes, read Chapter 5 in the Windows section.

Although not all of DeBabelizer Toolbox's functionalities are covered here, a good overview is provided. It should help you to navigate the tricky interface, while providing a general scope of what DeBabelizer Toolbox can do. Chapter 11, "Overview of DeBabelizer Toolbox," discusses the interface and helps you navigate through the more difficult parts. Chapter 12, "Batch Processes," covers the Batch Processes DeBabelizer Toolbox offers.

Overview of DeBabelizer Toolbox

DeBabelizer Toolbox (1.6.5) for the Macintosh is the predecessor for DeBabelizer Pro for Windows. DeBabelizer Toolbox offers some extra functionality you cannot find in DeBabelizer Pro. Equilibrium intends to release another version of DeBabelizer Pro for the Macintosh and maintains that it will support DeBabelizer Toolbox.

In this chapter, DeBabelizer Toolbox's basic functions and tools are explained, and you will learn about its interface. This chapter is a general overview of what the program can do for you. The functions are broken down and grouped together under their larger general task heading. The following list shows the main tasks DeBabelizer Toolbox can do for you:

- File Conversions
- Color Depth
- Image Manipulation
- Batching
- Scripting

Before discussing these functions, you need to become more familiar with DeBabelizer Toolbox's unique interface.

A Word About Modes

DeBabelizer Toolbox can be run in two modes, Simple and Advanced. Simple Mode enables you to open a single file and change its format with no Batching. It actually offers very little. Unless you are completely new to the Mac, you probably would not want to use this mode.

The menubar under Simple Mode has only File, Edit, and Misc. The Advanced Mode is the mode that you use to do everything; it really is the heart and soul of the program. You can switch back and forth between modes by going to the **Misc** menu and selecting **Simple Mode**. If you find that all your menus are missing things that you need, you most likely have stumbled into Simple Mode.

Watch Your Settings

Settings are automatically retained by DeBabelizer Toolbox. If you quit the program and then start it again, DeBabelizer Toolbox retains the settings from the previous time you used it. Also, settings in one dialog box can affect the settings in another. This will be explained more in Chapter 12, "Batch Processes." The way to clear all settings is to go to the **Misc** menu, select **Preferences**, and then choose the **Set Factory Defaults** option, automatically clearing all settings you may have chosen.

Saving your own custom settings is especially productive for situations in which more than one user is using the same version of DeBabelizer Toolbox but for different processes. You can save your personal settings by going to the **Misc** menu, selecting **Preferences**, and choosing **Save Preferences As**.

DeBabelizer Toolbox can be launched by double-clicking any Preferences file. Double-clicking automatically launches DeBabelizer Toolbox with the custom settings you saved, including scripts, palettes, and catalog styles. If you want to use another person's script without having to recreate it, for example, you can save that person's preferences and transfer the file containing those preferences to your machine—a nice way not to have to recreate everything.

> **TIP**
>
> If you have more than one user on a computer using DeBabelizer Toolbox for different reasons, you can save your Preferences file to the desktop with each user's name. You can easily launch the program from the Preferences file, retaining the settings you need.

The Interface

The interface of DeBabelizer Toolbox is challenging. Part of this is due to the program's power and the number of choices you have. The options, however, repeat themselves throughout the interface, and the key to mastering the interface is to understand the choices you are being asked to make.

Toolbox Help at the Ready

Online Help is always available to you, should you need it. Help brings you immediately to the Help section that applies to the DeBabelizer Toolbox option you are using. For example, if you click Help at the Open dialog box, you land in the Help section entitled "Open." You can access online Help by pressing Help on your keyboard.

When launching DeBabelizer Toolbox, you get a standard Mac menu bar and a Toolbar to the left. Like most software packages, you can move the Toolbar wherever you like within the screen. The menu bar lists five options: File, Edit, Palettes, Misc, and Scripts. Although DeBabelizer Toolbox has only five menus, don't let this fool you. These menus are filled with submenus and subsubmenus. The organization of functions within these menus is not as straightforward as it first appears. For example, some of DeBabelizer Toolbox's image editing functions appear unexpectedly in the **Palettes** menu, and others appear on the **Edit** menu, where you would expect them.

251

NOTE

DeBabelizer Toolbox requires that your monitor be set to 256 colors in order for certain functions to appear on your monitor.

Besides housing the tools, the Toolbar has other important file information. In Figure 11.1, the Toolbar contains the name of the file that is open, its width, height, color depth, and resolution. It also tells you the color values of where the cursor is placed on the image. The bottom of the Toolbar describes whether a selection marquee has been made and displays its dimensions.

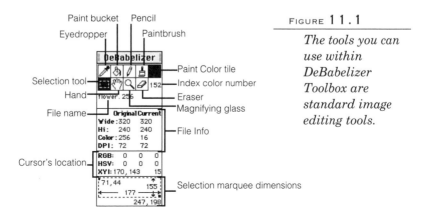

FIGURE 11.1

The tools you can use within DeBabelizer Toolbox are standard image editing tools.

The selection in Figure 11.1 is 177 pixels wide and 155 pixels high. The numbers on the top left corner (71,44) tell you the x,y coordinates for the upper-left hand corner of the selection. The numbers in the bottom-right corner are the x,y coordinates for the bottom-right corner. This selection is 247 pixels in from the left and 198 pixels down from the top. This characterization of images by the width and height is used again and again, as are the x,y coordinates. DeBabelizer Toolbox's uses this interface in other dialog boxes.

If you want to check whether an action has occurred, the Toolbar tells you. In the File Info section you have two columns, one for the Original file information and a second for the Current file information. Original reflects the file as it was when it was first opened by DeBabelizer Toolbox, and the Current column reflects the file after it has undergone an operation. You can check here to see what has changed in the file. For example, if you have a file that is in millions of colors when you open it and then you change the pixel depth to 8-bit, 256 colors would be listed in the second column.

The Tools

The tools work in the same way they do in most imaging software. The tools are:

- **Eyedropper:** This tool enables you to select certain colors by clicking them. The color goes into the Paint Color tile.

- **Paint bucket:** This tool fills an area of one contiguous color with the selected Paint Color.

- **Pencil:** This tool selects one pixel and replaces it with the Paint Color.

- **Paintbrush:** This tool enables you to paint over the image with a user-defined size. If you double-click this tool, you find another menu that enables you to select from eight different brush sizes. Generally, you aren't going to want to use DeBabelizer Toolbox for its painting tools because Photoshop has a more elegant tool set.

- **Paint Color tile:** This tool displays the selected color that the paint tools use. If a number is listed below the paint color, then it is a color captured from an indexed image. If no color is listed, then the captured color is from a 24-bit image. The number displayed here is useful for working with palettes directly. If you double-click the color, the standard color wheel appears and you can modify the color by entering new values or by choosing a new color, as shown in Figures 11.2 and 11.3.

TIP

Hold down the Tab key with any tool and you get the Eyedropper tool.

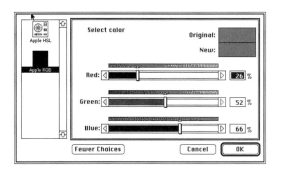

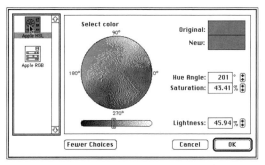

FIGURES 11.2 AND 11.3

Two different ways to adjust color within DeBabelizer Toolbox. This is the same color wheel used when you double-click directly on a palette color.

253

- **Selection Tool:** When using the Selection tool, click and drag with the mouse, and the marching ants appear. You can select a portion of an image based on the size you draw. After this selection is made, you can further manipulate it. The arrow turns into a box with arrows when a selection is made. If you hold the Option key and drag, an instant copy is made of the selection. If you hold the Command key down, the box with arrows icon changes to a plain box, and you can simply move the selection borders and not the part of the image inside it. The width, height, and x,y coordinates of your selection are displayed in the Toolbar, as shown in Figure 11.1. Holding the Shift key while dragging a selection constrains the selection to a square. Holding the Shift *after* making a selection constrains the movement of the selection to the horizontal or vertical axis.

You can set the marquee to a certain size by double-clicking the tool. As shown in Figure 11.4, you are given some choices about creating the selection.

From within the dialog box, you can set the selection marquee size. The selection size can then be used to manipulate images. Under the New section to the right of the dialog box, you can set the size of your selection. You can also Stash the selection, which comes in handy for writing scripts. Stashing the selection is like storing the selection size into short-term memory. You can set the selection to the entire image or to what the current selection is, as is displayed on the image by the marching ants. (More on the selection marquee later in this chapter.)

FIGURE 11.4

You can set your marquee to a particular size, which is useful when creating scripts.

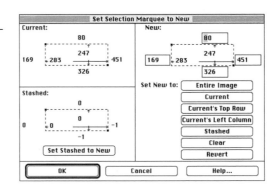

- **Eraser:** This tool replaces the image with whatever color is in the 0 position of the palette, the top left position when looking at a palette. If you double-click this tool, the entire image is erased. An unusual quirk of the Eraser tool is that its size is relative to magnification of the image. For instance, if you at a 1:1 view of the image make an erasure, then go to a 2:1 view and make an erasure, the 1:1 erasure mark will be bigger.

TIP

Hold down the Spacebar with any tool and you get the Hand.

- **Hand:** Click and drag the image with this tool and you can move the image so more is visible, if the image is bigger than the image window.

- **Magnifying Glass:** This tool enables you to zoom into a specific part of the image by clicking. Holding the Option key gives you the de-magnifying glass, a magnifying glass with the minus sign in the middle.

Interface Examples

Two good examples of the interface are the Open and Save As dialog boxes. Both perform easy straightforward operations. From each dialog box, you can click the buttons to reveal additional options.

Opening Files

The Open dialog box is a good example of navigating through DeBabelizer Toolbox's unique interface. DeBabelizer Toolbox only enables you to open one file at a time. If you have a file open and then go to open another file, it automatically asks whether you want to Save As, Cancel, or Discard the original file if changes were made. If no changes were made, it goes directly to the Open dialog box (see Figure 11.5).

When opening a file already in 256 colors, it automatically pulls up that file's palette. If the file is in millions of colors, no palette is displayed. The palette window can be made smaller or larger by clicking the max/min box to the right of the window, but you can never make it go completely away.

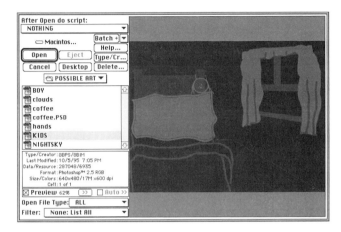

FIGURE 11.5

The Open dialog box gives you several options, one of which is to apply scripts upon opening a file.

255

From the Open dialog box, you have the following options:

- **After Open do script:** You can apply a script immediately upon opening a file. The pull-down menu lists all the scripts you have created and saved in DeBabelizer Toolbox.

- **Batch+:** You can add a file directly to a BatchList, either a new BatchList or the active BatchList, which is last BatchList used in a batch process. You can also view the active or new BatchList from this button; all the files in a BatchList appear in a separate window. Clicking the arrow beside the Batch+ button gives you the option of creating a new BatchList or adding to the active Batch- List.

- **Help:** You have access to DeBabelizer Toolbox's online help engine.

- **Type/Cr:** On the Macintosh, a file has both a resource and data fork in it. The file's creator and type are stored in its resource fork. DeBabelizer Toolbox reads this information and displays it at the bottom of the window. 8BIM is listed at the bottom of the dialog box as the Creator, the code for Photoshop. Hackers may want to designate a different creator and type, forcing DeBabelizer Toolbox to read a file format that is not supported, which can have unexpected results.

- **Delete:** You can delete a file from the desktop.

- **Preview:** You can choose to preview your files to be certain you are opening the desired file.

- **Open File Type:** You can specify a specific file type to search for. Only those files matching the specified file type are displayed.

- **Filter:** This option applies to the Open File type. The selected format that you are filtering for can scan the files Fast or Slow. Actually, a Slow Filter quickly analyzes the content of the files before it displays them as choices.

TIP

Remember your settings. If you applied a script the last time you opened a file, this setting is still set to run the next time you open a file. This also holds true for applying a script as you save.

Saving Files

The Save As dialog box offers another example of some things that are unique to DeBabelizer Toolbox in comparison to other programs. For instance, it doesn't have a Save option; it only has a Save As. Why? It assumes that you are saving the file into another format. The Save As dialog box, shown in Figure 11.6, appears, giving you the option to change format. The Save As dialog box lists several other options as well.

FIGURE 11.6

You can also apply a script as you are saving a file.

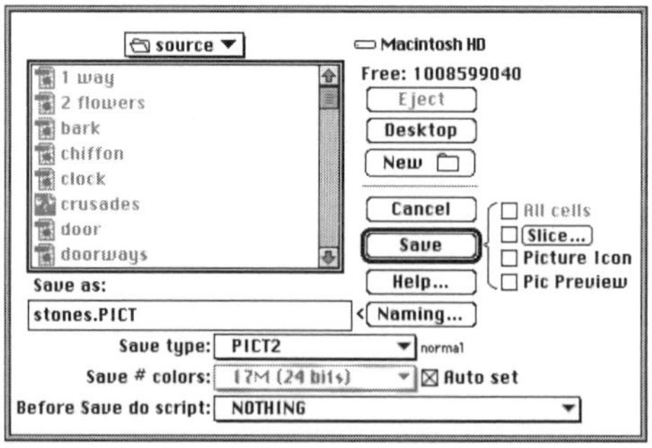

You have several options in the Save As dialog box:

- **Save type:** This option selects the new file format you are saving your files as.

- **Save # colors:** You can change the number of colors a file has. If you increase a 256 color file to millions of color, no new color information is added to the file. If you select the Auto set checkbox, the number remains the same as the file's current number.

- **Before Save do script:** You can apply a script as you save a file. The pull-down menu lists all the saved scripts.

- **Naming:** You can change the naming convention of your file.

- **Save:** You have a few different ways you can save the file. The All cells checkbox in the Save As dialog box is grayed out unless you are saving a QuickTime movie or animation. It is only available for a multiple cells file format. You can select a range of frames to be saved instead of saving the entire file. Slice cuts up your image according to the values you have set. Picture Icon option saves your file with a picture icon of your file. Pic Preview is a preview image viewed in the Open dialog box.

Making Selections

Another interesting example of DeBabelizer Toolbox's interface is the Selection tool dialog box. You can access this option by double-clicking the Selection tool. DeBabelizer Toolbox, at first glance, looks very mathematical. For those who are mathematically challenged, this can be a frightening thing. When you become familiar with the way DeBabelizer Toolbox uses numbers, however, it isn't really all that intimidating. Figure 11.7 shows the Selection tool's dialog box.

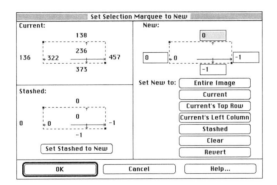

FIGURE 11.7

The Selection tool dialog box is a good example of DeBabelizer Toolbox's interface.

257

Several dialog boxes have a similar look to this one, such as the Catalog Styles dialog box. DeBabelizer Toolbox always expresses dimensions in pixels and uses diagrams like the one in Figure 11.7 to convey what they measure.

Break the dialog box into sections. First, look at the diagram titled "Current" in the upper-left hand corner. It has numbers on the inside and numbers on the outside of the diagram. The inside numbers are the dimensions of the selection. In Figure 11.7, the selection is 322 pixels wide and 236 high.

The outside numbers tell you how many pixels you are in, or down/up, relative to the edges of the file. In the example, the selection is 138 pixels down from the top. The selection ends at 457. If you add 136 (the number of pixels in from the left side) to 322 (the width of the selection), you get a total of 458, but the edge number says that the selection ends at pixel 457. Remember these numbers are inclusive; they begin with the number 0. In a nutshell, that is how DeBabelizer Toolbox displays dimensions. You will see these dimension diagrams pop up elsewhere.

From within the Selection tool dialog box, you can make several different selections. You have a current selection displayed in the Current diagram. The goal of this dialog box is to set a New selection area or to designate a Stashed selection area. A Stashed selection is useful when creating a script involving pasting and copying. Your options to set a New selection are:

- **Entire Image:** You can select the entire image as a New selection size.

- **Current:** Whatever active selection you drew on the image appears in the Current selection diagram. You can set this to be your New selection.

- **Current's Top Row:** The very top scanline or field in your active selection becomes the New selection. It defaults to the entire width of your image despite your original selection. It has a width of one pixel.

- **Current's Left Column:** The very first pixel vertically in your active selection becomes the New selection. DeBabelizer Toolbox defaults to the entire height of your image despite the original selection. It has a height of one pixel.

- **Stashed:** Your stashed selection becomes the New selection, which can be viewed in the lower left diagram entitled "Stashed."

- **Clear:** This selection clears any settings from the New selection diagram.

- **Revert:** You can revert back to the setting that was entered under the New selection when you opened the dialog box.

- **User-defined:** You can enter in your own values into the New selection fields.

The Set Stashed to New button enables you to use the values in the New selection diagram as the Stashed selection. Setting a selection as opposed to drawing one enables you to make selection with a precise size and location. If you are doing multiple copying and pasting, a set size can be an integral part of the process. For example, if you are copying a smaller part of one image to go onto another background, you can select just the part you need and paste it into the background file.

Setting DeBabelizer Toolbox's Preferences

DeBabelizer Toolbox has an entire submenu under the **Misc** menu devoted to preferences. In Figure 11.8, you can see that these preferences range from General preferences to how specific file formats work in the **Readers** and **Writers preferences**.

FIGURE 11.8

The Preferences submenu enables you to set DeBabelizer Toolbox to your own liking.

Settings are crucial to DeBabelizer Toolbox working the way you expect. You can automatically clear all settings and return to the default factory settings from the **Preferences** submenu by using the **Set Factory Default Prefs** option. Some of the preferences shown in Figure 11.8 are covered in more detail in the next chapter. For now, take a look at the five most important preferences.

Startup Preferences

The Startup Preferences are default settings that are launched every time DeBabelizer Toolbox opens. Figure 11.9 shows the Startup Options dialog box.

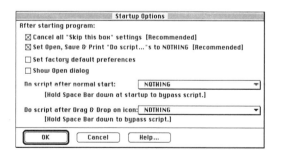

FIGURE 11.9

The Startup Options dialog box offers many of the pull-down Preferences choices.

Some of the startup options are:

- **Cancel all "Skip this box":** This is a checkbox found in several different locations, most having to do with Batch Processes. Skip this box enables you to override a prompt or dialog box that may have to appear during a process. This process is explained further in the next chapter. If you check this preference, then all dialog boxes or prompts are set to appear.

- **Set Open, Save & Print "Do script..."s to NOTHING:** All these dialog boxes have an apply script pop-up menu. If this preference is checked, it tells DeBabelizer Toolbox to do Nothing, so you don't run a script by accident.

- **Set factory default preferences:** Because customized settings are retained from session to session, this checkbox automatically sets DeBabelizer Toolbox to its original factory settings. The customized settings are then cleared when DeBabelizer Toolbox launches.

- **Show Open dialog:** This preference, when checked, automatically brings up the Open dialog box when DeBabelizer Toolbox is launched.

- **Do script after normal start:** You can have a script automatically start to run as DeBabelizer Toolbox is launched. This option can be overridden by holding the spacebar down at startup.

- **Do script after Drag & Drop on icon:** You can immediately launch a script when you drag and drop files over the DeBabelizer Toolbox icon. This option can be overridden by holding the spacebar down at startup.

Open/Save Dialog Preferences

These preferences affect the Open and Save dialog boxes primarily. Figure 11.10 shows the options available.

FIGURE 11.10

Preferences for the Open and Save dialog boxes.

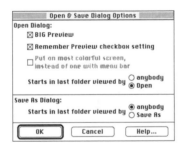

- **BIG Preview:** This option affects the size of the dialog box for opening. DeBabelizer Toolbox offers you two sizes for the Open dialog box file previews, large and smaller.

- **Remember Preview checkbox setting:** The file's preview image comes up as you click files to open them.

Altering Preferences

Most of the preferences can be changed here and also in most of the main dialog boxes. For example, there is a Preview checkbox in the Open dialog box. If you uncheck it, no preview image is shown despite what is set in the preferences.

- **Put on most colorful screen:** If you are working on a computer system that has more than one monitor hooked up, this option is available to you. Otherwise, it appears grayed out. It sets the Open dialog to go to the monitor with the most colors.

- **Starts in last folder viewed by (for Open):** For this option, you can choose anybody or Open. The anybody choice means the Open dialog starts in the folder you last opened from or saved to. The Open choice refers to the last folder you opened from.

- **Starts in last folder viewed by (for Save As):** For this option, you can choose anybody or Save As. The anybody choice means the Save As dialog starts in the folder you last opened from or saved to. The Open choice refers to the last folder to which you performed a Save As.

General Preferences

These preferences deal with how DeBabelizer Toolbox operates in general (see Figure 11.11.) The preferences are for the general running of DeBabelizer Toolbox instead of specific functions.

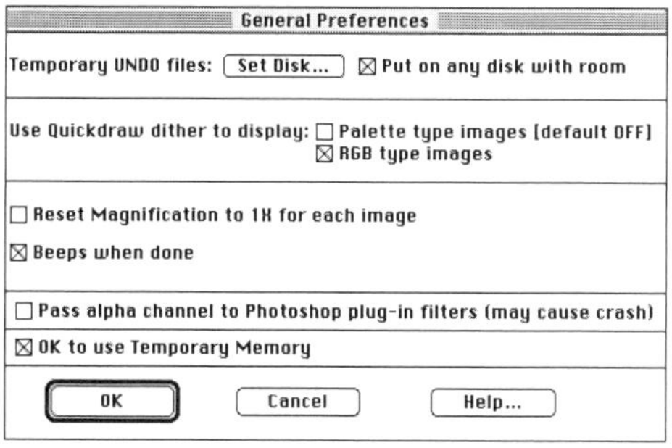

FIGURE 11.11

The General Preferences set DeBabelizer Toolbox to run the way you want.

The options are:

- **Temporary UNDO files:** This option tells DeBabelizer Toolbox where to store temporary files. Click the Set Disk button and you can choose the hard drive, or a particular hard drive if you have more than one on your computer. The checkbox next to it enables DeBabelizer Toolbox to find the hard drive with the most room. It is necessary to have ample room when using DeBabelizer Toolbox for long complicated scripts and Batch processes.

- **Use QuickDraw dither to display:** QuickDraw is how the Mac displays colors on the monitor and it displays your images onscreen as accurately as it can. The RGB option is for images that are not indexed and more than 256 colors. You can also use QuickDraw to display the indexed images in more accurate color.

Indexed or Palletized images can be viewed with a monitor set at 256 colors, because they are generally indexed to either 256 colors or fewer.

- **Reset Magnification to 1X:** When you open a file, it opens the file at 1:1. If this box is checked, DeBabelizer Toolbox opens at the magnification you were last using.

- **Beeps when done:** DeBabelizer Toolbox beeps when a process is complete, which is helpful when you are running a process unattended. For example, if you run a Batch Catalog, DeBabelizer Toolbox beeps when all the pages are spooled.

- **Pass alpha channel to Photoshop plug-in filters:** This option only works on images that are in 32-bit. Because the image has an alpha channel stored, the alpha channel is used to manipulate the image during a filtering function.

- **OK to use Temporary Memory:** DeBabelizer Toolbox can use part of the computer's RAM if it runs out of the memory allocated to DeBabelizer Toolbox.

Single-Option Preferences

These Preferences can be set directly from the **Preferences** submenu as well.

- **Photoshop Plug-ins Location:** You can tell DeBabelizer Toolbox where to find the Photoshop Plug-ins. DeBabelizer Toolbox uses the third party Plug-ins for filters and export/import modules.

- **Save As Preferences:** You can save your own personal preferences as a file, and that file can be stored for future use. You cannot bring it back into DeBabelizer Toolbox, but you can double-click it as if it were an alias. It launches DeBabelizer Toolbox with the settings you saved.

- **Set All Factory Preferences:** This option sets all preferences to factory defaults, and all customized preferences are cleared.

- **Cancel All Skip Boxes:** All skip box checkboxes are unchecked.

- **Check All Skip Boxes:** All skip boxes are marked.

That is the basic information regarding the interface and setting DeBabelizer Toolbox to run the way you want. The next section discusses each function in DeBabelizer Toolbox and groups it under its main task.

File Conversions

DeBabelizer Toolbox is an expert at handling file conversions. It can read and write in 70 file formats. These file formats include multiple platforms such as Macintosh, IBM, SGI, Unix, and Amiga. DeBabelizer Toolbox can also read and write files from non-platform dependent file formats like Avid since its file format abilities are quite diverse.

DeBabelizer Toolbox can open file formats that include still images, digital movies, and animations. However, DeBabelizer Toolbox can read and write bitmapped formats only—it can't handle vector images. At this time, DeBabelizer Toolbox can only support RGB files and cannot read CMYK files.

Some file formats DeBabelizer Toolbox supports have submenus of their own to offer additional options. For example, GIFs can be saved with or without interlacing.

As the computer industry grows, the demand for file formats also continues to grow. Being able to work on files that can be used on many platforms is an important facet of life in the production world. The digital world requires that all these different platforms be able to work together, and with programs like DeBabelizer Toolbox this is a real possibility.

When working with various file types in DeBabelizer Toolbox, a number of options are available to you:

- **Readers and Writers:** Certain file formats can be set to be read and written with special circumstances. These file formats can be edited under the **Misc: Preferences Readers** or **Writers** submenu. The file formats listed on both the **Readers** and **Writers** submenus offer additional options when the file is being read or written. For example, you can open a Photoshop file that has more than four channels and can tell DeBabelizer Toolbox how to open these extra channels.

TIP

File conversions can be combined with a Batch process or with a script. The power of DeBabelizer Toolbox lies in the combining of these powerful functions and making them work together.

- **Acquire and Export:** DeBabelizer Toolbox can acquire and export files by using third-party Photoshop Plug-ins. When you export a file, a Progress Meter appears showing you that the file is being processed. You need to tell DeBabelizer Toolbox where the Plug-ins reside on your hard drive, or it prompts you the first time you use either function. Generally, the Plug-ins can be found in your Photoshop folder.

- **Extension and File Type:** DeBabelizer Toolbox enables you to change a file's extension and file type. A Macintosh file has three parts to it: a data fork, a resource fork, and a finder file. The finder file contains the application that created it and the format information. This is why when you double-click a file's icon, it will automatically launch the application that created it. If you change this information, the file may no longer be readable because the computer cannot figure out what it is.

- **Convert MacBinary:** The **Convert MacBinary** option enables you to convert modemed files that have been sent in the MacBinary format. In order to be sent via modem, a MacBinary file puts all three parts of a Mac file into one part. This options converts that one file back into three parts, like a normal Macintosh file. When you select this option from the menu, it asks you to find the file.

- **Swapping CRs for LFs:** In a situation where a file is going from platform to platform, sometimes files can be converted to text. For example, say a file is going from Unix as text as opposed to being sent in Binary mode. When this happens, carriage returns are converted to line feeds. Using the **Swapping CRs for LFs** option on the **Misc** menu corrects this.

The main way DeBabelizer Toolbox converts files from format to format is using the Batch Save process. You can take a series of files and convert them to another file format *en masse*. More on this in Chapter 12.

Color Depth

DeBabelizer Toolbox offers many options for changing a file's color depth. Color depth is the available colors that can be used to display an image, movie, or animation. The palette is a swatch of the available colors. There are several standard palettes that come with DeBabelizer Toolbox, such as the standard Macintosh or Windows default palettes.

DeBabelizer Toolbox's Color functions fall into two main categories (with some overlap): creating custom palettes and the applying of palettes, or the reduction of color in files. You can create a custom palette to use with your files, or you can apply one of the default standard palettes to your files. You can also reduce the colors in a file without applying a specific palette. For example, you can change the bit depth of a 24-bit file to 8-bit. The original file's colors are reduced to 256 without applying a specific palette.

How to Work with Palettes

DeBabelizer Toolbox automatically displays a palette for indexed images. If you open a file and no palette is displayed, you know your file is greater than 8 bits or 256 colors. You can view a palette's information by selecting the Palette Info option from the **Palette** menu. For more information about Color Depth, see Chapter 5, "Working with Palettes." The Windows interface is different, but the functionality for palettes is similar.

DeBabelizer Toolbox is incredibly good at creating custom palettes. If you are going to be using a series of images, you will want to consider all of those images when creating the optimal palette for your project. You can do this by using DeBabelizer Toolbox's Batch SuperPalette. DeBabelizer Toolbox polls all the images, movies, and animations in the BatchList to create a SuperPalette from their colors.

The metaphor DeBabelizer Toolbox uses for constructing a palette is called voting. DeBabelizer Toolbox analyzes the image and takes a vote on the colors in the image and creates a palette based on the more popular votes. If you are working with a series of files, the votes carry over from image to image.

After palettes have been created, you can modify them further by using one of the palette modification options DeBabelizer Toolbox offers. Some palettes include colors not used in the image, because they are used in the computer's interface. For example, the Windows palette has 20 colors designated for this purpose.

Creating Palettes

You can create and save palettes in a couple of different ways from within DeBabelizer Toolbox. You can create a SuperPalette that is based on a series of files, or you can save a palette directly from an indexed image.

The SuperPalette

The **SuperPalette** option is for creating the best possible palette based on a group of files. It bases the choice of colors for the SuperPalette by how much a color is used and by how much of it is in a file.

You can run a batch for this option, but you can also open the images one at a time and use the option of **Factor this picture in** on the **SuperPalette: Options** from the **Palette** menu. You can also use this method to add a file to batch SuperPalette if you forgot to add it the first time around.

Saving and Deleting Palettes

To save a palette in DeBabelizer Toolbox, open an indexed image and select **Palette: Save** from the **Palette** menu. The hitch is that the image must already be indexed so that it has a palette associated with it. Files that are in millions of colors will not bring up a palette to be saved; **Palette: Save** is grayed out. After the Save Palette dialog box appears, you can name it and indicate how many colors will be included in the palette.

TIP

> When saving the palette, you do not have to save all the colors in the palette. For example, you can save the first 16 colors to create your own version of a base palette.

You can choose to delete a palette directly from the **Palette** submenu, which brings up another dialog box showing you the palette you want to delete. A better method to purge your system of unused palettes is to use the **Export** option from the **Misc: Scripts-Palette-Etc** menu choice. From the **Misc: Scripts-Palette-Etc** option, you can also delete scripts, palettes, BatchLists, and catalog styles. Using export, you can save the palettes and archive them somewhere, so you can use them again.

Stashed Palettes

You can **Stash** a palette from **Palette: Stash** from the **Palette** menu. Stashing a palette means saving a palette to memory without naming it specifically. It is a shortcut but can be confusing if you have more than one person working on a machine at a time. DeBabelizer Toolbox uses that palette whenever you select the Stashed Palette.

Palette Info

After you have created and saved your palette, you can access its Palette information by going to the **Palette** menu and selecting **Palette Info**. **Palette Info** is only available for indexed images. If an image is in millions of colors, it cannot show you the **Palette Info**. Palette Info displays all the colors polled to create the palette. It also can give you information about what colors are specifically used in the image. Figure 11.12 shows the Palette Info dialog box with all the color information for the palette. You can get the RGB values for each index color. It also displays how many palette colors are used in the image. In this example, only 83 colors are used.

FIGURE 11.12

You can use the number of palette colors to know that you can remove unnecessary colors from the image and reduce your file size.

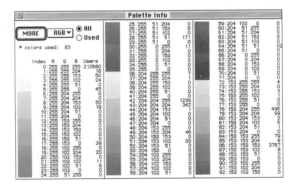

The Palette Info dialog box lists the colors sequentially by index number. Next to each index number is the RGB value for the color. This information is very useful for tweaking palettes. If you want to have a specific color used and you know its RGB, HSB, and YIQ (color model used in TV/video) values, you can see whether it is included. You can view the list of all the colors used in the image. If it isn't in the palette, you can make sure it gets added. The Palette Info can be printed as well.

Modifying Palettes

You can double-click the index number within the palette to modify its color. When you double-click it, the color wheel dialog box appears, as shown in Figures 11.3 and 11.4. This is an excellent way to ensure your client's logo color is included, for example. With your Eyedropper tool, click the image where the logo is, and the "captured" color's index number is displayed in the toolbar. Find the index number in the palette and double-click it, to make certain the RGB or HSL formulas match your client's logo color.

After a palette has been created, you can edit it or tweak it with DeBabelizer Toolbox's options. You can apply a number of built-in changes to a palette. The following options deal with the physical placement of the color within the palette.

Removed Unused and Duplicates

You can remove colors that are unused or repetitive within a palette. This function streamlines your palette. Applying this function to your images decreases your their file size, which is especially useful when you are dealing with Web graphics.

For example, in Figure 11.12, the Palette Info dialog box reported that only 83 palette colors were used in the image. You could use the **Removed Unused and Duplicates** option from the **Palette** menu to reduce the palette to 83 colors.

Sort Palette

You can use DeBabelizer Toolbox's **Sort Palette** submenu from the **Palette** menu to organize a palette. This option has a number of ways you can sort a palette. This option does not change the colors in the palette; it simply rearranges their order.

You can sort the colors in the palette according to their RGB values, Brightness, HSB, HBS, or Popularity. You can also go from the lowest to the highest value in all these categories, which is useful to determine the range that a palette is covering, to be assured that it is the optimum palette for your project.

Macintize

To *Macintize* a palette means you have placed white in the first position, the 0 position, and have placed black in the final position, 255. The Macintosh needs the palette to be stored in such a way for software programs running on the Macintosh. The software programs will be looking for black and white in those specific positions. Other platforms store black and white in the opposite positions. DeBabelizer Toolbox offers several methods of Macintizing a palette. You can use the Smart, Shift, or Default methods.

By clicking either **Smart** (recommended) or **Shift** in the **Default Set** dialog box, you can establish a Default setting. The Smart method scans the palette and determines two colors that can be replaced by black and white with the least disruption to the image and replaces them. The Shift method moves all colors one position to the right and replaces the last color with black, removing two colors from the original palette. You can do this if you know those two last colors aren't important, because they are the ones to go.

Palette Rearranging

You can also rearrange the palette colors by moving the index colors to new positions. You can affect the colors alone or the pixels associated with the colors. You can do this by using the **Rearrange** option from the **Palette** menu. Figures 11.13 and 11.14 show the Rearrange dialog box and how easy it is to move index colors around.

FIGURE 11.13

From the Rearrange dialog box, you can affect the palette, the image's pixels, or both. You can click and drag a color to its new position.

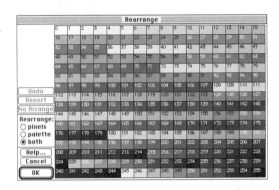

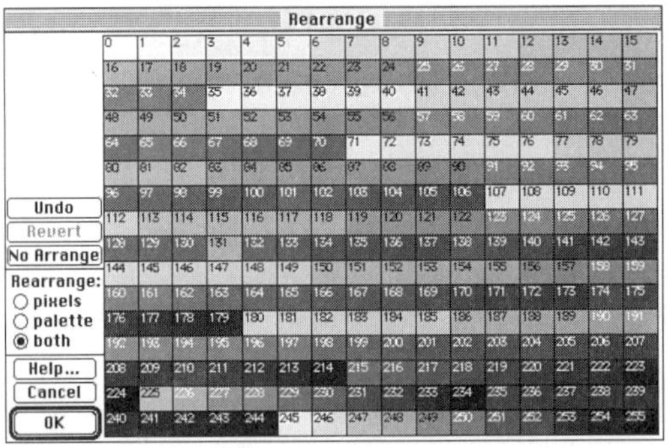

FIGURE 11.14

Index number 17, shown in Figure 11.13, was moved to its new position of index number 131. This move affects both the palette and the pixels in the image associated with it.

You can select one color to move or a range of colors to move by clicking and dragging a selection. This option comes in useful for creating a palette that includes colors needed in specific locations. For example, if you are modifying a palette so it can be read in the PC environment, it requires that black and white be in certain index positions. You can use the **Rearrange** option to achieve this.

Merging Palettes

The **Merge Palettes** option enables you take color tiles from other existing palettes. For instance, if you have two custom palettes that you want to Merge together, you can use the Merge option to do this. You can specifically choose the colors needed from each palette to be combined into the final merged palette You can select the desired colors by clicking and dragging or by entering in an index color number. Figure 11.15 shows the Merge Palettes dialog box.

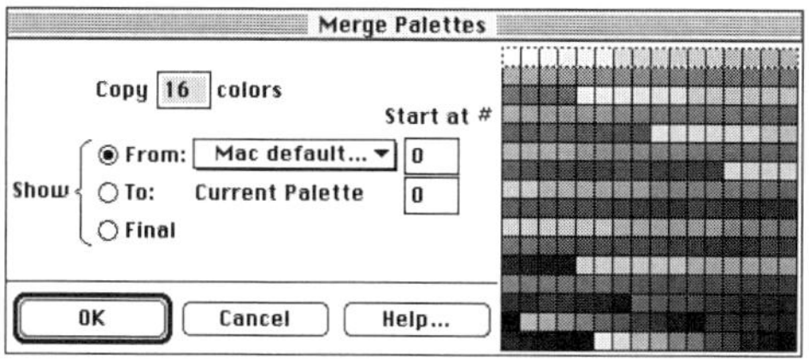

FIGURE 11.15

You can combine two palettes to create an optimized final palette.

The key to this option is selecting the Palette. You have these choices:

- **From:** The palette you are taking colors from.

- **To:** The palette to which you are taking colors. It should be the palette currently displayed with the open file on your desktop.

- **Final:** The final palette. It should display the color(s) you have copied in their new positions in the current palette.

You can select the tiles of the palette directly by clicking and dragging. You can also enter the index number of the colors you want to copy in the Start at # boxes. This box also designates what index number the borrowed colors will begin at in the Final palette. Using the index number boxes enables you to dictate where you want the new colors to begin in the final merged palette.

As you cycle down the From, To, and Final options, you can see the palettes change. Your choices for the From menu are from all the palettes available in DeBabelizer Toolbox. You can pull down the menu and choose the one you want. The palette you choose is displayed to the right.

Manipulating Palettes

You have learned how to move the colors around within the palette, but you can also change the actual colors in the palette. There are a number of ways to adjust the palette colors. DeBabelizer Toolbox gives you many options to manipulate a palette. These options are useful for finding the palette color information and using that information to modify a custom palette.

Equalize Palettes

The **Equalize Palettes** option manipulates the palette by adjusting its Brightness and Saturation. DeBabelizer Toolbox refers to Hue, Saturation, and Brightness (HSB) as HSV. You cannot view the changes onscreen unless your monitor is set to 256 colors. The Equalize Palettes option not only changes the image but the palette as well.

> **TIP**
>
> Remember that your monitor has to be 256 colors in order for you to see the dynamic Preview option work.

Invert

Another way to manipulate the palette is to invert it. **Invert Colors** can be found on the **Palette** menu. Invert flips the order of the index colors. If you have a Macintized Palette, this option will de-Macintize it. This option also inverts the RGB values for the colors in the image. This function applies to both the image and palette. In effect, it creates a negative of the image.

Translate

The **Translate** option also can adjust the palette and/or image pixels. You can access **Translate** from the **Palette** menu. You can actually convert the pixels from one color to another by clicking the index colors. You can change only one color or an entire range. The Translate dialog box has the index colors all represented by their numbers, as shown in Figure 11.16.

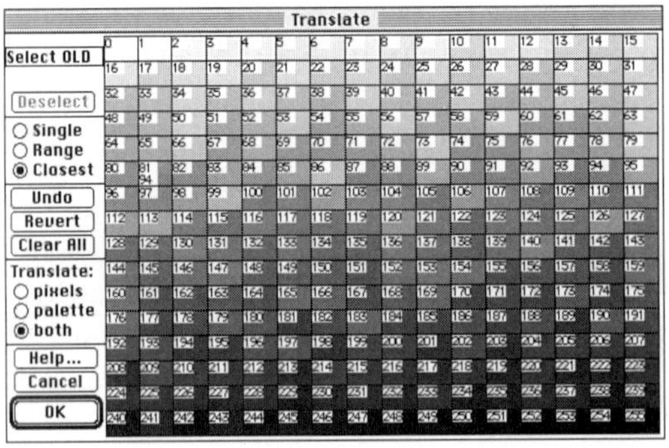

FIGURE **11.16**

From the Translate dialog box, you can click a color and DeBabelizer Toolbox locates its closest equivalent from within the palette. Look at index number 81 to see this option in action.

The Translate option enables you to go in and move a color to another index location precisely. In Figure 11.16, notice that the index numbers are listed for each color. You can swap out colors in three ways:

- **Single:** One color is changed for another.

- **Range:** By clicking and dragging the mouse, you can select more than one color at a time. When you designate the new position, that is the first position of the first selected color.

- **Closest:** This option searches the palette for the closest equivalent color, which is useful for optimizing graphics for the Web and reducing their palettes.

You have the option to manipulate the pixels, the palette, or both. You can convert the image's pixels from one color to another by clicking the index colors with the both option selected.

The dialog box works by clicking the first index color, which becomes the new color. After you have clicked the new color, you'll see "Select Old" flashing to the left. You can now click on the second tile (the old tile); you'll see the new tile's index number appear below the old tile's index number. You have told DeBabelizer Toolbox to reassign a new color (first tile) to the old color (second tile). If both is checked, the palette and the image are both manipulated. This option only works on indexed images.

Translate RGB

For images in millions of colors, you can manipulate the colors by using the **RGB Translate** option from the **Palette** menu. **RGB Translate** converts one RGB color into another. The Translate RGB Value enables you to select a range of color values and designate a new color. This option is also available for 8-bit images.

Clicking the From button tells DeBabelizer Toolbox what range of colors you are converting. To the right are the RGB levels for this range. You can be very specific here, if you know the values, by entering in the RGB values. You can also click directly with the Eyedropper tool on the image for the From values. In the To section, you can perform the same techniques or double-click the color tile and get the standard color wheel. This option is also available in the From section.

Converting one RGB color to another can be done with three levels of preciseness. The strictest option to choose is "Red and Green and Blue are all satisfied"; the RGB values are met exactly. The other two options are "Red or Green or Blue is satisfied" and "Red or Green or Blue is not satisfied." These two options only require that one of the RGB channels is loosely met. They are not as discriminating as the Red and Green and Blue are all satisfied option.

Palettes Safeties

Television monitors display color differently than your computer monitors do. For movies or images going out to video or television, you can apply the **NTSC Hot Pixel Fixer** option found on the **Palette** menu. This option protects the colors in the palettes and files from peaking or appearing hot. Each pixel in the file is given an NTSC-safe or PAL-safe color.

Color Reduction

Color reduction is conforming an image or movie to a specific palette. Generally, you are taking a file that has a higher number of colors, such as millions of colors, and converting it into fewer colors, such as 256 colors. You are taking the colors present in the file and remapping them to new, similar palette colors.

Dithering

Dithering is the technique DeBabelizer Toolbox uses to remap an image's colors to new colors. Dithering is the ability to fake your eyes out. When you have an 8-bit image that has only 256 colors, using dithering creates the illusion that more colors are present than really are. Dithering pulls this off by placing adjacent colors in such a way that they look like more than just those two colors. You can notice dithering if an image is very magnified, if you are using low-resolution files, or if you dither too much. Too much dithering can create a soft, fuzzy appearance.

You can access the **Dithering and Background Color** option by going to the **Palette** menu and selecting **Options**. The Dither Options & Background Color dialog box controls the amount of dithering applied during the palletizing of an image (see Figure 11.17). You can also select the method of dithering DeBabelizer Toolbox uses. After these options are set, whenever dithering is required it does so according to the preferences set here, except in scripts. Scripts retain their specified dithering percentage; if you change the method of dithering in the options submenu, your scripts are not affected.

FIGURE 1 1.17

You can say how much dithering DeBabelizer Toolbox applies from the Dither Options & Background Color dialog box.

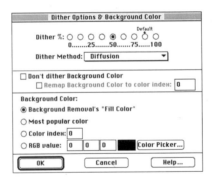

DeBabelizer Toolbox can dither by two methods, Diffusion and Albie. The Diffusion method gives the appearance of more than one level of brightness. The Albie method of dithering results in images with slightly more contrast than Diffusion.

When dithering an image or an animation, the background can be very important. DeBabelizer Toolbox provides an opportunity to protect the background. You can also designate a new color for the background, as shown in Figure 11.17. You can select a color from the palette by entering a Color index number. This is great option when you have applied a blue screen process to your images.

Options to Reducing Colors

There are a few ways in DeBabelizer Toolbox that you can reduce the colors of a file. This section describes the different methods you have available to you. You will want to use them in different circumstances.

For example, you will want to use Set Palette and Remap when you have a palette already created and want to apply it. This is the method to use when you have a specific palette that you want to apply, such as a custom project palette that you want to apply to your images.

Changing a file's pixel depth through the Change Pixel Depth command also creates a palette, but it does not apply a specific palette. You may want to use this method when you are troubleshooting an image that does not remap well to the project's custom palette. You can then compare the two palettes to see what colors are problematic.

Change Pixel Depth

You can change the color depth of a file by using one of DeBabelizer Toolbox's preset values. You can apply these to animations, movies, and stills. You can access **Change Pixel Depth** by going to the **Palette** menu. There is a list of set values to change your image to, as shown in Figure 11.18. Some options in Figure 11.18 are grayed out because they are the color depth the image has currently.

273

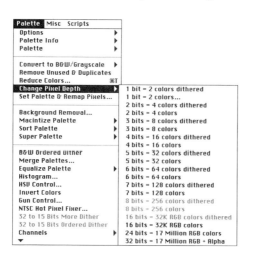

FIGURE 11.18

You can change a file's pixel depth by a preset value.

Using **Change Pixel Depth** changes the colors in the image based on the colors already present in the file. For example, if you take two different files and apply the option to them individually, you create two different palettes. This option creates palettes based on the original colors in the file. You can increase color depth, but no new color information is added to the file.

If you wanted to reduce the number of colors in your files without applying a specific palettes, this is the option for you. For example, you may want to use this process to reduce your artwork to 4 bits. You can then run a script to palettize the 4-bit images to the Netscape palette. After they are palettized using the Netscape palette, you can add the Remove Unused and Duplicate command to them.

Reduce Colors

The **Reduce Colors** option on the **Palette** menu brings up another dialog box, as shown in Figure 11.19. This option is useful to reduce the colors in a file to a designated number. You can use one of the preset values or specify your own value.

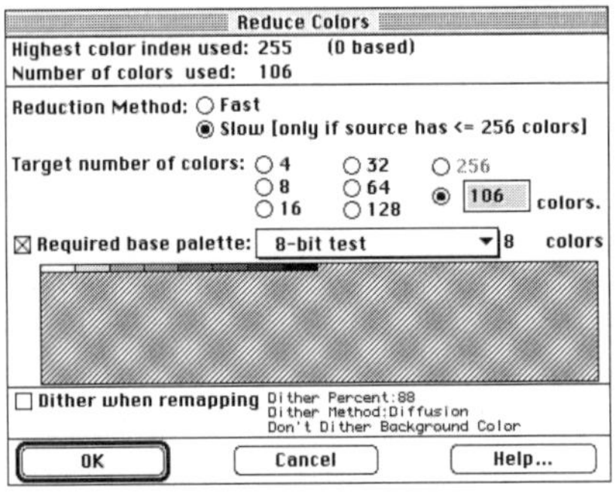

FIGURE 11.19

You can make a quick custom palette for an image by entering 256 for the target palette.

This is a very useful option for optimizing graphics for the Web. The more colors you have, the larger your file size. Reducing the number of colors in a graphic and palette can lower your file size.

In reducing the colors, you can include a Base Palette. Including a Base Palette is useful if you know your file is going to the Windows platform. You can use the pull-down menu to select a Base Palette. Any palette you have saved into DeBabelizer Toolbox is available from the pull-down menu. You can apply dithering if you want by checking the Dithering option. It lists the current dithering settings, a useful way to see that your Dithering preference is set to the amount you want.

Using Reduce Colors changes the colors in the palette based on what is already in the file. With the exception of the Base Palette option, the file is creating a palette based on the color information already present in the file.

Set Palette and Remap

Unlike the two previous options, the **Set Palette & Remap Pixels** option enables you to apply a specific palette to your files. The palette you select to remap to is displayed in the palette choices, as shown in Figure 11.20. You can pull down the **Palette** menu and select one of the defaults or one of your own saved palettes. DeBabelizer Toolbox remaps the colors present in the file to the closest equivalent in the target palette.

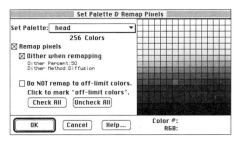

FIGURE 11.20

Using the Set Palette & Remap Pixels option enables you to apply a specific palette.

The characteristic that makes this option distinct is that you designate a palette to which you remap the image. If you just created a SuperPalette, you would be able to apply it from this dialog box.

The Set Palette and Remap function is one of the most common scripts to write. You can create your custom palette and then save it; using a script you can set your BatchList to be converted to the new palette by using the Set Palette and Remap command to the script. You use this command to convert files to your desired custom palette. For example, you would use this function to convert all your graphics for a CD-ROM title to the new custom palette.

Other Color Reductions

You don't only have to have colors in a palette. A palette can include shades of gray as well. In DeBabelizer Toolbox, there are two ways to turn your file into black and white. Your options are Black and White Dithered and Black and White Threshold. You can access these options from the **Palette** menu by selecting **Convert to Black and White/Greyscale**.

Black and White Dither enables you to dither an image to black and white according to the options set in the **Dithering and Background Color** dialog box. You can also convert images to black and white values via the dialog box shown in Figure 11.21. You can set a percentage of the image to become black, or you can set a limit or Threshold value where any index color level higher than the threshold value is designated as black.

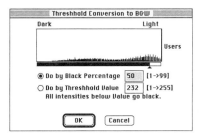

FIGURE 11.21

The Black and White conversion techniques are useful for color images that are going to be used in a newspaper.

Several options can change your color pixels into greyscale values. The **Convert to Black and White/Greyscale** option has several preset values for you to choose from. These options are convenient when you need to convert color images to greyscale for print.

Another use for **Convert to Greyscale** is if you are creating Duotone artwork for the Web. For example, often magazines or newspapers have Web pages as well. You can take existing graphics and convert all the files to greyscale in DeBabelizer Toolbox. After they are in greyscale, you can bring them into Photoshop to create your Duotones.

Image Manipulation

DeBabelizer Toolbox offers many options for manipulating images, movies, and animations. Most of these functions can be combined with Batches or Scripts to automate them.

Cut, Copy, and Paste

Within DeBabelizer Toolbox you can Cut, Copy, and Paste an image or a selection. Unlike other programs, DeBabelizer Toolbox requires you to drop your selection before you can paste your selection. The command for dropping your selection is the same as Photoshop, Command+D. If you don't drop the selection, you won't be able to paste.

Place

The **Place** option is similar to Paste. The **Place** command enables you to place an image onto another open image. The placed image automatically goes to the center of the image, unless the image you are placing is wider or taller. When placing an image into another image, the placed image automatically remaps to the palette of the image into which it is placed. You can use this function to composite images. If you have an image that was digitized against a blue screen, you can remove the blue screen process and then place the image on to its background.

Selections

You can create your own selection areas in DeBabelizer Toolbox, which enables you to designate the size of a selection by entering values and double-clicking the Selection tool. You can also designate a selection by drawing the selection directly on an image. You can select all (Command+A) and deselect (Command+D) using the same commands as found in the more popular image editing software. After you release those marching ants, it's permanent. Pasted selections can be manipulated as well. You can manipulate images just inside the selection leaving the unselected area untouched. You can also use selections to crop or trim.

Selection Transparency

After you paste a selection into another image, you can tweak the appearance of the pasted selection. There are various ways to manipulate a selection with **Selection Transparency** options:

- **Not Transparent:** This option clears any transparency setting from the selection.

- **Color 0:** The color in the first (0) palette position becomes transparent. In a Macintosh palette, this is white.

- **White:** This option makes white transparent in the pasted image, which is good to use on images remapped to the Windows palette. Figure 11.22 is an example of using this method.

- **Black:** This option makes black transparent in the pasted image.

- **Alpha Channel:** If you have an alpha channel saved with the file, the alpha channel acts as a mask. You can use this to manipulate areas inside the masked area.

- **Background Color:** The background color is transparent, which is useful for images with a blue screen process applied.

- **Even Lines:** Images are broken down into fields of Even and Odd lines; the Even lines are transparent.

- **Odd Lines:** Images are broken down into fields of Even and Odd lines; the Odd lines are transparent.

277

FIGURE 11.22

An example of pasting a selection with the White transparency option applied. Notice that where the image is not pure white, it is not knocked out.

NOTE

When the Undo Status is set to off, Undo is grayed out on the Edit menu.

Crop and Trim

Crop is a way of cutting the image based on the active selection. You can combine this option with Batches and scripts. You can also Trim to a selection and, in essence, crop the image, but the **Trim** submenu gives you more options than To Selection.

You can use **Trim** to crop an image according to the image's values around its borders. For example, the image in Figure 11.23 has a white border around it and in between the panels. After you apply the **Trim: White Edges**, the white border is removed, as in Figure 11.24.

The original image has a white border.

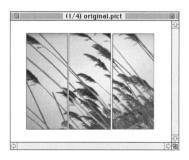

FIGURE **11.24**

The image's white border has been trimmed away. Notice that the white between the panels still remains. Trim only affects the edges of an image.

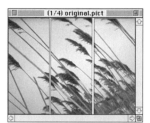

Shave Outline

Similar to Trim is the Shave Outline option. Shave Outline removes one pixel around every object in the image that is surrounded by the background color. You can designate the background color from the Dithering and Background Color dialog box. This is helpful to combine with the **Background Removal** function. The Background Removal function removes the blue screen that an image was digitized against. Combining the **Shave Outline** command ensures that an all the blue is removed around an object digitized against a blue screen; it ensures you will not blue halo effect when you composite the image onto another background.

TIP

Similar to the Command+F in Photoshop is DeBabelizer Toolbox's Repeat Last Menu Item option, except that it applies to more than filters. DeBabelizer Toolbox lets you repeat the last menu item you selected.

Slice and Flipbook

You can slice or cut up an image by choosing the Slice option from the Save As dialog box. Slicing an image is basically telling DeBabelizer Toolbox to cut up the image into cells. The primary use for the Slice feature is generating animation storyboards for animators. You define the cell size and also designate the number of cells to create. If you say how many cells you want DeBabelizer Toolbox automatically divides the image for you by hitting the small "?" mark next to Cell Size.

Cells can have a border as well. DeBabelizer Toolbox gives you the option of panning the cells. For example, you might have a landscape-oriented image. The height is the entire image, but you can make the cell slice the image across. Then, if the sliced files are brought into an animation file later, they give the appearance of panning or stepping through the cells of the original image, which is a very nice way to give the illusion of movement to your files.

Flipbook is another way of slicing an image. This option is great for slicing up an image and making an animation of it, except that a Flipbook only displays onscreen. You can specify the sizes of the cells and how quickly they run to screen. Remember that slower computers act differently, depending on their processing speed and the size of image you are Flipbooking. The Flipbook option is a good way to create test files for Video Walls.

TIP

Click the question marks when in the Slice option dialog box and have DeBabelizer Toolbox do the math for you. For example, you know that you want four cells with a border of five pixels. If you hit the ? marks near the across and down section, the number of pixels is automatically entered based on the values you selected.

The different slicing options available in the pulldown menu are:

- **By using the current catalog style:** The style set in the Batch Catalog dialog box. You have to make sure your image is big enough to accommodate the cell sizes.

- **Values from the flipbook:** In essence, the values you set in the Flipbook options are reflected in the Slicing dialog box and used to slice up the image.

- **Use values from below:** User-defined values you set yourself.

279

- **Save the fields:** You can slice an image according to its image fields. You can select either even or odd fields by which to slice the image.

Scale

The **Scale** option enables you to resize an image, change the aspect ratio, scale to half size, double size, and perform other tasks related to the image's size. These options are also useful in scripts.

Rotate and Flip

You can manipulate the image by rotating it. There are a few standards and, of course, you can set your own degree of rotation. The Flip option enables you to flip the image from left to right and from up to down. If you have text on an image, the left to right flip makes it backward. DeBabelizer Toolbox will rotate the image including the entire image or rotate it so that parts of the image falling outside the dimensions of the image will be truncated.

Histogram

A Histogram is a graphical interpretation of the colors represented in the file. DeBabelizer Toolbox breaks down the image information into RGB and intensity. This option is convenient for analyzing images before you apply a manipulation to it.

Adding to the File

In DeBabelizer Toolbox, you can add certain functions to an image, such as changing the size of your document. You can use these functions in other programs, as in the Grid function and in scripts.

Document Size

You can change the dimensions of the overall file itself by selecting **Document Size** from the **Edit** menu. You can add to an image or cut away from an image depending on the values you set in the options. If you add to the image, you can determine what color to use to pad the image. You can also indicate where the padding goes and borders can be given to the image as well. The interface of this dialog box uses that inside/outside numbering discussed earlier.

Text Overlay

Text Overlay enables you to place user-defined text over the image. It offers the same keywords to be included as the Log Entry text (see Figure 11.25 for the Text Overlay dialog box). You can determine where you would like to position the text, the color of the text, and the color of the background. You can make a selection on the image and the text appears within the selection. This is a good option when you are posting art to online services, as shown in Figure 11.26. You can even type in whatever you want, such as your name and the copyright mark or telephone number.

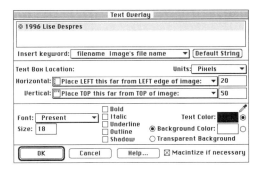

FIGURE 11.25

FIGURE 11.25

You can choose the color and placement of the text. This text is a user-defined line.

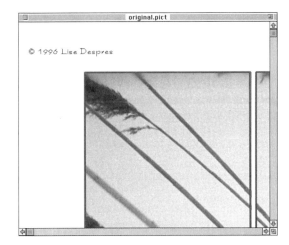

FIGURE 11.26

The Text Overlay information can help to protect your work if you distribute it digitally.

281

Offset

The Offset option enables you to reset the upper left corner's X and Y coordinates, which is sometimes necessary for some files formats to be read correctly in DeBabelizer Toolbox. Changes to the offset are not visible onscreen.

Grid

You can place a grid over an image at a user-defined size by using the **Grid** option from the **Edit** menu. You can choose different units as well; you are not locked into pixels. The nice thing is that you can save an image with a grid, then go back and remove it. You could use this for placement in another program like Photoshop. If you have a background image that you want to line up bullet text onto, you could save the text background in DeBabelizer Toolbox with a grid.

Set Resolution

The **Set Resolution** option is useful for writing scripts and doing Batch Processes. You can change an image's resolution from several standard settings listed in the submenu. The listed resolutions are the most common ones for multimedia and print. You can also set your own specifications.

Filters

You can apply any filters that you have for Photoshop because that is where DeBabelizer Toolbox gets the filters from. This option is great for image manipulation scripts and batching. You need to tell DeBabelizer Toolbox where the Photoshop Plug-ins folder resides on your hard drive to make use of the filters. Using filters in a script is a convenient way to apply filters consistently to your images. You could take a series of scans and apply the KPT Sharpen Intensity filter. Unlike the Photoshop Sharpen filter, it does not enable you to set the amount you sharpen. Most of the third party filters only work on files in 24-bit color.

Intensity and Contrast

The **Intensity and Contrast** option manipulates the image and its palette and enables you to change the RGB and brightness and contrast of an image. The settings are retained so the next time you use this option, the settings are the same. This is not the same as modifying intensity elsewhere, because it is not isolated in that it does affect brightness and saturation.

Accessing Sharpen in Photoshop

Photoshop's Sharpen filter is not an outside filter; it is actually a part of the software and for this reason you cannot access it. Photoshop 4.0 has also included its Gallery Effects filters as part of the software, so they are not available to use DeBabelizer Toolbox as well.

Using Channels

Every image contains channels and they are represented as RGB, despite the image's color depth. A 32-bit image has four channels, the fourth being an alpha channel. Since it is 32-bit and it has four channels, each individual channel is 8 bits. The **Channels** option enables you to manipulate the individual channels, RGB, or the alpha. You can use this to affect each channel individually. For example, the blue channel often contains a lot of shadow information. You can make subtle changes to the blue channel to change the shadow information in a file.

The **Open Channels** option on the **File** menu enables you to open an image's individual channel and by using this, you can open an image's alpha channel.

After you load the alpha channel, you can apply it to a batch of images. Under the Selection transparency, set the paste to alpha. All three channels combined make the image that appears onscreen.

You can also affect a series of images by also checking the **General Preferences** of Pass alpha channel to Photoshop Plug-ins. The alpha channel will be used to apply the filter to the images. For example, you may have alpha set to highlight the area around a corporate logo for a business presentation. The logo is always in the same position so you can use the KPT Sharpen filter to draw more attention to it.

Manipulating Movies

You can apply a few of DeBabelizer Toolbox's options directly to movie files. You are not limited to applying these option to movies, however; you can also apply them to still images, with the exception of Frame Rate.

- **Frame Rate:** You can change the frame rate of a movie from within DeBabelizer Toolbox. The frame rate of a movie is how many frames are displayed per second. The DeBabelizer Toolbox default is 15fps. If a movie has sound, you do not want to do this; it will become unsynchronized.

- **Skew Fixer:** This option fixes damaged movies or stills from movies that have blurred lines going through them.

- **Fields:** Images are divided by fields; they are horizontal lines the width of the image and the height of one pixel. Fields are broken down into Odds and Evens, alternately down an image. DeBabelizer Toolbox enables you to manipulate images by their fields. You can swap Odds lines for Evens and so on. You can also Interpolate them, so that if an image is blurry due to motion blur, you can try to compensate for it.

Printing

You can choose to print directly from DeBabelizer Toolbox. The Print dialog box has an additional feature; it tells you the number of pages across and the number of pages down, for tiling files. In Figure 11.27, the numbers read 2 across and 1 down. It takes two printed pages to print the image's width and one page to print the image's height.

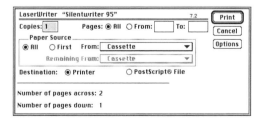

FIGURE 11.27

You can tell if your image will be tiled. By changing the orientation of the page, you may be able to remove the tiling.

283

Page Setup

Page Setup is the standard page setup you see in most programs, except for one twist—you can run a script from this location. You could scale or crop an image before sending it to the printer, for example. Some of the standard scripts that ship with DeBabelizer Toolbox apply to printing to laserwriters, but you could increase the resolution of your file via a script before the file gets printed.

Page Setup enables you to select the orientation of the page; this is useful later when discussing the Batch Catalog. You want to know the orientation of your page when printing a Batch Catalog; it also specifies whether you are printing in color or black and white. If you are doing a straight print without batching, you can mark the Fill the Page with Picture checkbox, and the entire printable area of the page is used. The Monochrome option temporarily converts an image to black and white for better printing on a black and white laser printer.

Batching

Batching is at the heart of DeBabelizer Toolbox. Batch Processes enable you to automate certain functions, such as saving, and apply them to a series of files. After you set up the specifics of the Batching, it can be done while the computer is unattended.

The nine Batch Processes DeBabelizer Toolbox offers are Catalog; Compare; Export; Save; Save Simple; Slideshow; SuperPalette; Place and Save; and Place, Acquire, and Save. All these Batches require that a BatchList be created. (These Batch processes are discussed in further detail in the next chapter.) A BatchList consists of a list of files that are processed. All the file names and the type of files are included in the BatchList. You can create new BatchLists or edit existing ones, and in order to save one, you must first name it.

TIP

You can have a BatchList as a text file. As a text file, the BatchList can be printed and used as a proofing device.

You can rename the files after they have undergone the Batch Process. Sometimes the new file names reflect their changes. For example, for a Batch Save of converting images from PICTs to BMPs, you could change the extension of the file name from PICT to BMP. This way you know what file format they are in and that they have been converted because they will sport the DeBabelizer Toolbox preview icon.

Drag and Drop

You can launch DeBabelizer Toolbox by dragging and dropping a file or a group of files onto the DeBabelizer Toolbox icon or a Preferences file. When a group of files is dropped over the icon, DeBabelizer Toolbox automatically adds these files to a Drag and Drop BatchList. The files are then treated as any other BatchList. When using the drag and drop method to launch DeBabelizer Toolbox, it automatically launches the Slide Show Batch Process. You can hit the Cancel key and the Drag and Drop BatchList stays intact to be used in another batch process.

Learn To Ignore

This advanced option is mainly used for batching a large number of files. DeBabelizer Toolbox "learns" what files to ignore (up to a total of 128) and then ignores those as it is batching. This process can get tricky, so you have to be careful that files you don't want ignored aren't added to the Ignore List. You can set Learn To Ignore to exclude certain types you know you do not want to be ignored and you can ignore ambiguous files or unknown file formats and text files. The Ignore List is not a report; it is simply a list DeBabelizer Toolbox compiles internally for its own purposes. The Ignore List is not retained from session to session.

285

Log Entry and Error Logs

Log entry is used to generate Error Logs. The Errors Logs can be printed or saved to disk. You can customize the Log entry with the provided selection of information, such as file name, file size, and so on. Figure 11.28 shows the default text string that DeBabelizer Toolbox offers you to modify.

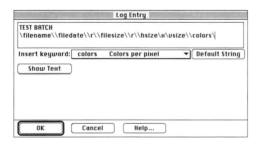

FIGURE 11.28

A Log is a useful tool to keep track of what occurs in DeBabelizer Toolbox, especially during batch processes.

You can display the text string you have customized by clicking Show Text. If you want to set up an Error Log, remember to place your own Error Log title before the text string. For example, "TEST BATCH" was used in Figure 11.28. Figure 11.29 is the end result.

FIGURE 11.29

You can print an Error Log or save it to disk from the Error Log submenu from the Misc menu.

Scripting

Scripting is another of DeBabelizer Toolbox's powerful tools. It can be combined with Batch Processing to automate several functions at a time, while being applied to a series of files.

Basically, a script is a customized list of tasks you tell DeBabelizer Toolbox to do automatically. Creating scripts is similar to creating a Macro. You can create scripts and edit existing scripts. You can also save scripts for future use by exporting them. You can import and export scripts from the **Script-Palettes-Etc** option on the **Misc** menu. The best part is that, like Batch Processing, these scripts can run unattended. For example, you could set the machine to run overnight.

There are two ways to create scripts. You can go to the **Scripts** menu and select **New** or the **Watch Me** mode. By creating a script using the New command, you can pull down on the actions in the main menus to add them to the script. A question mark will appear before each action that has settings. Double-click the action and the Actions dialog box comes up. From the dialog box, you can set the action to work how you want it.

The **Watch Me** mode records what you do to a file as you physically manipulate the file from the pull-down menus and click options in dialog boxes. DeBabelizer Toolbox records your actions and saves them into the Edit Script dialog box shown in Figure 11.30. You can then tweak the script and save it.

FIGURE 11.30

Scripts are retained within the DeBabelizer Toolbox program. If you want to bring a script with you to another machine, you must export it.

You see line by line the tasks the Script is set to do. You can create as many scripts as you need; the only problem is real estate on the submenu. You can only delete customized scripts.

You don't need to overlap your script functions with Batch Processing. For example, if you are going to dither a group of images, set the script to do the dithering and remapping portion only. The Batch Process handles opening and saving of the files.

Scripts can include anything that you can think of that is a pull-down menu option. For example, it can include Photoshop filters, Readers or Writers, Acquire Modules, and so on; the list is endless. To run a Script, select **Execute** on the **Script** menu and choose one of the Scripts listed.

Scripts can also be accessed in the Open, Save As, and the Batch Processes dialog boxes. Just remember when you set a script to run from these locations, the next time you open a file or save a file it will automatically launch the script. It may take you a while to remember you had a script set to run.

TIP

Setting the script option in the Open, Save As, and the Batch Processes dialog boxes to do Nothing is also a preference setting.

The Scripts dialog box gives you extra parameters such as loops or delays. The parameters help the script's functionality. You can also add other commands to your scripts such as delays and pauses. For example, adding a pause can be useful to add to a script so that you can watch the changes happen to the file onscreen to ensure the process is going successfully.

It is always an excellent idea to troubleshoot and test a script. It is very easy to miss one step and forget a setting needs to be a certain way. Before applying the script to an entire BatchList, you should apply it to one or two images. This way you can be certain the script is doing exactly what you want.

If the script is not doing what you want, go back and analyze the steps you added and the settings they have. You need to think in a very concrete and linear way when writing scripts. For example, if you are creating a script to remap images to the Netscape palette and you want to add a command to remove unused and duplicate colors to optimize them for the Web, you would need to create the script in this order.

The script should have Set Palette and Remap listed first. The Remove Unused and Duplicates command should be listed after Set Palette and Remap. The order of events is important. You need to have the correct palette colors in the file before you can remove the file's unused and duplicate palette colors.

Export AppleScript

DeBabelizer Toolbox can be run by AppleScript (Macintosh's own scripting or macro language) or QuickKeys (a separate macro and scripting language). It can also export DeBabelizer Toolbox scripts in the AppleScript format. You can also execute an AppleScript from within DeBabelizer Toolbox.

If you had created a QuickKeys macro, for example, that could run several Batch processes overnight, the macro would include the list of DeBabelizer Toolbox functions you wanted. You would also have to be certain everything was set up to run. The files would be in a BatchList and the scripts to be used would be set in DeBabelizer Toolbox for the Macro to use.

Batch Processes

Batch Processes enable you to automate a series of events, letting your computer do the work for you. This is one of the reasons why DeBabelizer Toolbox is so popular. Another benefit of Batch Processes is that you get very consistent results.

DeBabelizer Toolbox comes with nine standard Batch Processes: Batch Catalog; Batch Compare; Batch Export; Batch Save; Batch Save Simple; Batch Slideshow; Batch SuperPalette; Place and Save; and Place; Acquire; and Save.

A brief description of each Batch Process follows:

- **Batch Catalog:** From a BatchList, you can create Catalog pages, which are DeBabelizer Toolbox files that can either be printed or saved to disk. On the Catalog pages are the images included in your BatchList. The Catalog pages can include one or more images per page, depending on your settings. For example, you could have six images per page. This is an excellent tool for archiving a project or getting client approval.

- **Batch Compare:** Images are compared to one another on the basis of image information. This is an excellent tool for purging your project of duplicate files.

- **Batch Export:** This process is an automated save function using Photoshop Plug-in formats. It gives DeBabelizer Toolbox added functionality by borrowing third-party file formats. Using this process enables DeBabelizer to work with file formats that DeBabelizer Toolbox does not support directly. Also by using the export Plug-ins, you can also write to a special hardware device.

- **Batch Save:** This process can save the BatchList in different ways but is most commonly used for file conversion or in combination with a script. This is a quick way to convert Photoshop files to a format your authoring program can read.

- **Batch Save Simple:** This process is the same as Batch Save with fewer options. You can also use this Batch Process in combination with a script.

- **Batch Slideshow:** Images are displayed for a user-defined amount of time to the screen. If you are searching for a file, but do not remember its exact name, you can drop the suspected files onto the DeBabelizer Toolbox icon and watch the screen as DeBabelizer Toolbox displays each file until you find the one you need.

- **Batch SuperPalette:** This process creates a SuperPalette, which is an optimized palette, based on a list of files. It is one of the most popular Batch Processes. It can create one optimized custom palette for all the files in your project.

- **Place and Save:** Places an image over a series images or just one image. This Batch Process can act as a compositing tool, pasting a file onto another background image.

- **Place, Acquire, and Save:** This process is similar to the Place and Save process except that it adds Acquiring the file. It can also act as a compositing tool with the added benefit of using file formats not directly supported by DeBabelizer Toolbox.

Similarities in Batch Process Settings

Although the Batch Processes handle different functions, their interfaces have some similarities. The Batch Processes dialog boxes also have some similar options. These options are described in this section. Later in the chapter, each Batch Process's unique features are discussed in detail.

All these Batch Processes are similar in that they all require a BatchList and some processes require two BatchLists. An example can be seen on the left side of Figure 12.1. This list contains the files that will undergo the process you have selected. At the top there are three buttons: New, Edit, and Delete. These buttons all refer to creating or editing BatchLists.

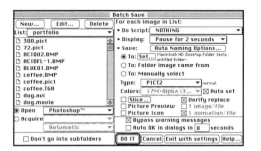

FIGURE 12.1

You can create BatchLists directly from the Batch Process window.

Using Error Logs

An Error Log records all the actions your do in DeBabelizer Toolbox that generate errors. For example, if you try to edit a default Catalog style and save over it, an error will be generated in the Error Log.

If you are running a Batch Process the Error Log keeps track of any errors that occurred during the process and provides you with additional information. For example, if you are running a Batch Compare, the Error Log contains the file's differences. The Error Log can be saved to disk or printed.

To display the Error Log choose Error Log: Show from the Misc menu. You can also save, print, and clear an Error Log. You can save the Error Log as a separate text file. Error Logs also have options. The Error Log options are:

- **Automatically show Error Log *only* if running Batch:** This option automatically displays the Error Log when a Batch Process is running.

- **Show Error Log instead of Error Alert Boxes:** This will display the Error Log instead of a warning box.

- **Display date and time of each error:** This will display the date and time of the error in the log. This can be useful to use when running a batch unattended.

Error Logs are an excellent way to keep track of the Batch Process and to ensure it is running successfully. You can use the Error Logs in all the Batch Processes, but the most important one to use it in is Batch Compare.

Creating BatchLists

The New button enables you to create a new BatchList, Edit enables you to edit an existing list, and Delete enables you to delete a list that you no longer need. If you select New or Edit, another dialog box appears, as shown in Figure 12.2.

On the left side of this dialog box is a list of the files from which you can choose. As you add files, they move into the right panel of the dialog box which becomes your BatchList side.

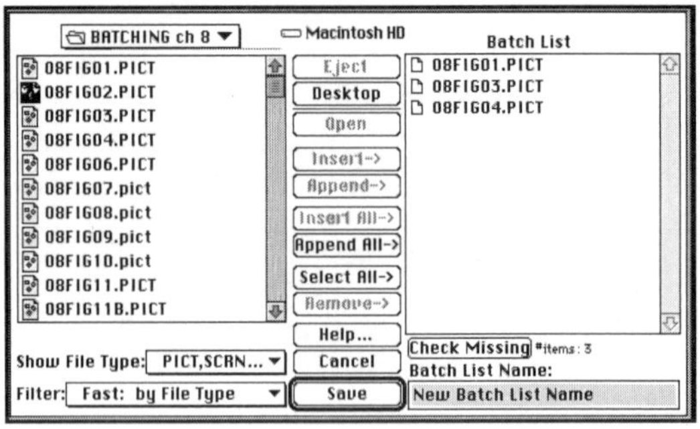

FIGURE 12.2

You can append an entire list of files to your new BatchList from the BatchList creation dialog box.

On the bottom left side of the dialog box is the Show File Type menu. Show File Type selects the format of files you are processing. It acts as a filter to allow only that particular file format to be shown in the window above. Selecting All from the Show File Type submenu displays every file format in the folder.

If you pull down this menu, you can see the entire list of file formats that DeBabelizer Toolbox reads. You can be selective and choose one specific file format to read if you want. This can speed up the process by purposely ignoring files that you know you do not want to include in your BatchList. For example, if you are editing a BatchList and it already includes BMPs, you may want to search for a QuickTime movie to add to the BatchList. By selecting QuickTime as the Show File Type, only files that are QuickTimes will be displayed in the left side of the window.

NOTE

On the Macintosh, you can create aliases for documents, folders, and programs. If you select an alias of a folder when adding files to your BatchList, it treats the folder's alias as a document instead of the folder for which it is an alias. You won't be able to open the alias folder because the Open button is grayed out. To open the folder, you need to find the original.

TIP

A quick way to create a BatchList is to select a series of files and drop them on the DeBabelizer Toolbox icon, instantly creating a "Drag and Drop" BatchList. The Drag and Drop BatchList becomes available from the BatchList menu. The Batch Slideshow process is automatically launched, but you can exit from it by hitting Cancel. The files are retained in the Drag and Drop BatchList until you create a new Drag and Drop BatchList using the same method. You can then choose any Batch Process and the Drag and Drop BatchList will be available to you.

Show File Type is only for creating a BatchList. In the main Batch Process dialog box, you are asked again what file format to use. This can be confusing, but the Show

File Type deals only with displaying files for you to add to your BatchList. It helps you to navigate through folders on your hard drive that have many different file formats. It also helps DeBabelizer Toolbox to quickly find the files you want to add to your BatchList, by acting as a filter.

The Filter type option deals with how DeBabelizer Toolbox filters out the possible file formats chosen under the Show File Type. As DeBabelizer Toolbox filters out possible files, the files that match the selected file format in the Show Format Type are listed on the left side of the window.

There are three options under Filter:

- **None: list all:** DeBabelizer Toolbox displays all files on your hard drive, regardless of the file format overriding the file format selected.

- **Fast: by File Type:** DeBabelizer Toolbox displays all files on the hard drive that could possibly be the file format selected in the pop-up menu based on the information stored in the file's resource fork.

- **Slow: by file contents:** This filter looks at the entire contents of each file to be certain it is the selected file format. This filtering takes longer because DeBabelizer Toolbox actually opens and scans each file.

293

In the center of the dialog box (refer to Figure 12.2) are the options from which you can choose. All these options deal with selecting files for the BatchList:

- **Eject:** You can eject a disk from your drive if you are trying to find a file on a floppy disk to add to the BatchList.

- **Desktop:** You can go to the desktop to find a file to add to your BatchList.

- **Open:** You can open folders or hard drives to find the files you want to add to your BatchList.

- **Insert:** You can add a file in a particular order to a BatchList. Highlight the file you want to add and highlight the file in the BatchList you want the new file to come before and select Insert. For example, look at Figure 12.2. The file **08FIG02.PICT** is not added to the BatchList. If you highlight **08FIG02.PICT** on the left side then highlight **08FIG03.PICT** on the right side and hit insert, **08FIG02.PICT** is inserted in the correct order in the BatchList.

- **Append:** Highlight the file you want on the left side, click on Append, and the highlighted file is added to the BatchList. You can only highlight one file at a time; you cannot Shift-click and highlight multiple files.

- **Insert All:** You can Insert all the files from the left side window into a BatchList at a designate position.

- **Append All:** You can add all the files from the left side window into the BatchList, which is convenient if you are adding an entire folder into a BatchList.

- **Select All:** You can select all the files in the batch list at once with this command. You usually use this in combination with one of the other choices. For example, you may select all and then remove. Your BatchList is cleared for any new files you want to add, which is helpful when editing an existing BatchList. You can use the Shift key to unhighlight selected batch list files.

- **Remove:** Highlight the file that you no longer want in the BatchList (right side window), click Remove, and the file is taken off the BatchList.

- **Delete:** You can delete a file from the BatchList. You must highlight the file and press Delete.

You also have the choices of asking for Help and to Cancel from the BatchList dialog box.

Figure 12.3 shows the Check Missing button. In the BatchList, notice that **08FIG02.PICT** is grayed out. Next to the Check Missing button is the number of total files in parentheses, and next to it the number missing. This function is available only for editing an existing BatchList. It shows the number of files missing in the folder from which the Batch is created. This is a good proofing device for using the same BatchList over and over again.

294

FIGURE **12.3**

You can quickly find out if any files have been deleted from a folder since the last time you ran the Batch Process by using the Check Missing option. The missing files are grayed out in the BatchList.

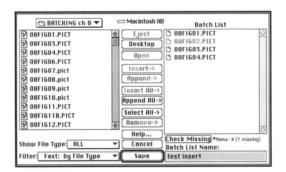

Creation Alternatives

You can also create new BatchLists and add to existing BatchLists from the Open dialog box by using the Batch+ button. This is a quick way to modify or create BatchLists.

At the bottom of the right side of the dialog box, in a highlighted state, is where you will name your new BatchList. Click Save and another dialog box appears, prompting you to give a name to the BatchList. DeBabelizer Toolbox does not let you close without saving, even if you have to replace the default BatchList. If you pull down the BatchList there is a choice of existing BatchLists, as shown in Figure 12.4. BatchLists remain in DeBabelizer Toolbox until you delete them.

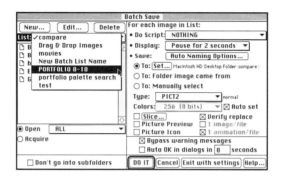

FIGURE 12.4

BatchLists available to choose from; your new batch list should be listed.

All the Batch Processes have these options. After the BatchList has been saved, you can return to the Main dialog box. The BatchList is on the left side now. On the right side are more options that are specific to each Batching Process.

File Type

In Figure 12.1, you see that below the BatchList is the **Open** submenu giving the similar options available for a direct open. You can specify the exact type of files that are to be opened in the BatchList and then processed. For example, in Figure 12.1 the Open filter is set to Photoshop; only files saved in the Photoshop format in the BatchList can be opened and processed. You can filter the BatchList for a particular format and apply a process to only those files. The Open option should not be confused with the **File format** submenu found in the BatchList creation dialog box. They serve two different purposes.

Below the **Open** submenu is the **Acquire** submenu. The **Acquire** submenu enables you to use third party Photoshop Plug-ins to open files. These are generally formats not directly supported by DeBabelizer Toolbox. The **Acquire** submenu can also be used to access scanners.

File Hierarchy

The last item on the left side of the main dialog box is the Don't go into subfolders checkbox; only the folders in the BatchList can be processed. If there is a folder within a folder, the subfolder cannot be opened, and the files inside it cannot be processed. In Figure 12.1, only files are added, but you could append an entire folder to have it processed.

Displaying as You Batch

Moving to the right side of the dialog box, all the Batch Processes have a Display submenu, enabling the user to see onscreen the action that is taking place. The viewing options for Display are:

- **Display Off:** This option turns off the image display. You can run DeBabelizer Toolbox in the background while using the computer for another task.

- **Display Off Fast No Background:** This option turns the display option off. You cannot use computer for any other task; it will only process the files. This option runs the quickest.

- **Stop and Wait:** This option displays the image and waits until you click the Next Image button to go to the next image. This option gives you an opportunity to manipulate the image. This option, however, requires someone to watch over the Batch Process. Figure 12.5 shows the Next Image button.

FIGURE 12.5

The Toolbar grows to include the Cancel, Options, and Next Image buttons during a Batch Process.

- **Pause for 1 second:** The images are displayed for 1 second.

- **Pause for 2 seconds:** The images are displayed for 2 seconds.

- **Pause for 10 seconds:** The images are displayed for 10 seconds.

- **Pause for a user-defined period of time:** You can designate a specified time for the image to be paused. This may give you enough time to apply certain manipulations to the image.

The quickest option to use is the Display Off, but, if you want to ensure that you set up your script or batch is processing correctly, then displaying it for 1 or 2 seconds is a good safety.

TIP

By holding down the spacebar, you can pause the image display, but only if you have a display time chosen from the **Display** submenu. When you release the spacebar, the next image is displayed.

Batch Warnings

Another similarity for all the Batch Processes is the Bypass warning messages checkbox. If DeBabelizer Toolbox is running unattended, you need to check the Bypass warning messages checkbox, or when you return to your computer to see if your BatchList is done processing, the computer is waiting for a response to a dialog box from the user.

The Auto OK checkbox is another useful option directly below the Bypass warning messages checkbox. To use the Auto OK option in dialog boxes, you need to set a user-defined amount of time. The specified amount of time acts as a timer. If no response is given to the dialog box in the user-defined amount of time, DeBabelizer Toolbox automatically says OK to any prompt. The only possible hitch with this is that you have to make sure that you really want the OK button to be hit.

Getting Ready to Begin the Batch Process

Along the bottom of every Batch Process dialog box are four options: DO IT, Cancel, Exit with settings, and Help. The DO IT option means you have checked everything, and BatchList is ready to go. After clicking it, the Batch Process begins. Cancel cancels the batch without retaining the settings you created. Exit with settings is very useful because when you need to go check something in the Finder; you can exit and retain the settings you created.

DeBabelizer Toolbox does not let you click back to the Finder when a dialog box is up. If you need to check something, you have to click either Cancel or Exit with settings. Help is also found at the bottom of the dialog box, which is very useful and is topic-driven.

The Progress Meter

After you choose the DO IT button, the Batch Process begins, and you are now batching. If you have a display on, you can see the images whizzing by. If you have no display selected, another way to check that your Batch Process is processing is to look at the Toolbar. As mentioned earlier, after the Batch Process has begun the Toolbar grows. Below the Selection Marquee Info is a white bar called a Progress Meter. That Progress Meter turns black to mark the progress of the process, as shown in Figure 12.6.

The Progress Meter is only available during a Batch Process. Below the Progress Meter are three more options: Cancel, Options, and Next Image. Clicking Cancel brings up a dialog box that asks if you want to Cancel the Batch. If you decide Not to Cancel the Batch, you can click the Do Not Cancel batch, and then select the Next Image and the Batch continues processing.

An alternative is to select the Options button. Selecting the Options button returns you to the main dialog box for that particular Batch Process. From here, you can check or change your batch settings. If you did not Cancel completely, you need to click the Next Image button in order to begin the Batch again.

FIGURE 12.6

Checking your Progress Meter makes certain that your computer hasn't crashed if the "no display" option is on.

Auto Naming Options

The Auto Naming Options button is part of most Batch Process dialog boxes, but not the SuperPalette and Slideshow dialog boxes. Even the Batch Catalog dialog box provides access to the Auto Naming Options from the Save Setup button. Naming your files after they have gone through a Batch Process is an important step. For example, you can set up a naming convention that denotes whether a file has been processed; or, applying an extension to the file can let you know you have applied a palette. Figure 12.7 shows the Auto Namer dialog box.

FIGURE 12.7

The Auto Namer dialog box enables you to change the names of your processed files.

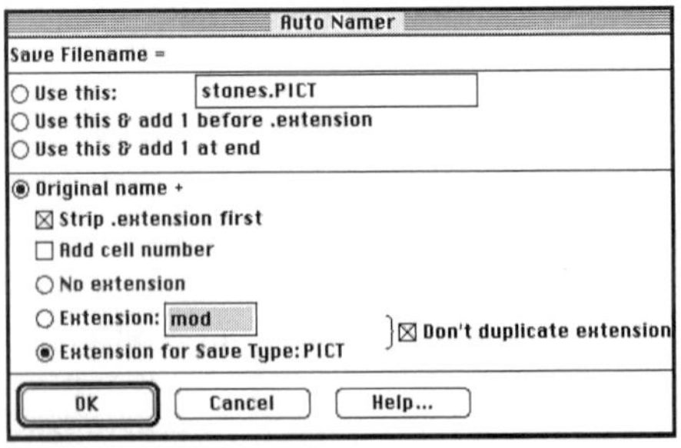

These options are similar to the options available from the Naming button in the Save As dialog box:

- **Use this:** This option enables you to type in a name that you would like the file to be renamed and saved as. DeBabelizer Toolbox, by default, automatically places the file's original name in this box, but retains the name you enter here from session to session.

- **Use this & add 1 before .extension:** This option uses the name typed in the space above and adds a sequential number to the files in the BatchList. This is a convenient option for naming and saving an entire folder of images. The sequential numbering is done according to the file's order in the BatchList, for example **FILENAME01.PICT**.

- **Use this & add 1 at end:** This option uses the name and places a sequential number at the end of the file without an extension, such as **FILENAME01**, or **FILENAME02**. This is a convenient method for working with individual PICS files to create an animation later.

The second section shown in Figure 12.7 deals with keeping the original file name and adding to it:

- **Strip .extension first:** This option removes the original extension letters and then adds whatever else you may check.

- **Add cell number:** You can use this option to save multi-celled file formats. Each cell within the file is named with the original name plus its sequential cell number.

- **No extension:** You can choose to not add an extension to the file name with this option.

- **Extension:** You can attach your own extension (maybe some internal code that you use to identify where an image is in a long a process of steps). Codes should be only three characters in length for transferring over to the PC platform.

- **Extension for Save Type:** This option automatically places the extension that corresponds to the selected file format. In Figure 12.7, PICT is displayed because it is the code that DeBabelizer Toolbox uses for the PICT file format.

These last two options offer a second feature of not duplicating the extensions so that your file does not read **FILENAME.PICT.PICT**. To avoid this problem, make sure the Don't duplicate extension checkbox is marked.

The Destination of Your Processed Files

The Set option enables you to determine the destination for the renamed or converted files. Click on this button to find the folder or create a folder for DeBabelizer Toolbox to save the processed files. You can choose for the file to return to the folder it came from, but unless you change the naming convention, you run the risk of overwriting your original files as they are processed.

Additional Options for the New Files

You can also apply extra options to the files as they are processed:

- **Slice:** Slice takes an image and cuts it up into segments called cells and saves the pieces as individual files or into one master file like a PICS format. The primary use for the Slice feature is generating animation storyboards for animators. You can set the parameters of the cell size in the Slice dialog box.

299

DeBabelizer Toolbox also gives you the option of saving the image's fields. Within the Slice picture setup dialog box there are other option to choose from, as shown in Figure 12.8.

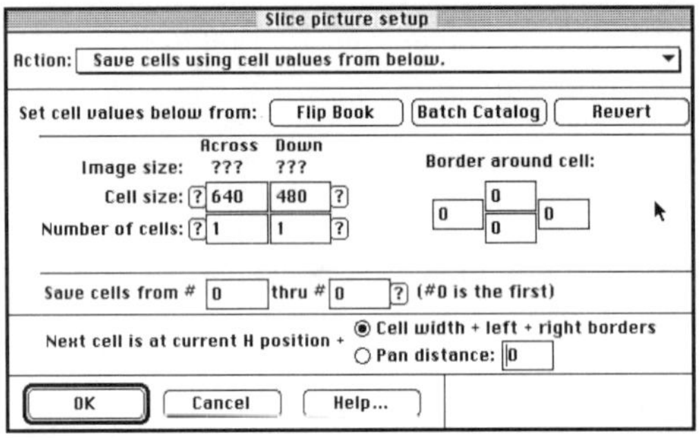

FIGURE 12.8

You can create your own Slice specifications or use one of DeBabelizer Toolbox's own preset values.

- **Picture preview:** This option creates a preview of the file to use in the Open dialog box. You can create Picture previews for the files listed in the BatchList. Animations and QuickTimes will use the first frame as the preview. It is an actual image that is saved with the original.

- **Picture icon:** This option creates an icon for the image. You can see it when the file is on the desktop. It is the finder icon.

The rest of this chapter is dedicated to detailed descriptions of each of the Batch Processes individually. Explanations of what they do and how they can be used are included. The right side of each of the Batch Processes dialog boxes is different.

How to Batch Catalog

Batch Catalog is a catalog of the images in the BatchList. The images are placed sequentially from the upper left corner to the right side of the page. You can set up the page to have several images or just one. Depending on the size of your page and how many images you want to place on it, you can adjust the size of the images being cataloged.

A Catalog page can also include other information: name, file size, date, and time. The Catalog pages can be printed, saved to disk, or displayed on your monitor. Depending on whether you have a color printer or not, they can be printed in color or in black and white.

DeBabelizer Toolbox comes with four default catalog styles: Thumbnails for Black and White Printer, Thumbnails for Color Printer, Thumbnails for Screen, and Thumbnails for a Grayscale Printer. All these Catalog Styles are useful for printing catalog pages to printers. You can edit these as well, and they provide a good start for the Catalog styles you create for yourself.

Why Batch Catalog?

Batch Catalog is useful because it shows you what you have and what it looks like. In a visual medium, these are important criteria.

In a multimedia title, you can have a group of Source Images or assets from which to draw to create art for the title. If you run a Catalog, the art director and production artist can easily pick the best images to use in creating the artwork.

It also can be crucial for file management. You can Catalog all the pieces that make up a project for archival purposes. In projects where there are numerous files in numerous locations, you can use the catalog to keep it all straight. You can quickly keep track of images no longer in the show or when archiving a project.

You can also create Catalog pages to pass finished indexed art files along to a programmer. After all the art has been palletized and saved in the final file format, a Catalog helps the programmer keep track of various assets. You could also submit the Catalog pages to a client for approval, especially if text is something that needs to be checked for accuracy.

Whether it is print or multimedia, Catalog pages keep your work organized as the project passes hands, whether it is to a programmer or a printer.

Creating Catalog Styles

The interface for creating Catalog styles may be tricky, but it isn't so scary. It uses the diagrams you learned about in Chapter 11, "Overview of DeBabelizer Toolbox." Figure 12.9 shows the main dialog box for Batch Catalog. Mathematically challenged individuals might avoid creating catalog styles like the plague until they realize DeBabelizer Toolbox can do the math for you.

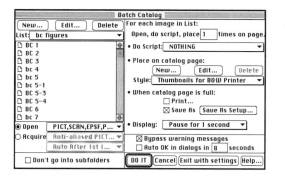

FIGURE 12.9

The Batch Catalog dialog box.

Above the **Style** submenu are the three buttons that should look familiar from creating BatchLists: New, Edit, and Delete. If you choose New or Edit, the dialog box in Figure 12.10 appears. This is where it starts to get fun!

FIGURE 12.10

*The dialog box for
creating new
Catalog Styles.*

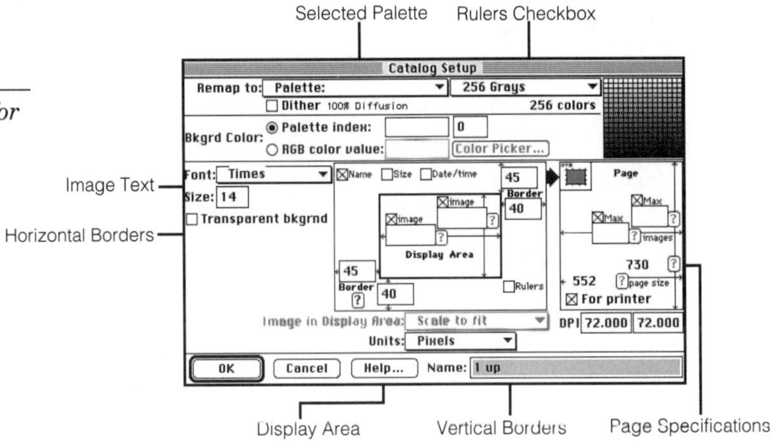

Selected Palette   Rulers Checkbox

Image Text

Horizontal Borders

Display Area   Vertical Borders   Page Specifications

TIP

You can edit the default Catalog pages, but you cannot delete them.

The Remap To Options

As you can see, not all options in the Catalog Setup dialog box are available to you. The first option is the **Remap to** submenu. The Remap to option refers to the color range used in displaying the images. It can be based on a specified palette, the palette of the first image or a Macintized palette of the first image in the BatchList.

You can also change the pixel depth for optimum printing. For example, if you are going to print to a black and white printer, you remap the images to a palette of 16 grays. The Remap to options only apply to the Catalog page; you are not remapping or changing the color depth of the original files.

The options for Remap to are:

- **Palette:** This option enables you to specifically pick an existing palette to use, by pulling down the submenu next to it. When this option is selected, a pull-down menu of palettes becomes available.

- **Palette of the 1st image:** This option automatically uses the palette of the first file in the BatchList. All the images to follow are remapped to that first image's palette. This is fine if all the images are already indexed to one palette. If not, you may get some heavy banding and dithering.

- **Palette of 1st image, Macintized:** A Macintized palette has white in the 0 position and black in the 255 position in a palette. This option uses the first image's palette, but as a Macintized palette.

- **RGB: 32768 colors:** This option enables you to have a fuller color range without taking a hit on time and RAM. It still requires more RAM than 256 colors. This option uses thousands of colors to display the images.

- **RGB: 17 million colors:** This option is the best way to print or display color but it requires the most RAM. This option uses as many colors as you can possibly have.

TIP

If you are printing to a black and white printer, you don't need all the color range of millions of colors, using a grayscale palette is more efficient.

Using a Palette for the Remap To Option

To the right of the **Remap to** submenu are the palette choices. As you see in Figure 12.10, you can pull down this submenu and see more choices. The **Palette** menu only becomes available if you select the Palette option for the Remap to option. The palettes in boldface are customized palettes you created in this DeBabelizer Toolbox session. If you close DeBabelizer Toolbox and relaunch it they are no longer in boldface. The chosen palette is displayed next to the Palette pull-down menu, as shown in Figure 12.11.

303

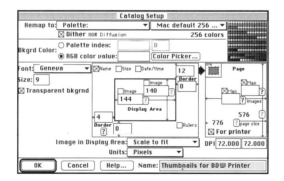

FIGURE 12.11

The palette chosen to remap the images is displayed.

Using Dithering with Catalog Images

Working your way down the Catalog Setup dialog box, the next item is the Dither checkbox. The Dither checkbox is the setting for the amount of dithering to be applied to the images as they are remapped. Remember that the files themselves are not being dithered, but their Catalog page images are being dithered for display purposes.

The amount of dithering currently set in the **Dithering and Background Color** options is listed next to the Dithering checkbox. In Figure 12.11, the dithering is set to 88 percent with the Diffusion method selected. The default setting for DeBabelizer Toolbox is 88 percent dithering, but you can change this, if you feel you need more, by going into the Dithering and Background Color dialog box.

The amount of dithering you apply to file depends on the image itself. If your files become fuzzy you dithering too much; banding and artifacts also appear in images that have been dithered too much. Photographic images tend to handle dithering better than line-art or computer-generated art. The best way to make sure you are applying the right amount of dithering on your images is to do tests. If you are applying a dithering amount to a BatchList of files, keep in mind the images you are dithering to find a balance so all images look good.

Background Color

You can designate a background color in the Catalog Setup dialog box. Background Color is the color of the background against which the images appear. The default setting is white. For printing, the background color is best if set to white, but if you are going to screen with your Catalog pages, white or black will do nicely.

You can set the background color to whatever color you may need. You can set it in three ways: by using the color wheel, knowing the exact index number of the color, or by using the Eyedropper tool and clicking the selected palette to find the color.

Image Description

You can print file information with the images on the Catalog pages. The text information can include the image's name, size, the date, and time. You can select the font used in displaying the information from the **Font** submenu. You can also designate the font size used. Another related option is the Transparent bkgrnd checkbox. Transparent background refers to the background of the text information, as shown in Figure 12.12.

FIGURE 12.12

A comparison of Image text on a transparent background and on no background.

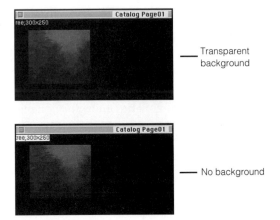

—— Transparent background

—— No background

The image information prints on white despite what the background color is, if Transparent bkgrnd is not checked. Next to the **Font** submenu are the checkboxes for Name, Size, and Date/time. One of these checkboxes has to be checked in order to have access to Font and Size; otherwise they are grayed out. This information is printed *above* the image, as shown in Figure 12.12; you cannot vary the position.

You need to designate a border around the image using the diagram in the Image Display area. If no border is designated, the text information writes over the top left portion of the image, as shown in Figure 12.13.

FIGURE 12.13

The images are butted up against each other because no border was set.

Display Area

The two most important and intimidating parts of this dialog box are Display Area and Page Specifications. As shown in Figure 12.14, in the center of the dialog box is the Image Display Area.

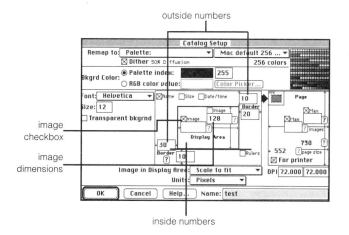

FIGURE 12.14

The Image Display Area diagram with inside and outside numbers.

The Display Area indicates the area on the page an image appears. You can give the image borders. The borders create space for the text information to be written. Borders also provide space between the images. In Figure 12.13, no borders were given, so there is no space between the images. The outside numbers of the diagram are for designating borders. The inside numbers are for sizing the image on the Catalog page.

If you have the horizontal borders set to 0, the images butt up against each other. A five-pixel border set in both Horizontal borders gives *each* image its own five-pixel space, a total of 10 pixels inbetween. This number is reflected in the Image Display Area, because it reduces the area for image display by 10 pixels/image.

TIP

Clicking the Border ? button automatically gives you the ideal border settings for the amount of text information you want above the image. When images butt up against each other and a lot of text is chosen, the images' texts can cancel each other.

Clicking the image checkbox sets the size of the image to an automatic setting that is based on the Page Specifications entered. If you want to manually set these numbers, you need to uncheck the image box, as shown in Figure 12.14. In Figure 12.14, one image checkbox is marked and the other isn't. The unmarked image checkbox enables you to enter your own values into the Image size field.

You can add in your own numbers; you can enter in your own values. You can pull-down the Units submenu to see the size displayed in other units. (DeBabelizer Toolbox defaults to pixels.) In Figure 12.14, the image is 128 pixels in height.

A very useful function is to let DeBabelizer Toolbox do the math for you by clicking the ? button. DeBabelizer Toolbox then enters the values based on the Page Specifications and border values. The Page Specifications is the size page you are working with.

After the image checkbox is marked, you see the Image in Display Area submenu become active (see Figure 12.15). The choices nestled under Image in Display Area submenu are as follows:

- **Scale to fit:** This option enables the entire image to be displayed. It scales the entire image to the specified size.

- **Crop to center:** This option crops the outside of the image if it is larger than the size specified in the settings.

- **Crop to upper left:** This option crops that part of the image that falls to the right and bottom of the settings.

Ruler Marks

You can have ruler marks printed and displayed on the outside of the image by clicking the Rulers checkbox in the **Image Display Area**. This option is helpful when trying to determine where a portion of the image is in relation to the another image. When Rulers is checked, you have four choices to make as to where the marks begin. Figure 12.16 shows a Catalog page with ruler marks.

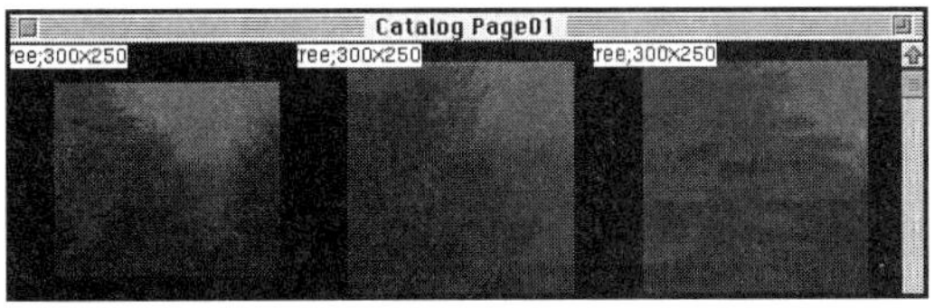

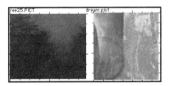

FIGURE 12.15

The different ways to size the image from L to R: Scale to fit, Crop to center, Crop to upper left. You cannot combine all three on one Catalog page as the figure suggests.

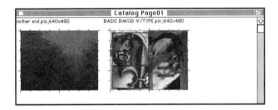

FIGURE 12.16

Rulers options on a Catalog page.

You can designate the ruler measurements by the **Units** submenu. You can choose from pixels, inches, centimeters, millimeters, picas, and points. On either side of the Ruler checkbox are two boxes that designate the distance between ruler marks; you can enter your own values (see Figure 12.17). You must first activate the Rulers checkbox before the two boxes for the distance between rulers appear.

307

FIGURE 12.17

Ruler mark increments surround each image. You can use this option to compare the relative sizes of the images.

Page Specifications

Page Specifications is the size of your page and its orientation. Page Specifications also uses a diagram to describe its dimension. Figure 12.18 shows how the Page Specifications defines the size of page you are displaying or printing. There are two parts to the Page Specifications diagram, the page size, and the number of images you want to print to the page.

FIGURE 12.18

Page Specifications section of the Catalog Setup dialog box.

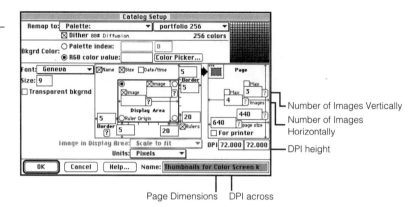

Number of Images Vertically
Number of Images Horizontally
DPI height

Page Dimensions   DPI across

Based on the numbers, you can determine the number of images you place on the page. How many images you fit per Catalog page depends on the size of your page and the borders you have selected.

The Max checkbox, when checked, enables the maximum images to be placed on the page according to the size of the images and the borders set. When the checkbox is unchecked, you can enter a specific value.

Clicking the For printer checkbox automatically brings up the dimensions associated with the printer selected in the Chooser. When the image checkboxes are checked, the ? button in the page size section becomes unavailable because it is used for manual settings only. DeBabelizer Toolbox can do the math for you and come up with the number of images that can be printed, based on the borders and page size specified. This function is initiated by clicking the ? button.

TIP

It is a good idea to preview to screen a new Catalog style before doing an entire page. Not only does it save paper, but it also ensures that you set it up the way you intended.

Changing the dpi of the images changes the size of the images as well. For example, if you have an image that is 72 dpi and you enter in 144 in the dpi value field, the image prints at half its size. This is a quick way to make your images print smaller.

After you have gone through all these various settings, you are now ready to name your newly created Catalog style and begin Batch Cataloging.

Options in the Main Catalog Dialog Box

There are a few more options in the main Batch Catalog dialog box (refer to Figure 12.9):

- **Open, do script, place *X* times on page:** This option is useful when you would like to have the file displayed more than once on a page. You can specify how many times. It can apply a script as it places the image on the page.

- **Do Script:** You can select a script to run while you Batch Catalog your images.

- **Place on catalog page:** This is the option to choose or create your Catalog style.

- **When catalog page is full:** With this option you have two choices. You can have the Catalog page automatically printed, or you can save the page to disk when it is complete. The Save As Setup button is for naming the Catalog pages. Figure 12.19 shows the dialog box for naming the Catalog pages via the Save As Setup option.

FIGURE 12.19

Automatic Save Setup dialog box for naming Catalog page files.

- **Display:** You can display the Catalog page as it is created, even if it is going to be saved to disk.

From the Automatic Save Setup dialog box, you can name the Catalog Page file. You are given three choices where to save these files. The first is to click the Set button, then you have to find or create a folder as a destination folder.

The second is to click To: Folder image came from. This option sends the files to the same folder that houses the BatchList files. The third choice is to manually select the folder and tell it to save in a certain destination folder. If this choice is marked during the Batch Catalog, the Save As dialog box comes up asking you to select a destination. DeBabelizer Toolbox uses "Catalog Page" as the default name for the files.

You can tell what file format to save the Catalog page as. You can give it a certain color depth or use the Auto Set to use the color depth the file is currently using. You can also Slice, create a preview, and create a finder icon for the files. The choices are similar to the options found in a Save As dialog box.

The Verify replace checkbox should not to be overlooked. This is a safety option to prevent you from writing over your files with the same name. If you have run another Batch Catalog, it prevents you from writing over the files, especially if you have chosen the default name. You should, however, only use this option for still-images and not use it for animation formats or QuickTime movies.

Batch Compare

The Batch Compare process compares files to one another. The files are set in the BatchList and then compared to files set in a Comparison List. You create both these lists by the standard BatchList creation.

Comparisons are based on image information, which can range from color information to pixel depth to resolution and dimensions. A report in the form of an Error Log can be generated to tell you the differences. This report can be saved to screen or printed. You can also save a comparison image file, which stores information about the differences between the images. To use this option, you need to mark the Save differences image checkbox.

Batch Compare can be a handy tool when there is a palette conflict or to proof your work for minor image manipulations. It can also be used to solve file management problems, where you discover a folder that has duplicate files. If Display is chosen in the Main dialog box, the modifications or image differences, if any, are visible on your screen in white highlighted area. Figure 12.20 shows the main Batch Compare dialog box.

FIGURE 12.20

You can compare BatchLists in different ways.

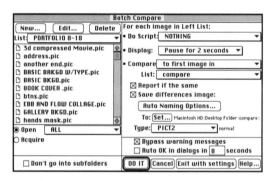

Why Use Batch Compare?

There are a number of reasons you would want to explore the Batch Compare process. It could be useful in maintaining good file management. When working with a large number of different files, it is helpful to be able to keep track of the most current and up-to-date files.

Comparing files for their palettes to find which palette works best on what image or QuickTime movie is another possibility. Some images have banding effects when palettized. If you can compare the differences between images, you may discover the problem areas in the images that need to be tweaked. For example, if you do some tests on the images with different palettes you can then compare them to see their differences.

You can also use it to compare different file's sizes and color depths for file formats. For example, you may want to compare how a GIF file is saved via Photoshop as opposed to the way DeBabelizer Toolbox does it. Discovering the lowest file size with the best display is important for images going to the Web.

Different Ways to Compare

You cannot select the same batch list for both the BatchList and the Comparison list. There are five different Compare styles to apply to batch list images; all are different ways to compare the images against each other. These options can be seen in the pop-up menu under Compare styles. The following list describes the different Compare styles:

- **Compare image with same name:** This option is ideal for a situation where you find files and are not sure if they should be used or thrown away. You have two folders (or possibly more) with identical file names. Going by date can help solve the problem, but it may not be the most accurate way. Create a BatchList out of one of the folders and then use the extra folder for the Comparison List. Each image is compared to the image with the exact same name. The only hitch here is to make sure they are completely identical in name and extension. For example, when comparing a file from the BatchList named CH180SA.pic, make sure that the file name in the Comparison List reads the exact same name for this option to work correctly.

- **Compare image in same position in list:** This option compares images in a sequential order as opposed to file name so that the third file in the BatchList is compared to the third file in the Comparison List. This is a good way to compare images that have undergone a process and whose file name extensions may have been changed to reflect the change.

- **Compare to previous image in left list:** This option compares the images based on the image directly preceding it in the BatchList. Notice that when this option is selected, the Comparison List becomes grayed out because the files in the BatchList are comparing themselves to each other and not to another list. This is useful for animation sequences where each frame should be consistent in color and pixel depth to the frame preceding it.

- **To first image in left list to next in:** The first image in the BatchList is compared to each image in the Comparison list on the right to make sure that all changes have been made. For example, if the brightness levels were tweaked, then you could make sure that it was done according to the image that was approved.

- **To first image in:** The first image in the Comparison List is compared to the files listed in the BatchList. You may need to check for consistency in the image's information so it can proof the files for you by creating an Error Log that (hopefully) reports they are all the same.

Error Log

Error Logs report information on pixel depth, color differences, and dimensions. The Error Log conveniently tells you if the image is from the left (BatchList) or right (Comparison List).

You can tell if the settings you want for the file are correct by the information it gives you. If the Report if the same checkbox is marked, DeBabelizer Toolbox will tell you on the Error Log that the images were the same (see Figure 12.21). This is a useful option for clearing out duplicate files.

FIGURE 12.21

A Comparison Error Log enables you to decide if an image has an unnecessary duplicate.

NOTE

When comparing GIFs, they must be saved in the same format either interlaced or with or without background transparent. If either side of the list is not matched up, it tells you a "parallel file does not exist" in the list.

Options in the Main Compare Dialog Box

Many of the options from the Compare process are similar to the options offered in every Batch Process. From the Batch Compare dialog box, you can also run the following options:

- **Do Script:** You can select a script to run while you batch compare your images.

- **Compare:** You have several ways to compare files with one another.

- **List:** This option is used to compare the BatchList against the Comparison list.

- **Report if the Same:** DeBabelizer Toolbox lets you know if the files being compared are identical and it reports it in the Error Log.

- **Save differences image:** DeBabelizer Toolbox saves an image that shows the differences between the two files being compared. It only saves a file if there are any differences. DeBabelizer Toolbox uses the default name **Diff.FILENAME**. You can use the Auto Naming Options to change the differences image's name.

You then can open up the differences file and see the areas of difference between the files being compared.

- **Auto Naming Options:** You can give a naming convention to each of the differences images created from the Compare batch run.

- **To: Set:** You can say where the differences images are saved.

- **Type:** You can select the format the differences image are saved in.

Batch Export

The Batch Export processes files by saving them into a third party Photoshop format. These are formats DeBabelizer Toolbox does not support directly, for example the anti-aliased PICT format. It is difficult, however, to imagine that any file formats are not supported by DeBabelizer Toolbox. You would use this option, for example, if you have exported an anti-aliased PICT from Persuasion and wanted to apply a script or save it in another format.

Why Batch Export?

Batch Exporting beats opening each individual file in Photoshop to get the desired file format. This way you can spend more time on some other aspect of the project.

For example, Persuasion exports files as anti-aliased PICTs. You would have to acquire these files into Photoshop and save them individually as PICTs. With Batch Exporting, you can borrow the Photoshop Plug-in through DeBabelizer Toolbox and create a Batch.

It is a quicker process to use DeBabelizer Toolbox's Batch Process, and you can apply a script to immediately remap them to a specified palette. Using the Batch Export increases the flexibility of DeBabelizer Toolbox by using file formats it doesn't normally support. In the Persuasion example, if you used the standard PICT format to open the files from within DeBabelizer Toolbox, their text would appear garbled.

How Batch Export Works

You need to tell DeBabelizer Toolbox where the Photoshop Plug-ins folder is located to support the Export file formats you need. You can do this by going to the **Misc** menu, selecting **Preferences**, then choosing the Plug-ins folder on your hard drive. Figure 12.22 shows the main Batch Export dialog box.

You can process the files and then export them in the format they need to be in. As usual, these options are allowed: scripts, display, naming conventions, and so on. From this dialog box you can:

- **Do Script:** You can select a script to run while you batch export your images.

- **Display:** You can display the images as they are being processed.

- **Export: Auto Naming Options:** This option enables you to give a naming convention to the exported files.

- **To: Set:** You can designate the destination of the exported files.

- **To: Folder image came from:** You can return the exported files to the original folder. If the name has not changed in anyway, you run the risk of overwriting them.

- **To: Manually select:** As the Batch Process runs, a dialog box prompts you to create or select a folder for the exported files to be saved into.

- **Type:** This pull-down menu is the file format to which you are converting the exported files.

- **Slice:** You can slice up the exported files into smaller segments either by cells, fields, or a user-defined size. The primary use for the Slice feature is generating animation storyboards for animators.

- **Picture Preview:** You can create a preview picture for the exported files. It is an actual image that is saved with the original.

- **Picture Icon:** You can create a picture icon for the exported files.

- **Verify replace:** This option sets a prompt to come up to ask you if you want to replace files with the same name. This option provides a safety for preventing you from writing over your files.

314

FIGURE 12.22

The Main Batch Export dialog box for supporting borrowed file formats from Photoshop.

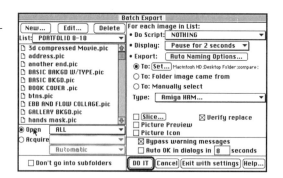

Batch Saving

You can automatically save files after you have either done a script or run a process on them. The files can be saved with a new name or with a new file format. This enables a large group of files to be converted or manipulated. This is the handiest of processes and is used in more than one way. Figure 12.23 shows the main Batch Save dialog box.

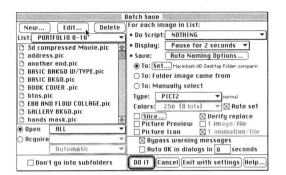

FIGURE 12.23

You can change the file format and apply a script from the Main Batch Save dialog box.

By using DeBabelizer Toolbox's Batch Save, you can convert an entire BatchList of files into another file format. The list of the file formats DeBabelizer Toolbox supports is long and growing. After the target file format has been established, for better file management, you can change the file extension to reflect the new file format.

Now that the computer world is truly cross-platform, the 8.3 has become a standard in the industry. The .3 is usually where the file format is represented; for example, .PCT for a PICT file and .TGA for a Targa file. The standard allows for the quick identification of files, and, in some multimedia firms, you can tell where the file is in the process. For example, a certain file's extension (.3) tells you it is a flattened Photoshop file.

You can also replace the images here if the file naming convention does not change. This is generally used to update files. If you have changed the palette, instead of having two folders with two different palettes, you can replace the old palette files with the new palette files. You can also use the Manual save if you know there are a only a few files that need to be saved in a special location. For example, you have a file hierarchy in your company that separates palettized PICTs from palettized movies. You can set your Filter to open only QuickTimes and use the manual save to save the QuickTimes to the specified QuickTime folder.

Why Batch Save?

Batch saving is often combined with customized scripts. It is at the heart of DeBabelizer Toolbox and probably the most used Batch Process after Batch SuperPalette. It can be used to palletize a series of files as you convert them to another file format. At that point, the files are ready to be programmed.

Saving to other file formats is important for CD-ROM titles, print, or Web pages. Every facet of the industry has its own optimum format that works or doesn't work. DeBabelizer Toolbox makes the digital world a lot easier by managing all these file formats.

Options in the Batch Save Dialog Box

As in all the Batch Processes, you can make several choices from the Main Batch Save dialog box. Many of these are familiar from other Batch Processes:

- **Do Script:** You can select a script to run while you batch save your images. For example, you can apply a script for remapping your images to a new palette.

- **Display:** You can display the images as they are being processed.

- **Save: Auto Naming Options:** This option enables you to give a naming convention to the saved files.

- **To: Set:** You can designate the destination of the saved files.

- **To: Folder image came from:** You can return the saved files to the original folder. If the name has not changed in anyway, you run the risk of overwriting them.

- **To: Manually select:** As the Batch Process runs, a dialog box prompts you to create or select a folder for the saved files.

- **Type:** This pull-down menu is the file format to which you are converting the BatchList files.

- **Colors:** You can set the color depth of the new files. The Auto set button automatically uses the color depth from the original BatchList files. You can set the color depth to one of the standard DeBabelizer Toolbox settings; if the Auto set checkbox is checked, the Colors pop-up menu is grayed out.

- **Slice:** You can slice up the saved files into smaller segments either by cells, fields or a user-defined size. The primary use for the Slice feature is generating animation storyboards for animators.

- **Picture Preview:** You can create a preview picture for the saved files. It is an actual image that is saved with the original.

- **Picture Icon:** You can create a picture icon for the saved files.

- **Verify replace:** This option sets a prompt to come up to ask you if you want to replace files with the same name. It provides a safety for preventing you from writing over your files. Do not use this option with multi-celled image and movie files.

- **1 image/file:** The 1 image/file checkbox writes out individual, single-celled files for each frame in the multi-image file.

- **1 animation/file:** The 1 animation/file option is used when you have more than one animation in your BatchList and you don't want to write out one large animation, but separate animations for each animation file.

Batch Save Simple

This option is similar to Batch Save except that there are fewer options. This process can also be used with a script. It is like using the Batch Save in a Simple mode. See Figure 12.24 for the options offered in the Batch Save Simple process. Batch Save Simple is mainly used for processing single or still frame images. You would not use this operation to process animation files.

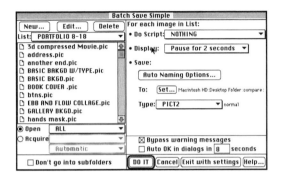

FIGURE 12.24

You have fewer choices, but the process can convert files and apply a script.

317

Why Batch Save Simple?

If you know exactly what you need and do not have to change the color depth of your files, then Batch Save Simple is right for your purposes. You may want to use this process rather than the Batch Save, because the interface is simpler. It is used primarily for still images and not to do Batch runs on movies or animation files.

Options for the Batch Save Simple

Although you are not given as many choices as other Batch Processes, you do still have some options:

- **Do Script:** You can select a script to run while you batch save your images. For example, you can apply a script for remapping your images to a new palette.

- **Display:** You can display the images as they are being processed.

- **Save: Auto Naming Options:** This option enables you to give a naming convention to the saved files.

- **To: Set:** You can designate the destination of the saved files.

- **Type:** This pull-down menu is the file format to which you are converting the BatchList files.

You cannot change the color depth of your files. You also cannot change the saved files in appearance or create sliced images from them. If you need to do any of these options, Batch Save Simple is not the choice for you.

Batch Slideshow

Batch Slideshow displays images to screen for a specified period of time. It offers the standard Display options listed at the beginning of this chapter. If you are planning to apply a script during the Batch Save process, you could use the Batch Slideshow process first as an intermediary step for proofing. If no display is designated, then no Slideshow appears onscreen. Figure 12.25 shows the main dialog box for Batch Slideshow.

FIGURE 12.25

The main dialog box for Batch Slideshow.

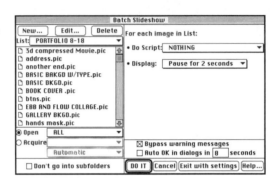

318

Why Batch Slideshow?

Batch Slideshow can be used in reviewing artwork for final approval. For example, you can have the art director or a client review each frame one at a time, depending on the Display option chosen, to give the final okay to artwork before it goes to the programmer. You can also check to make sure all the client or art director revisions were made to the files.

Because this Batch Process also has the Acquire option, you can acquire a BatchList of images and display them to determine which images you want to use. For example, if you exported several anti-aliased PICTs from Persuasion but weren't certain which one to use, running a Batch Slideshow could verify the correct file.

The last way you can use Batch Slideshow is to test a script. If you have images that have been difficult to palettize because of banding and so on, you could test the palette to screen before using the Batch Save process.

Options for Batch Slideshow

You only have two options for this process:

- **Do Script:** You can select a script to run while your images are displayed.

- **Display:** You can display the images onscreen.

Batch SuperPalette

Batch SuperPalette reads a series of images or movies in a BatchList and creates an optimized palette based on their color information. This is a vital component in any multimedia title, unlike the Web where a palette is provided by a service, and unlike a CD-ROM title that develops its own palette based on the artwork in that title. Oftentimes when working with QuickTime movies, you may use a default palette such as the Indeo palette, if the files are going to the PC environment. Figure 12.26 shows the main Batch SuperPalette dialog box, which offers some new options.

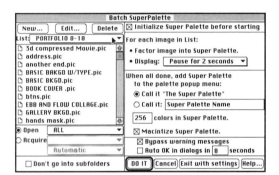

FIGURE 12.26

The main Batch SuperPalette dialog box offers some new options.

Why Batch SuperPalette?

Creating and using SuperPalettes is an incredibly vital part of putting together a multimedia title. The issue of palettes is up there in importance with file space.

Using a custom palette ensures that you can display your artwork in the best possible way. Using palettes also decreases the size of a file and increases how quickly an image can display onscreen. Load times of images or movies in millions of colors is not a possible feat. Smaller files increase end-user access times, and that is always a desirable goal.

After you have the custom palette in place, you can bring it into image editing software and use the colors to create art. This is generally used for text colors or so on. It sounds like you are working backwards, but if you have all the backgrounds worked out with a palette, adding text to the screens using one of the palette colors is an easy solution.

TIP

To ensure that DeBabelizer Toolbox creates the best SuperPalette for your project, you can stack its deck. You can include images with the desired colors more than once in your BatchList, so they are polled more than once, giving extra weight to those colors during polling. You can also cut up the artwork into smaller pieces. If there is a constantly unchanging background, such as an interface, by cutting it into smaller pieces, DeBabelizer Toolbox does not overuse the background colors.

Options in the SuperPalette Dialog Box

Within the Batch SuperPalette dialog box, you have several options available to you:

- **Initialize SuperPalette before starting:** This option clears any previous SuperPalette that may have been created and saved with the default name "SuperPalette."

- **Display:** You can display the images to screen as they polled for their color information.

The next two options deal with naming the newly created SuperPalette.

- **Call it "TheSuperPalette":** This option uses DeBabelizer Toolbox's default name of "SuperPalette."

- **Call it:** You can give a specific name to your SuperPalette by using this option. This is very useful for project management. If you are working on more than one project at a time, you can have each project's palette saved with the corresponding project name. Giving a SuperPalette a specific name avoids confusion.

- **Colors in SuperPalette:** You can designate the number of colors you want in your SuperPalette (256 is the most you can have).

- **Macintize SuperPalette:** This option creates a SuperPalette with white at the 0 index position and black at the 255 index position. The Macintosh software requires these placements.

After you click DO IT, the SuperPalette Batch Process begins. After all the files in your BatchList have been processed, another dialog box appears asking you to name your SuperPalette. Figure 12.27 shows the dialog box for naming your SuperPalette.

FIGURE 12.27

You get a second chance to name your SuperPalette.

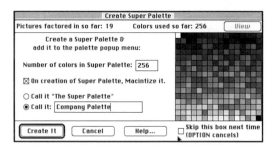

Naming the SuperPalette

The Create SuperPalette dialog box displays your newly created SuperPalette. The dialog box also gives you some important information, such as the number of images used to create the SuperPalette and how many colors were polled in the images to create the SuperPalette. In Figure 12.27, 19 images were used to create the SuperPalette, and 256 colors were polled.

You can reduce the numbers, if you decide that 256 is not the ideal size. If you do change the number of colors the palette has, the View button becomes available. You can see the reduced palette by clicking the View button.

You have the opportunity to confirm or alter your choices previously set in the main SuperPalette dialog box. For instance, you can change your option to have the SuperPalette a Macintized palette by using the On creation of SuperPalette, Macintize it checkbox.

You can also confirm or alter the choice of the SuperPalette name by giving it your own name or going with DeBabelizer's default "SuperPalette" title. Of course, it should all look familiar, because it is based on the settings you checked previously. But once again, it serves as a proofing device to make sure all is set the way you really intended. After you click Create It, the SuperPalette is added to the list of palettes either as the SuperPalette or by the specific name you gave to it.

Batch Place and Save

The Place and Save Batch Process places an image or images over a series of images. This option is useful in situations where you are compositing images. For example, you have a standard background and you want to add a blue screened image into its foreground. Figure 12.28 shows the main dialog box for the Place and Save Batch Process.

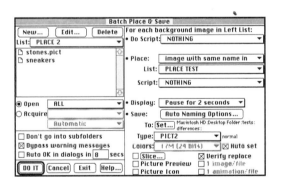

FIGURE 12.28

The Batch Place & Save main dialog box offers an option you haven't seen yet, applying a script to two BatchLists.

Why Use Place and Save?

The Place and Save Batch Process can be used when compositing images that have been through a blue screen process. You can composite the blue screen images onto the background images. You need to create a script for removing the blue screen background from the foreground images. This option can also be applied to QuickTime or animation files.

To use the Place and Save with the blue screen images you need to set the blue used in the blue screen as the Background color in the Dithering and Background under the **Palette** menu. You can use your Eyedropper to capture the color and get the RGB formula for the blue screen color.

After you have the color, you need to enter the RGB formula into the Dithering and Background dialog box. If your images are palettized, enter in the index number. If they are in 24-bit, you need to enter the RGB formula. If you are using an index number, remember that the files you are placing into must have the background color in its palette. This is important because if the background color is not present in the palette, DeBabelizer Toolbox will remap the blue screen to another color and the Background color set in the Dithering and Background dialog box will no longer apply.

When you place the image into the background file, you can choose Selection Transparency under the **Edit** menu. From the Selection Transparency submenu, choose the background color. The placed image's blue screen should disappear. If there is a halo of the blue, you can choose Shave Outline from the **Palette** menu. From the Shave Outline submenu choose Outline, and the blue halo should disappear. You can create a script to do all this for you.

Options for Place and Save

In this Batch Process, like the Compare Batch Process, you are working with two BatchLists at a time. You are taking images from one BatchList and placing them into another BatchList of images.

The unusual option that this process offers is the ability to run a script on both the Left BatchList and the Right BatchList. This option is significant because it enables you to manipulate the image before it is placed.

> **NOTE**
>
> The placed image automatically remaps to the palette of the image into which it is placed.

The Left BatchList displays the files into which the images form the Right BatchList are going to be placed. The Right BatchList is the files to be placed. The Left BatchList is the background upon which the images are placed. The options you can choose from the Place and Save dialog box are:

- **Left list Do Script:** You can select a script to run while you batch Place and Save your images. For example, you could scale your background images to the IBM aspect ratio or apply a particular palette to them.

- **Display:** You can display the images as they are being processed.

- **Place:** You can place the images in several different ways. See the list in the next section for the best choice for you.

- **List:** You can select the Right BatchList, the images that are placed into the Left BatchList.

- **Right list Do Script:** You can apply a script to the images as they are placed. For example, you may want to write a script with Background Removal in it to remove the blue screen process.

- **Save: Auto Naming Options:** This option enables you to give a naming convention to the saved files.

- **To: Set:** You can designate the destination of the saved files.

- **Type:** This pull-down menu is the file format to which you are converting the BatchList files.

- **Colors:** You can set the color depth of the new files. The AutoSet button automatically uses the color depth from the original BatchList files. You could set the color depth to one of the standard DeBabelizer Toolbox settings; if the Auto Set checkbox is checked, the Colors pop-up menu is grayed out.

- **Slice:** You can slice up the files into smaller segments either by cells, fields or a user-defined size. The primary use for the Slice feature is generating animation storyboards for animators.

- **Picture Preview:** You can create a preview picture for the files. It is an actual image that is saved with the original.

- **Picture Icon:** You can create a picture icon for the files.

- **Verify replace:** This option sets a prompt to come up to ask you if you want to replace files with the same name. This option provides a safety for preventing you from writing over your files.

- **1 image/file:** The 1 image/file checkbox writes out individual, single-celled files for each frame in the multi-image file.

- **1 animation/file:** The 1 animation/file option is used when you have more than one animation in your BatchList and you don't want to write out one large animation, but separate animations for each animation file.

There are several different ways of placing the images into the background images. Some of the options require two lists and others require only one list; it is similar to the comparison style pop-up menu covered earlier.

The following is a fuller description of each option:

- **Image with same name in:** This option requires that both image lists have the same exact names. It places the images with the same name, moving the right side file onto the left side image. Even though they have the same names, there must be two BatchLists.

323

- **Image in same position in:** This option pairs the image from the left list in the same sequential order as the file from the right list.

- **Next image from Left list in pairs:** This option has no right list. It only uses the left list and breaks it down in pairs. The first image in the pair is used as the background image and the second image is placed into it. When this option is checked, the right side list submenu is grayed out.

- **Onto first image in left list:** This option only uses the first image from the left list as the background and places every image from the right list over it.

- **First image in:** This option places only the first right side image on every left side image.

Place and save offers all the same options for saving and naming as the other Batch Processes.

Place, Acquire, and Save

Place, Acquire, and Save is similar to the Place and Save except that it adds Acquiring the file to the mix. You may need to acquire files, then do the place function and save. Using the Acquire option allows greater flexibility in the file formats used. You can use a file format not directly supported by DeBabelizer Toolbox. This Batch Process is useful for acquiring images via a Photoshop Plug-in and need to be manipulated in various ways. Figure 12.29 shows the main dialog box for Place, Acquire, and Save.

FIGURE 12.29

The main dialog box for Place, Acquire, and Save.

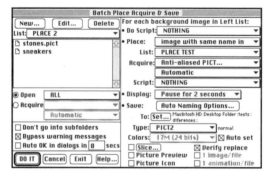

Why Place, Acquire, and Save?

You would want to use this Batch Process over the standard Place and Save when you need to acquire a file format not directly supported by DeBabelizer Toolbox, an animation file format that DeBabelizer Toolbox doesn't handle, for example.

Options for Place, Acquire, and Save

You have several choices to make in the Place, Acquire, and Save Batch Process. Many of these are similar to the Batch Place and Save process options.

Once again, the Left BatchList is the files into which the images from the Right BatchList are going to be placed. The Right BatchList is the files that to be placed. The Left BatchList is the background upon which the images are placed. The options you can choose from the Place, Acquire, and Save are:

- **Left list Do Script:** You can select a script to run while you batch Place and Save your images. For example, you could scale your background images to the IBM aspect ratio.

- **Place:** You can place the images in several different ways. See Batch Place and Save for a complete break down of each choice.

- **List:** You can select the Right batch list, the images that are placed into the Left BatchList.

- **Acquire:** You can select the file format you are going to acquire for the process.

- **Acquire Option:** This option determines the method DeBabelizer Toolbox uses to load the Acquired files. See the following list for a complete list.

- **Right list Do Script:** You can apply a script to the images as they are acquired.

- **Display:** You can display the images as they are being processed.

- **Save: Auto Naming Options:** This option enables you to give a naming convention to the saved files.

- **To: Set:** You can designate the destination of the saved files.

- **Type:** This pull-down menu is the file format to which you are converting the BatchList files.

- **Colors:** You can set the color depth of the new files. The Auto set button automatically uses the color depth from the original BatchList files. You can set the color depth to one of the standard DeBabelizer Toolbox settings. If the Auto set checkbox is checked, the Colors pop-up menu is grayed out.

- **Slice:** You can slice up the files into smaller segments either by cells, fields, or a user-defined size. The primary use for the Slice feature is generating animation storyboards for animators.

- **Picture Preview:** You can create a preview picture for the files. It is an actual image that is saved with the original.

- **Picture Icon:** You can create a picture icon for the files.

325

- **Verify replace:** This option sets a prompt to come up to ask you if you want to replace files with the same name. This option provides a safety for preventing you from writing over your files.

- **1 image/file:** The 1 image/file checkbox writes out individual, single-celled files for each frame in the multi-image file.

- **1 animation/file:** The 1 animation/file option is used when you have more than one animation in your BatchList and you don't want to write out one large animation, but separate animations for each animation file.

The **Acquire** pop-up menu tells you the third party Photoshop Plug-ins you have loaded by the file formats that are available to you. Below the **Acquire** pop-up menu is another pop-up for how to load the Acquired files. The methods of acquiring are:

- **Automatic:** The files are acquired automatically. A prompt comes up to suggest how to acquire the file.

- **Auto after 1st image:** This option also has a prompt for the first image to determine the process.

- **Manual:** This option brings up the Acquire prompt for each image on the right side list.

Running Batches Unattended

The beauty of these Batch Processes is that you can run them unattended. Combine them with a script and it is like a team of people working for you simultaneously. If you are nervous about leaving a computer unattended to work for you on its own, you can generate an Error Log while you run the Batch Process.

You can also use the Skip this option dialog checkbox to help with unattended batches. For some Batch Processes a prompt comes up automatically. These prompts generally include a Skip this option dialog checkbox. If the Skip this dialog checkbox is marked, then it does not appear again for the whole batch run, and you do not have to monitor the computer for dialog boxes. For example, when palletizing a group of images, a dialog box pops up dealing with Macintizing the palette.

You can override the skipping of dialog boxes by holding down the Option key. If for some reason one of the images needs special attention, you can interrupt the automatic cycle of a Batch Process.

Ignore List for Opens Option

According to DeBabelizer Toolbox, this is an advanced option, mainly used for batching a large number files. DeBabelizer Toolbox "learns" what files to ignore. (It can ignore up to 128 files.) The learned list of files is then ignored while batching. It can get tricky, so you have to pay attention that files you don't want ignored aren't added to that list.

You can set this option to exclude certain types you know you do not want to be ignored. The ignore list is not a report; it is simply a list that DeBabelizer Toolbox compiles internally. List is not retained from session to session. Learn to Ignore is useful to scan Macintosh and non-Macintosh files. Figure 12.31 shows the dialog box for Learn to Ignore. You can ignore ambiguous files or unknown file formats and text files.

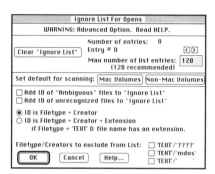

FIGURE 12.30

Make sure DeBabelizer Toolbox is not ignoring the files you want to be used.

Batch List Text Files

327

You can also Import and Export BatchLists as text files. This is a useful option for archiving a project. Figure 12.31 shows an example of a Exported BatchList text file. You can open these text files in a word processing program. The text BatchList file retains the path of the files in all BatchLists. If the files or folder no longer exist, the text file says so.

Batch lists can be generated using text. You can create, for example, a Macro in Word to generate lists, save them in text only format, and Import them back into DeBabelizer Toolbox. You can access these option under the **File** menu by selecting Batch.

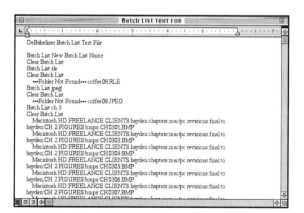

FIGURE 12.31

You can convert your BatchLists to text for archiving a project before you delete all the BatchLists.

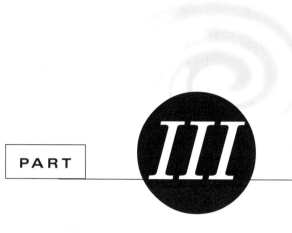

PART

III

Appendices

Appendices

This part provides reference information that can be referred to as you need it. Appendix A is a complete listing of the file formats DeBabelizer Toolbox and DeBabelizer Pro for Windows support. Appendix B is a glossary of terms. Appendix C includes interviews with experienced Toolbox users who offer tips, tricks, and their reasons for why DeBabelizer is a crucial part of their work.

File Formats Supported by DeBabelizer Pro and DeBabelizer Toolbox

Today a vast number of file formats are available for the many different applications and platforms available in computer graphics. DeBabelizer was originally created to help graphics professionals translate and utilize this multitude of formats in the industry and has established a reputation as a software "can opener" due to its unrivaled ability to read, write, and translate even the most obscure file types. DeBabelizer Toolbox currently supports the largest number of file formats by allowing additional types to be added via CCMs or Custom Code Modules as they become available (CCMs are located in the Custom Code folder).

The following list includes the latest CCMs that ship with Toolbox version 1.6.5. DeBabelizer Pro's file readers and writers are built directly into the program but currently handle over 90 different image formats. New file formats will be accessible via program updates. While both programs do not support vector file types, this is expected to be added in future versions of DeBabelizer Pro. This appendix provides a list of supported graphics formats, broken down by computer platform, along with a brief description. Default extensions are the extensions DeBabelizer automatically uses when saving each file type or the preferred extensions DeBabelizer expects when opening files (though correct extension names are not required to open files on either platform). Other extensions are additional extensions common to each particular file format.

 DeBabelizer Toolbox uses Custom Code Modules (CCMs) to add reader and writer functionality. The latest CCMs can be found and downloaded for free from the Equilibrium Web site (www.equilibrium.com) or BBS (415-332-6152). Place the CCMs in the custom code folder in order to update your readers and writers.

 Formats supported by DeBabelizer Toolbox version 1.6.5

 Formats supported by DeBabelizer Pro

Atari ST:

Degas

An animation file format created by Atari, used to store a single frame image at 2, 4, or 16 colors and 320 × 200 pixels.

 Default Extension: Pln

 Default Extension: PLN

Neochrome

An animation file format created by Atari, used to store a series of multiple images at 16 colors and 640 × 200 or 320 × 200 pixels.

 Default Extension: Neo

Other Extensions: ANI

 Default Extension: ANI

Other Extensions: NEO

Spectrum

Another Atari platform file format.

Read only

Extensions: SPU (uncompressed), SPC (compressed)

Read only

Extensions: SPU (uncompressed), SPC (compressed)

Commodore:

Amiga IFF/LBM

Electronic Arts Interchange File Format (IFF). A general purpose file format used on the Amiga platform supporting multiple images per file.

DeBabelizer Toolbox can read up to 32-bit color and write up to 8-bit color.

Default Extension: lbm

Other Extensions: HAM, HAM8, SHAM, and DHAM (read only)

333

DeBabelizer Pro can read up to 32-bit color and write up to 8-bit color.

Default Extension: IFF

Other Extensions: HAM, HAM8, SHAM, and DHAM (read only)

C64

Commodore 64 16-color image file format

Read only. Supports Koala format, packed, crunched, and uncompressed.

Digital F/X:

Digital F/X

A file format used by Video F/X and Titleman from Digital Effects, Inc., supporting 32-bit color.

TitleMan Default Extension: TDIM

Video F/X Default Extension: GRAF

TitleMan Default Extension: TDIM

Video F/X Default Extension: GRAF

DOS/Windows:

AVI

Audio-Video Interleaved. The most common desktop video format for Windows-based machines.

DeBabelizer Pro will open AVIs using the built-in movie window. Sound component is not openable/editable.

Default Extension: AVI

Dr. Halo™ CUT

A bitmapped image file generated by Dr. Halo supporting up to 256 colors. It is device-independent and used for transporting image data from one computer platform to another.

Default Extension: CUT

Default Extension: CUT

BMP

Windows and OS/2 Bitmap. A file type generated by the Windows Paintbrush program and used as the standard bitmap storage format in Microsoft Windows.

DeBabelizer Toolbox allows input and output of BMP/RLE files in compressed and uncompressed format at up to 24-bit color.

Default Extension: BMP (uncompressed), RLE (compressed)

DeBabelizer Pro allows input and output of BMP/RLE files in compressed and uncompressed format at up to 24-bit color. To output to RLE format, select the CompuServe RLE image format in the Save As dialog box.

Default Extension: BMP (uncompressed), RLE (compressed)

FLI/FLC

An 8-bit animation file generated by Autodesk Animator 3D Studio. It allows for multiple images in a single file.

Opening or previewing an FLI or FLC file brings up the FLI/FLC Selection dialog box, enabling you to choose the frame or sequence of frames to edit.

Default Extension: FLI, FLC

FLI/FLC files open to the Movie window in DeBabelizer Pro, enabling you to edit a frame or sequence of frames as well as preview the movie.

Default Extension: FLC

ICO

Windows Icon. A 16-bit color file used for creating icons for use in the Windows operating system.

Default Extension: ICO

IMG/GEM/Ventura Publisher™

GEM Raster File. A format created by Digital Research supporting up to 16 colors or 256 grayscale.

Option to save at grayscale or fixed colors

Default Extension: IMG

Option to save at grayscale or fixed colors

Default Extension: IMG

MSP Type 1

Microsoft Paint™ file.

Two color (b/w) input and output

Default Extension: MSP

Two color (b/w) input and output

Default Extension: MSP

PCP

Black and white mode for DOS PC Paint™ file format.

Read only

Default Extension: PCP

Read only

Default Extension: PCP

PCX

A file format generated by the PC Paintbrush™ program and used as an exchange and storage format in the Windows environment.

Default Extension: PCX

Default Extension: PCX

Pictor™

Another file format created by PC Paint. Supports up to 256 colors.

Read only

Read only

WPG

WordPerfect™ Graphics format. A graphic generated by the WordPerfect word processing program and supporting up to 256 colors.

Read only

Extensions: WPG

read only

Extensions: WPG

General/Cross-Platform:

Abekas

A digital video format from Abekas, Inc., a provider of digital video hardware. Files have an image size of 720×486 pixels at 24 bits in NTSC or PAL formats.

Write only

Default Extension: YUV

Read and write but file must use YUV extension to be read correctly.

Default Extension: YUV

BOB

A simple 8-bit raw image format used for images destined for ray-trace applications.

Default Extension: BOB

Default Extension: BOB

DBP

DeBabelizer Pro's proprietary file format for saving SuperPalettes. This is not an image format and is not compatible with DeBabelizer Toolbox.

 Default Extension: dbp

DBS

DeBabelizer Pro's proprietary file format for saving scripts. This is not an image format and is not compatible with DeBabelizer Toolbox.

 Default Extension: dbs

DBB

DeBabelizer Pro's default file format for saving BatchLists. This is not an image format and is not compatible with DeBabelizer Toolbox.

 Default Extension: dbb

DBL

DeBabelizer Pro's proprietary format for saving log files. This is not an image format and is not compatible with DeBabelizer Toolbox.

 Default Extension: dbl

FITS Astronomical

Flexible Image Transport System. A grayscale uncompressed image format used by NASA and many astronomical organizations for storing space and satellite image data.

 Default Extension: FITS

Default Extension: FITS

DeBabelizer Pro can extract any frame from a multiple frame image. FITS files can be saved at 8-bit only with only one image per file.

Default Extension: FITS

GIF

CompuServe Graphics Interchange Format. A lossless compression format for bitmapped images originally created by CompuServe and employing LZW compression. GIF files support up to 256 colors and are widely used on the Internet and online services because of the excellent compression ratios they allow.

DeBabelizer Toolbox allows reading and writing of interlaced, non-interlaced, interlaced plus transparency, and non-interlaced plus transparency GIFs. Support for reading multiple image files is available by selecting the appropriate reader options: **Misc:Preferences: Readers...:GIF**.

Default Extension: GIF

DeBabelizer Pro reads and writes all GIFs and allows options for transparency, interlacing, multi-image files, disposal methods, and embedded text comments.

Default Extension: GIF

JPEG/JFIF

Joint Photographic Experts Group/JPEG File Interchange Format. A commonly used file format providing lossy compression with excellent image quality, particularly for photographs. Supports 24-bit color or 8-bit grayscale only. DeBabelizer can save JPEG files with image qualities ranging from 1 to 100, the lower the number the greater the compression ratio, the higher the number, the better the image quality. Progressive JPEGs allow for incremental file streaming on the Web similar to interlaced GIFs.

Default Extension: JPG

Also supports Progressive JPEGs

Default Extension: JPG

Kodak PhotoCD™

An image format used for storing multi-resolution 24-bit photographic images on Kodak photo CDs.

 Read only

Default Extension: PCD

 Read only

Default Extension: PCD

OMF™ Interchange

Open Media Framework Interchange. A file format supported by AVID to facilitate cross-platform transfer of digital media.

 Default extension: OMF

PAL

 DeBabelizer Pro's proprietary file format for saving palettes. This is not an image format and is not compatible with DeBabelizer Toolbox.

Default Extension: PAL

Pixar™

A file format created by Pixar for use in high-end rendering applications. Supports up to 32-bit color, compressed and uncompressed.

 Default Extension: PXR

 Default Extension: PXR

Photoshop™

File format used by Adobe Photoshop. Supports up to 32-bit color.

 DeBabelizer Toolbox saves files in Photoshop 2.0 format and reads files up to version 3.0 (automatically flattens multi-layered images).

Default Extension: 8BIM

DeBabelizer Pro saves files in Photoshop 2.5 format and reads files up to version 3.0 (automatically flattens multi-layered images).

Default Extension: PSD

PNG

Portable Network Graphic file. A recently introduced lossless compression format sponsored by the W3C and created as a potential replacement for the GIF format, especially for Internet-based applications. It offers numerous improvements over GIF including resolution up to 48 bits, better compression, built-in gamma correction, multiple layers of transparency, progressive image display, and a better interlacing scheme. Browser manufacturers are beginning to support PNG, but it will take some time for this format to become widely used.

 Default Extension: PNG

 Default Extension: PNG

QDV

A simple general purpose color image format from Random Dot Software supporting up to 256 colors without any compression.

 Default Extension: QDV

 Default Extension: QDV

Raw Custom

This is a read only format allowing you to specify certain characteristics of a file in order to open it. Usually used to open files saved in unknown formats or otherwise difficult to open file types.

 Read only

 Read only

Raw RGB

The simplest format for saving RGB images. Supports up to 32-bit color.

 Default Extension: RGB

 Default Extension: RGB

RLE

Run-Length Encoded BMP file. A compressed format created and used by CompuServe and supported by most bitmap file formats.

 Default Extension: RLE

 Default Extension: RLE

Targa

A file format created by TrueVision. Supports up to 32-bit color, compressed or uncompressed.

 Default Extension: TGA

 Default Extension: TGA

TIFF

Tag Image File Format. A common bitmap file format originally created by Aldus supporting up to 17 million colors.

 DeBabelizer Toolbox supports most TIFFs, including uncompressed, compression type 32773 "Packbits," compression type 2 "CCITT," compression type 5 "LZW," and Thunderscan compression formats. Files can be saved as grayscale or color using Mac or PC encoding. Several compression options are available for output including: uncompressed, packed, LZW, and Group 4 faxes. CCITT and Thunderscan™ TIFFs are read only.

Default Extension: TIF

DeBabelizer Pro can read and write any TIFF file including uncompressed, compression type 32773 "Packbits," compression type 2 "CCITT," compression type 5 "LZW," and Thunderscan compression formats. Files can be saved as grayscale or color using Mac or PC encoding. Several compression options are available for output including: uncompressed, packed, and LZW. DeBabelizer Pro adds output capability for CCITT and Group 3 and 4 faxes.

Default Extension: TIF

Macintosh/Apple:

Apple II Series

File formats for the original Apple II series of computers

 Input and output for most Apple II GS, e, c, and + image formats

EIDI (Electric Image)

343

An animation file format generated by Electric Image supporting 32-bit color. This format allows for multiple images in a single file in which frames may be of different size or color resolution.

 Default Extension: EIDI

 Default Extension: EIDI

EPSF

Encapsulated PostScript File. A device-independent file format usually used to provide a bitmapped preview of an EPS PostScript vector image.

 Default Extension: EPSF

 Default Extension: EPSF

MacPaint™

B/W (2 color) file format used by MacPaint program.

Default Extension: PNTG

 Default Extension: MAC

PICT

The original format for defining bitmapped images on the Macintosh.

 Default Extension: PICT

 Read only

PICT2 Resource

A superset of the Macintosh PICT format offering better color support for up to 32-bit color.

 Default Extension: PICR

 Default Extension: PICT

PixelPaint™

A file format created by PixelPaint for the Macintosh. Supports up to 256 colors.

 Read only

RIFF

Old 32-bit color file format used by Letraset's ColorStudio for Macintosh. No longer in use. Not to be confused with the newer RIFF format–Microsoft Resource Interchange File Format.

 Read only

QuickTime™ Movie

Cross-platform desktop video format from Apple. Not currently supported by
DeBabelizer Pro for Windows 95/NT.

DeBabelizer Toolbox enables you to open and save QuickTime movies, simulate
animations, and edit individual frames. QuickTime must be installed on the
computer in order to read and write format.

Default Extension: Moov

QuickTime™ Still

A still image from a QuickTime movie. Not currently supported by DeBabelizer Pro
for Windows 95/NT.

DeBabelizer Toolbox enables you to open and save QuickTime stills. QuickTime
must be installed on the system in order to read and write format.

Default Extension: PIQT

Scrapbook

Macintosh system file.

Default Extension: ZSYS

Startup Screen

File format used to create startup screens for the Macintosh.

Default Extension: SCRN

Thunderscan

A file format created by Thunderware for their line of image scanners.

Default Extension: SCAN

Default Extension: SCN

Philips CD/I:

IFF

Compact Disc format invented by Philips. DeBabelizer Pro allows compliance with this format using the IFF format.

 Default Extension: IFF

Silicon Graphics:

Alias

A format created by Alias on the SGI platform supporting 8- and 24-bit color depth.

 Default Extension: PIX

346

SGI

A file format utilized on the SGI platform.

 Default Extension: SGI

 Default Extension: SGI

SoftImage

A single image file format used by the SoftImage 3D rendering program on Silicon Graphics and Windows NT platforms.

 Supports compressed and uncompressed formats

Default Extension: PIC

 Supports compressed and uncompressed formats

Default Extension: PIC

WaveFront

Run-length–encoded multiple image format created by WaveFront.

 Default Extension: RLA

 Default Extension: RLA

Sun Microsystems

SUN

A raster file format on the Sun platform used mainly for screen dumps. Supports up to 17 million colors, uncompressed.

 Default Extension: SUN

 Default Extension: SUN

Unix:

PBM/PGM/PPM

The Portable Bitmap/Greymap/Pixmap file types are simple file interchange formats utilized on Unix systems.

 Read only

X11 XBM Bitmap

X11 bitmap file supporting only two colors.

 Read only

Extensions: XBM

 Read only

Extensions: XBM

XWD Screen Dump

X Windows bitmap format used for screen dumps.

 Default Extension: XWB

 Default Extension: XWB

Glossary of Terms

A

ActionArrow™—An interface element in DeBabelizer Pro document windows composed of a tiny arrow in the document title bar. The arrow can be dragged and dropped on another image to allow the properties of the first document type to be applied to the second document type.

algorithm—A finite ordered equation or mathematical formula used to perform a calculation, conduct an operation, or solve a problem. JPEG and GIF formats, for example, use two different compression algorithms to compress images.

alpha channel—An additional 8-bit channel of available bitmap data in a 32-bit image. The alpha channel is generally used to store a black and white or grayscale image for creating image masks.

anti-aliasing—A method of removing jaggy edges from bitmapped images by setting pixels to intermediate color shades near the edges to make the edges appear smoother.

aspect ratio—The ratio of width to height of an image. When a new image is generated by changing the width and height of the first image in the same proportions, the new image maintains the same aspect ratio as the first image, even though it is of a different size.

B

banding—Unwanted bands of data or discoloration in an image, sometimes generated by dithering or digitizing processes.

BatchList™—A DeBabelizer Pro document including a series of files that can undergo a script or Batch Automation.

bit depth—A measure of how many colors can be contained in an image ranging from 1 to 32 bits. 1-bit = 2 colors (b&w), 2-bit = 4 colors, 4-bit = 16 colors, 5-bit = 32 colors, 6-bit = 64 colors, 7-bit = 128 colors, 8-bit = 256 colors, 16 bit = 65,536 colors, 24 bit = 17 million colors, 32-bit = 17 million colors plus an alpha channel. Also referred to as color depth or pixel depth.

bitmap—A graphic represented by individual pixels, from 1 to 32 bits, aligned in rows and columns to form an image. Also referred to as a raster file.

blue screen—A method used in film and video of shooting an object against a blue screen in order to easily extract the image from the background and aid in compositing.

brightness—In the HSB (hue, saturation, brightness (value) color model, brightness represents the amount of light reflected by or transmitted through an image independent of its hue and saturation and is measured as a balance of the dark and light shades in an image.

350

C

CD-I—A standard format created by Phillips for storing video and audio data on a compact optical disc.

channel—Images are broken up into separate channels in order to produce color variations. Each channel is represented by black and white to create the appearance of color. You can manipulate an image's channels individually or as a group.

chrominance—Referenced in NTSC and PAL television formats, it represents the color proportion of an image as a mixture of hue and saturation or the combination of RGB primary colors.

color model—The way colors are composed, specified, and utilized on a computer system or application. Also referred to as color space.

CMYK—A color space used in the printing industry in which images are composed of cyan, magenta, yellow, and black ink values. DeBabelizer Pro for Windows does not currently support CMYK images, although DeBabelizer Pro for Macintosh is expected to in a future version.

compare to—A command from DeBabelizer 1.6x for Macintosh used to compare separate images and report their differences. DeBabelizer Pro intends to implement this function.

compression—A software or hardware process used to reduce the file size of an image in order to save disk space.

contrast—The gradation between the light, medium, and dark tones in an image.

cross-platform—Refers to the ability to operate on more than one computer platform, such as Macintosh and Windows.

crop—To frame an image by cutting away portions of it via the Crop command.

D-E

density—The measurement of an object's ability to stop or absorb light. DeBabelizer Pro measures density in dots (pixels) per inch.

digitize—To convert an image into digital data that is usable by a computer.

dithering—The process of creating the illusion of more colors in an image by diffusing adjacent pixels to create the illusion of a new apparent color.

dpi—The measurement of the density of an image as represented by the number of dots per inch in the printed image.

F

field—An image or frame of digital video can be broken into fields. Fields are horizontal scan lines. An image or frame has two sets of horizontal lines represented by evens (0) and odds (1).

floater—A floating image in the selection marquee of a window that has been cut or pasted. The floater does not affect any of the underlying image pixels until it has been stamped onto the image.

frame—A single image in an animation or digital video. Multiple frames displayed successively produce an animation.

frame grabber—A hardware device that can, with proper software, digitize images from an exterior source, such as a video camera, and ultimately import them into DeBabelizer Pro.

G

gamma—Gamma is the amount of contrast found in the midtones of an image or movie file. Changing the gamma settings of a file affects the midtones without affecting the highlights or shadows. It gives the appearance of brightening the file.

gradient—(1) Another term for a blend, a gradual transition between two or more colors. (2) DeBabelizer Pro enables you to create a gradient within a palette by selecting a range of colors and holding the Shift key as you double-click the selected palette colors.

grayscale—Describes a black-and-white image with a range of up to 256 gray values (8-bit color). It is also possible to have grayscales at higher bit depths, but the term generally refers to images of 8-bit or lower depth.

H

hue—The quality of a color, as determined by its dominant wavelength, that distinguishes itself from other colors.

HSV—An acronym for hue/saturation/value that represents an image in terms of hue, saturation, and brightness. It is also referred to as HSB.

I-J-K

indexed color—Describes an image comprised of a palette, or color look-up table, containing 1 to 256 colors (1- to 8-bit depth).

interpolation—A method of increasing image resolution by mathematically inserting extra pixels into the image. Also called video interlacing.

L

log—A line by line historic record of the individual actions applied to a script, image, BatchList, or movie.

luminosity—A measurement of the color brightness of an image, expressed in percentages of red, green, and blue.

lossless compression—A compression algorithm or format that compresses an image without throwing out any image data. GIF is an example of a lossless compression format, where the image can be decompressed to its original level of quality.

lossy compression—A compression algorithm or format that compresses an image by stripping out data from the image. JPG is an example of a lossy compression format, where the image can never revert to its original quality, because the data is permanently lost.

M-N-O

midtone—The tone value of an image located halfway between the lightest and darkest values in the image.

monochrome—A 1-bit (2-color) image composed of either black and white or black and one additional color.

NTSC—An acronym for National Television Standards Committee. Refers to the type of video and television display signal that is standard in the USA.

P-Q

PAL—An acronym for Phase Alteration Line. Refers to the standard display signal for video and television used in most of Europe.

palette—The color table of a 1- to 8-bit color indexed image. The index values in the palette represent the location of the color in the palette, with the first location labeled index 0.

pixel—A single dot in an image, the smallest unit of the image used to display the image on a computer monitor.

pixel depth—*See* bit depth.

pixel packing—The storing of information into the empty spaces of a byte.

plug-in—A third party piece of software providing additional functionality to a program. DeBabelizer Pro can utilize most Adobe Photoshop Plug-ins.

polling—The process of analyzing a series of images to determine the most commonly prevalent colors.

R

raster image—A bitmapped image, or one that is created by a matrix of individual pixels aligned in rows and columns.

remap—To reassign the color value of one or more pixels to correspond to a new color palette.

resize—To change the height and width of an image without affecting its resolution.

resolution—The level of detail or density of an image, usually expressed as the number of dots or pixels per inch. Also used to describe the bit depth of an image.

RGB—A color space using red, green, and blue values to represent the color spectrum. The standard color model used by DeBabelizer Pro.

S

saturation—The purity of a color as measured by the amount of white present. A lower amount of white (purer color) reflects a higher saturation value, while more white reflects a lower saturation value.

scale—To increase or decrease the height and width of an image.

script— A series of DeBabelizer Pro user actions that can be stored and applied to a single image or succession of images (BatchList).

SuperPalette™—An optimized palette created by DeBabelizer Pro that is derived by polling the most common colors in a series of images.

T-U

threshold—A user-defined break-off point that represents the level at which an image's pixels are converted to either black or white, when reduced from a high color depth.

thumbnail—A miniature representation of an image.

V-W

vector image—An image defined by the end points of sets of lines that can be manipulated as objects. Also called an object-oriented image. DeBabelizer Pro does not currently support vector file formats.

X-Y-Z

X origin—The first point in an image along a horizontal axis.

Y origin—The first point in an image along the vertical axis.

YIQ—The color model used to display in television. Y represents the luminosity or lightness, I represents Red minus luminosity, and Q represent blue minus luminosity.

YUV—Native signal format of video for digital video compressed by either MPEG or Indeo codes. The compressed video is stored in YUV color space because it takes up less space than RGB.

DeBabelizer Toolbox 1.6.5 Interviews

This appendix features interviews with experienced Toolbox 1.6.5 users who discuss their use of DeBabelizer and offer tips for new users. These interviews are included to provide a better idea of how DeBabelizer functions in the real world and how crucial it is in many people's work. The information here can also serve as an aid to help you find new ways of taking advantage of DeBabelizer Toolbox's capabilities.

Lauren Schwartz

Title: Design Manager

Company: Outside The Box Interactive, New York, New York

Describe your position: Design and production of multimedia projects including CD-ROMs, kiosks, computer/disk-based presentations, and intranet/Internet sites.

How long have you been using DeBabelizer Toolbox? 1.5 years

Describe how you use DeBabelizer Toolbox: Primarily, we use DeBabelizer for batch processing the hundreds and sometimes thousands of images that go into a multimedia project. There is no better software when it comes to creating custom palettes for groups of images. The amount of time we save using DeBabelizer's scripting capabilities to scale, change resolution, and remap artwork to custom palettes is immeasurable. It's also a comfort knowing that because these scripts and palettes can be stored in memory, if any artwork is changed, or new artwork is added to a show, we can quickly and easily convert these as well.

We have scripts set up and saved that will downsample images to 72 dpi and can remap them to either the Netscape palette, adaptive palettes, or system palettes; save them as either GIFs, PICTs, or JPEGs; and can create thumbnail images of them for cataloging and quick retrieval later.

DeBabelizer is the first piece of software that we train new interns on. The learning curve is not very steep, and by teaching them to create their own scripts and to process files, our more experienced designers are freed up. The designers then can create their artwork and pass it to interns to process with DeBabelizer, who in turn pass it to programmers. This creates a really great work flow in the office and has become a major consideration in outlining proposals and estimating time frames on new jobs.

Any tips or tricks? We get a lot of use out of DeBabelizer's Merge Palettes command. Instead of putting a large textured background file, for example, into a Batch-list (which tends to use up more color spaces than necessary in the SuperPalette) or, if specific images need to be high-quality, we downsample those images to as few colors as possible while still retaining the best quality, and then reserve that many colors when batching the SuperPalette. Later, the different palettes are merged together.

Jon Bonne

Title: Senior Producer

Company (location): FOX News Internet, New York, NY

Describe your position: Oversight of long-term site-wide projects; producing feature packages; editorial guidance; various production responsibilities.

How long have you been using DeBabelizer Toolbox? 1.5 years

Describe how you use DeBabelizer Toolbox: It's absolutely invaluable for its JPEG codec alone. The JPEGs made with it are not only significantly more compressed than those made in Photoshop but also tend to look far better for their file size. I use this feature less now that I have greater freedom to use JPEGs, but its features for palette reduction make file size conservation for GIFs a remarkably easy task. Most notable among these features is the Translate utility, which enables me to manually edit and condense the color palette. When bytes count, the ability to pull colors from the palette one at a time is an absolute essential in reaching a balance between file size and image quality.

Two batch processes come to mind as truly useful. The first is the ability to batch process images into a single palette and to GIF them down when preparing frames for animated GIFs. It becomes as easy as creating a custom CLUT, preparing the frames, and running the batch process. Batch file type conversions are equally useful, especially when converting video grabs. Because we use a lot of video material from the FOX News Channel, we often end up with large folders full of bitmaps (our primary video capture stations are PCs running Premiere) that need to be resized and converted into JPEGs for use on the Web. A couple of clicks and a folder full of 60 or 100 stills can be made useable for Web publishing.

Finally, the Intensity & Contrast utility is invaluable in doing some very basic but necessary gamma correction to compensate for the darker gamma on PCs and the fact that we do most of our design work on Macs. A simple modification of the intensity and the images we do are ready for cross-platform viewing. When a graphical treatment needs to be done in mere minutes, as much of our work is, having known techniques to improve their quality proves a life-saver.

Any tips or tricks? Gamma correction on images to make them look good on both Macs and PCs can easily be made into a batch function. Set the Intensity & Contrast utility so that it has a batch value of between 10 and 15 (depending on the brightness of the images you like to create) under the Intensity setting. Run that over your images and you should have great-looking, gamma-balanced work.

Kalle Wik

Title: Web Programmer

Company (location): Blue Platypus, San Francisco, CA (www.blueplatypus.com)

Describe your position: As the CTO of the Blue Platypus, I produce rich media content for our Web site using many types of software tools.

How long have you been using DeBabelizer Toolbox? Three years

Describe how you use DeBabelizer Toolbox: I was first introduced to DeBabelizer while working on *The Adventures of Peter Rabbit*, an animation-intensive storybook project at Mindscape. We used its batch processing capabilities to quickly process immense volumes of frame-by-frame animation. Using DeBabelizer cut thousands of dollars in labor costs and time, and we met our production deadlines.

DeBabelizer can even process batches without tying up your processor, which enables a person to hone their Solitaire skills and perform work at the same time!

I still use DeBabelizer extensively when preparing graphics for use in Macromedia Director. The ability to create custom 256-color palettes from a batch of images in DeBabelizer is key for Director developers who want to reach the broadest audience. Custom palettes enable you to deliver high-quality visuals at 256-color monitor settings. If you can intelligently create and use multiple custom palettes, your CD-ROM and Shockwave projects will not have to sacrifice image quality to meet minimum performance and color-depth requirements. DeBabelizer facilitates creation of these custom palettes and I don't know of another program that can accomplish this feat.

I also use DeBabelizer to produce Web graphics. DeBabelizer will open *any* type of image file and saves to almost as many types. It compresses the file sizes of GIFs and

JPEGs extremely well while preserving image quality, making it an indispensable tool if you want to reach the modem-using consumer audience. There are multiple settings for dithering and color reduction, allowing the user far more control of the Web-preparation process than Photoshop. You can automatically set transparency, interlacing, and other properties of GIFs and JPEGs, making DeBabelizer the one-stop shop for translating a high-quality, large Photoshop or PICT file to something that can be distributed over the Internet.

Any tips or tricks? When designing for the Web, be sure to test your pages on low-end machines and at 256 colors. For photographic images or images that look terrible in the Netscape palette, use JPEGs. JPEGs are saved at millions of colors, and in many cases they dither themselves well at 256-color display settings.

Michael Kay

Title: Web Developer

Company (location): *Swoon* (CondéNet online publication), New York, NY (www.swoon.com)

Describe your position: I work with the editors and Art Director in developing interactive content for *Swoon*. I receive layouts from the Art Director and produce Web content.

How long have you been using DeBabelizer Toolbox? One year

Describe how you use DeBabelizer Toolbox: *Swoon* relies heavily on playful, high-quality Web graphics. It's my job to keep our page-loads quick while preserving the quality of the images. DeBabelizer is an essential tool for this.

DeBabelizer is an integral part of my daily production process. The Art Director supplies me with a Photoshop layout of each page, which he designs with the Netscape palette in mind. My usual strategy is to cut out the images, reduce the colors, and then remap the flat areas of color to the Netscape palette. DeBabelizer's color palette is intuitive, allowing me to click specific colors of an image's palette to modify them.

DeBabelizer is essential for creating animated GIFs. I use it to create a SuperPalette and then batch-save the frames of the animation to the palette.

DeBabelizer's "Watch Me" function has enabled me to create scripts that automate the processing of daily banner images. I open a PICT or GIF in DeBabelizer and execute a script that maps the image to a specific palette, trims it, removes unnecessary colors, and saves it to the appropriate directory on the server.

DeBabelizer's Batch and SuperPalette tools are also essential for serious Web production.

Any tips or tricks? Here are the steps I take when I want to maximize an image's palette:

1. Sample representative parts of an image into separate files to segregate flatter areas of color from gradations because the gradations need more colors.

2. Reduce the palettes of the clippings as far as possible.

3. Create a SuperPalette from those samples while reducing the colors even more.

4. Open the original 24-bit image and remap it to that SuperPalette.

Ylva Wickberg/Donna Slote

Title: Web Designer/Creative Director

Company: Maus Haus/NeoHouse, San Mateo, California (www.maushaus.com)

Describe your position: Web designer, conceptual artist/Information design and architecture

How long have you been using Debabelizer Toolbox: Three years

Describe how you use Debabelizer Toolbox: Maus Haus and NeoHouse keep a library of images for our numerous Web and multimedia projects, especially our most recent, Autodesk's *Picture This Home!* DeBabelizer helps us manage the overload of images in all of the various formats we work with. The Web site and applications we work on maintain the look and feel we want without compromising high standard imagery, thanks to DeBabelizer. We'd die without it!

When working on Web sites, we use DeBabelizer to check and process individual files in order to ensure the highest quality image using the least amount of colors possible. We also use DeBabelizer to batch process hundreds of images and at the same time organize them for easy accessibility.

Any tips or tricks? When working with lots of images, it's hard to keep track of their different specifications. A very simple, quick, and maybe obvious trick is to check image size, format, and colors in DeBabelizer's Open dialog box without having to actually open the image.

Tim Barber

Title: Creative Director

Company: CircumStance Design, San Francisco, CA (www.circumstance.com)

Describe your position: As creative director at CircumStance Design, a new media entertainment studio, I direct the development of consumer entertainment productions for the WWW, Enhanced CD, and CD-ROM.

How long have you been using DeBabelizer Toolbox? 1.5 years

Describe how you use DeBabelizer Toolbox: Like most new media studios we use Debab for production work that is either highly repetitive or calculation intensive—for the Web, CD-ROMs, and for Enhanced CD productions by processing animation and converting graphics to 8-bit color. Typically, we take animation sequences as PICT frames from After Effects or Strata that are anti-aliased to a green-screen and process them into either Director-ready sprites or GIF89a-ready frames.

For objects and characters that will eventually be "knocked-out" to a background scene this is accomplished by:

1. Scaling the image as required

2. Removing the background color

3. Shaving the outline (removes anti-aliased edges)

4. Re-stroking the outline with an aliased edge

5. Refilling the background with a color that will hold each frame's registration in either Director of a GIF animator

Then we use DeBabelizer to convert graphics to a Netscape-safe palette for the Web or to a Windows-safe custom palette for CD-ROM and Enhanced CD. These two solutions ensure the best color for the largest audience. DeBabelizer is the only tool that can accomplish all of these tasks effectively.

Any tips or tricks? Nesting Scripts. When things get repetitive, you can nest scripts within one another and even batch batches using scripts. For example, if you have four different characters that need to be processed with the previously described methods but each must be scaled differently, you might want to batch a batch.

Create a script that does steps 2, 3, 4, and 5. This will be the "clean-up cells script." Then, create a unique script for scaling each character appropriately. These will be "scale scripts 1–4." Next, create a script for each character that calls the appropriate scale script and the clean-up cells script. These might be called "character 1–4 full process." Then, the final script is one that simply runs four individual batch saves, each corresponding to a different set of source frames and each running the associated "character *x* full process script." Now the characters are ready to go in the morning!

Mick Wehner

Title: Art Director

Company (and location): Spray Interactive Media, Stockholm, Sweden (www.spray.se and www.sprayusa.com)

Describe your position: Concept and design for Internet/Intranet.

How long have you been using DeBabelizer Toolbox? One year

Describe how you use DeBabelizer Toolbox: At Spray, Sweden's leading Interactive design studio, we make extensive use of DeBabelizer. Most of our artists and production people swear by it. All of our projects destined for the Web get DeBabelized. Personally, I use it mostly for batch processing and when I want to make the smallest possible palettes for animated GIFs. We couldn't live without it!

Any tips or tricks? Save your work often!

D

J-K-L

M

377

U-V

DE·BABELIZER®

CONSERVES BANDWIDTH

AUTOMATICALLY

DeBabelizer makes Web graphics look better and download faster with automated ProScripts™ and exclusive SuperPalette™ optimization technology.

DeBabelizer® Pro for Windows® 95/NT™ 4.0 and DeBabelizer® Toolbox for Macintosh, is the cross-platform, automated graphics, animation, and digital video processor for your Multimedia, Web, and Desktop Productions. Imagine the power to apply many different editing functions, filter effects, color corrections, or text overlay to an unlimited number of images or frames with easy WatchMe™ scripting. Then output the entire batch to your choice of over 90 formats including Interlaced GIF and GIF89a (with or without transparency), PNG, and JPEG - *all optimized automatically!*

DeBabelizer will be at the center of your multimedia production.
Call your local software dealer or favorite Mac or PC catalog to order.

EQUILIBRIUM™
The Art of Automation™
www.equilibrium.com - 1·800·524·8651

MACMILLAN COMPUTER PUBLISHING USA

A VIACOM COMPANY

Technical Support:

If you cannot get the CD/Disk to install properly, or you need assistance with a particular situation in the book, please feel free to check out the Knowledge Base on our Web site at **http://www.superlibrary.com/general/support**. We have answers to our most Frequently Asked Questions listed there. If you do not find your specific question answered, please contact Macmillan Technical Support at **(317) 581-3833**. We can also be reached by email at **support@mcp.com**.

About the CD

The book's companion CD-ROM includes:

- Demo versions of both DeBabelizer Pro and Toolbox, third party filters you can use with DeBabelizer and Photoshop; GifBuilder and Drop*Name utilities.

- You can use one of the many digital images in creating CD-ROM or Web sites. Images from ArtBeats, Classic PIO Partners, and Image Club are included. (See licenses for usage-rights.)

- Several of the book's chapters (Chapters 4, 5, and 10) are also included on the disc for you to view the figures in color.